4/22/10

A Time to
FIGHT

For Sigourney Weaver —

With admiration.

Born Fighting

Lost Soldiers

The Emperor's General

Something to Die For

A Country Such as This

A Sense of Honor

Fields of Fire

A Time to FIGHT

RECLAIMING A FAIR AND JUST AMERICA

JIM WEBB

BROADWAY BOOKS

New York

Book design by Caroline Cunningham

Library of Congress Cataloging-in-Publication Data
Webb, James H.
A time to fight : reclaiming a fair and just America / Jim Webb.
p. cm.
1. Political planning—United States. 2. Political leadership—United States.
3. United States—Politics and government. I. Title.

JK468.P64W43 2008
320.60973—dc22

2008003598

ISBN 978-0-7679-2836-6

Hong Le
Warrior Queen
Love of my Life

"There is a time to pray and a time to fight. This is the time to fight."

—Pastor John Peter Gabriel Muhlenberg:
Sermon at Woodstock, Virginia, 1775

CONTENTS

PART THREE

Truth and Consequences

ACKNOWLEDGMENTS

A special thanks to Oleg Jankovic, Walter Anderson, Paul Reagan, Jessica Smith, and Amy Hogan (Famous Amos) for providing me with their varied and much-valued insights as I wrote and re-wrote the manuscript for this book.

And, since this is a book about problems, context, and solutions, it is as good a place as any to express my admiration for, and appreciation of, the quality of service that the members of my Senate staff have been giving to our nation.

PART ONE

Who Are We?

CHAPTER ONE

SCORPIONS IN A JAR

M ister President, on that I ask for the yeas and nays."

"Is there a sufficient second? There appears to be a sufficient second. The yeas and nays are ordered. The clerk will call the roll."

These final words calling for a vote on the Senate floor have been uttered by the presiding officer, from a chair that oversees the entire Senate chamber. If someone were watching the proceedings on C-SPAN or from the small visitors' gallery above the chamber, they would see a puzzlingly empty spectacle. In most cases, only a few senators are on the floor, having spoken while standing behind one of a hundred desks that form a semicircle in front of the elevated platform where the stiff, seemingly bored presiding officer sits behind a parliamentarian, two legislative clerks, and a journal clerk. With that, those observing might be forgiven for thinking that the debate they have just witnessed was nothing more than kabuki, a pantomime of stilted, false formality played out to deaf ears, as unheard and unremarkable as a tree falling in an empty forest.

But in almost every Senate office, indeed at almost every desk, the television sets and computer monitors are on, having followed the floor statements that precede the vote. And much more has been·done, well before the speeches began. Committee hearings have been held. Memos have been written. Recommendations have been drafted. Discussions and internal debates have taken place. All that remains is for the individual senator to decide which way he or she will vote. And within fifteen or twenty minutes, depending on the rule attached to the legislation, that vote must be cast personally, a yea or nay offered to the roll clerk sitting just below the presiding officer.

Some votes are easy, either because they are perfunctory, such as judicial and military nominations that have already been extensively scrubbed by trusted committee chairmen, or because they are procedural, calling upon a senator's loyalty to the party leadership, or because the philosophical arguments are clear. Some votes are enormously difficult. Many involve great stakes for the nation on issues that are far more complex than the inconclusive legislative answers that are being offered, a dilemma that many senators identify as "letting the perfect be the enemy of the good." Others involve deliberate traps by clever members of the opposing side, meaningless in their true impact because of procedural gimmickry but designed to soil the voting record of senators up for reelection and to provide fresh fodder for the bombast of the talk-show crowd. Casting such "gotcha" votes, one cannot help but think of Rudyard Kipling's knowing lament in the classic poem "If": *"If you can bear to hear the truth you've spoken / Twisted by knaves to make a trap for fools . . ."*

I am a junior senator, ninety-fifth on the seniority list, and so by Senate standards my office in the Russell Senate Office Building is less than splendid. But having spent most of my life outside of government, I know what splendid is, and how much it usually costs if you're paying for it out of your own pocket. From that perspective, my office meets the test—the high ceiling, the ancient fireplace along one wall, the classic furniture, the modern technology evident in the top-of-the-line computer on my desk, all bought and maintained with money that came from hardworking people who have paid for such emoluments through their taxes. And especially splendid, invisible but permeating, is the history that both haunts and inspires me every day. It is not always enjoyable to serve as a United States senator. But it never ceases to be an honor.

Members of my legislative staff, led by the legislative director, enter my personal office to go over the vote and to discuss other possible votes for the day. I sit on a hard-back, wooden-armed chair, facing them as they take their usual seats on the sofa that meets the wall. Above the sofa is a large print of George Washington in military uniform, kneeling in prayer next to his horse at Valley Forge during the Revolutionary War. The print is a personal possession. I brought it to the office when I entered the Senate, as one of a host of reminders designed to focus my sense of purpose as I carry out my duties. Samuel Cochran, one of my four times great-grandfathers, served in the Virginia Line as an enlisted soldier under General Washington. He crossed the Delaware under Washington's command. And Samuel Cochran was no "summer soldier": apropos of the scene in the painting, he kept the faith with Washington and suffered through the infamous winter at Valley Forge.

Across the room, amid a wall full of family pictures behind my desk, my mother's father, B. H. Hodges, stares out at me from a small picture framed in barn wood, as he has done in every office I have occupied for more than twenty years. My grandfather is just in from his patch of truck farm vegetables, wearing knee-high working boots and bib overalls. A cloth hat is pulled low over his ears to protect him from the scorching east Arkansas sun, which has already baked his face tobacco brown. The hat's brim is bent up in front, which along with his burning eyes gives him a defiant air. Defiant he was, and tragic, too. He was a fighter, a lonely champion of lost causes who himself lost everything because of the causes he championed. The picture doesn't show it, but he is lame from a busted hip, with a longtime wound that still seeps openly through breaks in his skin, and will soon die for lack of medical care.

Pictures and reminders fill my office. Samuel Cochran, B. H. Hodges, my parents, my wife, my brother and sisters, my fellow Marines from a time of brutal combat in Vietnam, my five children and one stepdaughter; those who went before me, those who were young with me and grew older by my side, and those who will be here long after I am gone. They look over my shoulder as I work. They give me balance, and also a sense of accountability. I owe those who went before me the kind of country they fought to create and wanted to perfect. I owe those who served alongside me the kind of country we tried to protect. And I owe my children the kind of country they want to see preserved and further greatened.

I have a world-class staff, made up of men and women who represent every aspect of American society, capable of researching and debating any issue that confronts our country. I know they are world-class because I personally interviewed and hired every one of them, after sorting for months through hundreds of talent-filled applications. The memos have been prepared by whichever staff member is responsible for the subject matter of the vote. On the more important votes, we will already have had numerous discussions. On every vote, I have received and considered their recommendations. On every issue, the approach I have demanded is that my staff focus on substance over politics. And on matters of substance, I have required that they focus on societal fairness above all else. I ask a series of questions about the issues embodied in the legislation. On the more complicated votes, I may ask them to debate the matter in front of me. And then it is time to vote.

A typical day in the Senate requires several trips to the Senate floor and back, although the journey is usually underground so that on some days once I arrive at work I never see the sun. I walk fast. I have an aversion to wasting time. My sense of constant motion is one of the reasons that my eldest daughter, Amy, nicknamed me "the Tasmanian Devil" when she was in her teens. Given the efficiency of my pace, it takes about five minutes to reach the Senate chamber from my office. Normally, I do so through a connecting corridor that begins in the basement of the Russell Building, passing underneath Constitution Avenue and ending up in the basement of the Capitol. If time is short, I can also catch the train—a small tram located in the same tunnel that shuttles continuously back and forth between the two buildings. Years ago, when I was serving as Assistant Secretary of Defense and then Secretary of the Navy in the Pentagon, I calculated that I had walked more than a thousand miles along the maze of corridors between my office and Secretary of Defense Cap Weinberger's. I have no doubt that I will surpass that mileage well before my Senate term expires.

I have lived a fairly complicated life, filled with unpredicted twists and turns. A phrase in "Gerontion," one of T. S. Eliot's greatest poems, frequently returns to my consciousness when I consider that journey: *"History has many cunning passages, contrived corridors / and issues . . . Think, now! "*

From the time I left the Marine Corps after serving as an infantry platoon and company commander in Vietnam, I decided that I would focus on immediate goals that inspired me to devote all of my energy to them, rather than putting together the more cautious and traditional building blocks of a predictable career. I've worked in government, first in the late 1970s when I was the youngest full committee counsel in the Congress, then in the 1980s as a Defense Department official, and now as a senator. I've written nine books, six of them novels, a process that allowed me to spend considerable time overseas and also among widely varying communities here in America as I researched and wrote. I've taught literature at the university level. I've worked on numerous film projects, some of them with Hollywood's top producers and directors. I've traveled widely as a journalist, writing from such locations as Japan, the Philippines, Vietnam, and Thailand. In addition to fighting in Vietnam, I've covered two wars—the Marines in Beirut for PBS in 1983, and then as an embedded journalist in Afghanistan in 2004. I've worked as a business consultant in Asia.

Financially and personally, my life has been one roll of the dice after another. I've had good years and bad years, but I've never lost my willingness to take a risk and I've never been bored. My curiosities have taken me down some pretty strange alleyways, to some of the darker, meaner corners of the world. And in that respect, when it comes to examining many of the issues of the day I have brought to the Senate a different set of experiences, and thus a different referent, from most of my colleagues. At the same time, I will admit that I acquired a certain level of cynicism along the way when it comes to the glitter-and-tinsel side of government and the trappings of power. And coming to the Senate after so many real-world, nonpolitical experiences, I will also admit that this well-honed skepticism is largely intact.

But the one connecting dot in all of my experiences has been a passion for history and a desire to learn from it. Not the enumeration of monarchs and treaties that so often passes for academic knowledge, but the surging vitality from below that so often impels change and truly defines cultures. The novelist Leo Tolstoy wrote vividly about war and peace, showing us the drawing rooms and idiosyncrasies of Russia's elite. But in reality, he was telling us that great societal changes are most often pushed along by tsunami-deep impulses that cause the elites to react far more than they inspire them to lead. And this, in my view, is the greatest lesson of political history. Entrenched aristocracies, however we may want to define them, do not want change; their desire instead is to manage dissent in a way that does not disrupt their control. But over time, under the right system of government, a free, thinking people has the energy and ultimately the power to effect change.

The American experiment, incomplete as it is in its evolution, is the greatest example of the possibility of balancing these two competing impulses. We ebb and flow, decade after decade, as the better minds among us seek to define the playing field of American success. And we are engaging in this debate, as best we can, under the principles of true representative government.

This leads me, perhaps surprisingly, to my innate distrust of the ornaments of power, because even an earned skepticism has its limits. If one has a sense of history and cares for the place of the United States of America as a unique, enduring model of the benefits of democracy, no amount of cynicism can diminish the largeness, and even the great-ness, that surrounds you when you walk the hallways and enter the chambers of the Capitol. Indeed, even when viewed from the outside landscape the Capitol dominates Washington, rising with an austere grandness above the skyline, and lit with a glowing majesty at night. The Capitol, quite frankly, humbles me, and for me it is a particular privilege to walk unescorted and unchallenged along its corridors.

Still walking, I reach the far end of the tunnel and ride an escala-tor up a floor, reaching the basement of the Capitol. From there I join several colleagues as we take one of the "Senators Only" elevators to the second floor. The elevator doors open. Almost as in a movie, I step from the solitude of the elevator into a scene of instant chaos. Dozens of senators have been exiting the four elevators that open at this nar-row corridor. They must now pass through a thick crowd of journalists who have interposed themselves along the corridor, which leads to the doorways of the Senate chamber. The news reporters wave micro-phones and notebooks, calling out to different senators, wanting print or radio interviews regarding their positions on different pieces of leg-islation or the latest hot issue that faces the Congress. Mini press con-ferences are being held in tightly knit groups as I move toward the chamber.

Back in their home states, each of these senators would be unique, commanding the full attention of every reporter in the room. Here, the reporters flit from one small grouping to another, looking for a series of quick quotes, or the best quote, and having their pick of any senator who will stop for a moment and give them some time. But the senators know the game as well. On any given vote, on any given day, a smart senator who has taken a bold or controversial position can reach far more media outlets between the elevator and the Sen-ate chamber than he or she could garner in a full press conference back home.

The doorway nearest the elevator opens into the Republican side of the Senate. I take a left turn in front of those doors, choosing not to enter them today, and walk along a side corridor that parallels the chamber, heading toward the Democratic side. Capitol police and floor assistants greet me as I pass. History surrounds me here. Those who have gone before us have left their mark, both visibly and spiritually. The beautifully colored tiles underneath my feet are muted with the passage of time, their patterns fading from the abrasion of a million footsteps. A wide bank of stairs falls to my left. Its marble steps are curved in the middle like mildly sagging cakes, the marble itself worn and polished from generation after generation of hard-soled shoes that have climbed them. The domed ceilings, the grand murals, the intricate, Renaissance-style artwork, the sculptured busts of great Americans, all surround me in this part of the Capitol. Their images are made more poignant by the whispered voices and echoing footsteps of others who are walking nearby in the hallway, reminding me that this is hallowed ground.

All of these feelings are accentuated when I enter the Senate chamber. The first time our newly elected group of senators was brought to the Senate floor, my good friend Senator Jon Tester commented that the experience gave him the same feeling as walking into his barn back in Montana. At first some thought this observation cheeky, but instead it was profoundly respectful. Jon Tester's great-grandfather built the barn. His point was that he cannot enter it without thinking of his heritage, and of the efforts of those who went before him, from which he benefits every day as he works the farm.

And so it is with the Senate chamber. It was conceived and built by ingenious leaders, and we are merely its latest set of temporary occupants, charged with the stewardship of our nation's standards and its continuity. I will always be a guest here, no matter how long I might remain in the Senate. The Senate floor is and always has been the great arena of our democracy. I spent eight years in my younger life as a boxer, and sometimes when I enter the chamber I think, *This is the ring. The American people can see us here, and listen to our arguments. This is where the fights matter.*

Traditions are preserved here: the somber aura of the chamber itself, the stilted phrasing of the parliamentary questions, the disingenuous but essential courtesies, the old-style furniture, the tobacco spittoons that remind us of other eras in our national journey, the names of those from far earlier times that have been carved by now-dead hands into the bottom compartments of the very desks we now occupy. This is a reminder for all of us, at the very moment of our greatest influence. Sit at your desk, open up the drawer, and stare directly not only into history but into the future, when you yourself will simply become a carved memory, even as the energy and the frustrations of the Senate and the nation move inexorably beyond your life.

I reach the entrance near the Democratic cloakroom, climbing two steps and heading toward a different set of double doors. They swing open as I near them, each door manned by a smiling, blue-suited page. I walk along a lush, royal-blue carpet past the rows of highly polished, old-school desks, stepping down from one wide platform to another until I am in the well, where I will cast my vote.

The Senate floor is alive now, dozens of senators milling about, buzzing with conversations. At the row of desks just below the presiding officer, off to his left, the roll clerk is calling the names, asking for the yeas and nays. Below the roll clerk in the well itself, the senators are milling around two separate tables. On the Democratic side, just in front of the majority leader's desk, two cloakroom aides sit behind one table, tallying votes. On the table are a summary of the amendment being voted on, a copy of the amendment itself, and a note giving the leadership's recommendation on the vote. A similar table sits just in front of the Republican leader's desk, providing their own aides and summaries.

I look around at my fellow senators, part of me again wondering at the unplanned personal journey that brought me here, and part of me surprised at how comfortable I have become in their midst. They are an eclectic bunch, this so-called Debating Club. More than a few harbor presidential aspirations. A large number are children of privilege, the product of great wealth and even of generations of ease and comfort. Many went to the best schools our nation has to offer. On the other hand, quite a few have reached this political zenith through more plebeian routes. And I have no problem saying without hesitation that almost all of them have impressed me with their love of this country, and with their sincere desire to preserve its greatness.

That doesn't mean that we are a big, happy family. Some of us believe that we were sent here to fix problems, and others believe that those who have come here to fix problems—at least the issues that we define as problems—are in fact the problem. So behind all the smiles and backslaps, and beyond the necessary courtesies that lend dignity to what otherwise would be a vulgar brawl, is the reality that in this room, right at this moment, are some of the shrewdest and most cunning creatures on earth.

There is an old joke that senators tell among themselves. Your first six months in the Senate, you spend a lot of time wondering how the hell you got here. After that, you look around at your colleagues and wonder how the hell any of them got here. But make no mistake—there are very few accidental senators. One might disagree with their priorities. Some might opine about which lobbyists and special-interest groups maintain a measure of influence over their political conduct. Others might dislike their personalities or criticize their ethical conduct. Every now and then, one of them suffers the misfortune of having their personal life spill over into the public consciousness, causing untold embarrassment. But at bottom these are people who have taken risks, exposed themselves to the public eye, and paid a certain price to reach the Senate floor. And one should never underestimate either their determination on matters that are important to them, or their mental toughness.

This is one of the great reasons for the elaborate courtesies that prevail on the Senate floor, and for the careful respect that is shown even to those with whom you adamantly disagree or even secretly dislike. There is always a tomorrow when one is serving a six-year term, dealing daily with ninety-nine other strong personalities. Whatever one's beliefs and loyalties to various political interests, and however loudly one wishes to argue about substance, this is no place for underhanded tactics or dissembling behavior when it comes to your colleagues, because the payback in such cases is usually paralysis. The Senate, more than any other body in American government, is a place where a very few people, and on occasion even a single member, can stop things from getting done.

The United States Senate is a venerable institution. It is also an odd kingdom with 100 fiercely protected fiefdoms. No, let me amend that, as they say in this place. In terms of volatility, behind all of its courtesies the United States Senate is composed of 100 scorpions in a jar. And one should be very careful in deciding how and when to shake that jar.

bring harmony and to honor our traditional notions of fair play. When such debates proceed from the starting point that, at least theoretically, every participant has an equal chance at the same type of future, they bring us together and reinforce the notion that we are the fairest and most creative society on earth. But this has not been so in recent decades. Vast changes have overwhelmed America, calling into question every aspect of our national identity and even the foundations on which our society was built.

Who are the Americans? Where did they come from, geographically and spiritually? What do they believe? What common good will they agree upon, work together to advance, or possibly even fight for? Indeed, what do they even owe one another, beyond the taxes they must pay and the laws that they, at least in theory, must obey? And speaking of laws and taxes, what do they owe their government, and what does their government owe them?

Over the past twenty-five years, these questions have become increasingly hard to answer. In fact, it would be challenging to find another time in our history—including the Civil War—when the country has been so filled with uncertainty about the very principles that define it. America today is overwhelmed by vagueness. We have entered a dangerous, unprecedented cycle of seemingly unsolvable unknowns. Our foreign policy is confused, without clear direction, increasingly vulnerable to such largely unexamined long-term threats as China's emerging power even as it has become bogged down in the never-ending struggles of the Middle East. Our demographic makeup has been altered dramatically and is set to keep on changing, through both legal and illegal immigration. Our economic policies, particularly in the age of globalization, have produced widely divergent results inside our own society, far beyond the ability of current government programs to design a fair formula for those who have unfairly benefited and on behalf of those others who have been unfairly hurt.

And as a result of this last point, our country has been increasingly calcifying along class lines, in a way we have not seen for more than a century and to an extent that may be unprecedented in our entire history. This is no longer a simple question of haves and have-nots. Every social and economic indicator shows that America now has an upper class that has swung exponentially away from the rest of society. To make matters worse, many of those at the very top now tend to view their inordinate success as simply a function of their innate talent in a brave new world of socioeconomic Darwinism, and have become openly consumed by self-justifying greed.

We are at risk of developing a permanent underclass. Millions of Americans are now propped up by government "safety net" programs that forestall open rebellion but at the same time neglect their well-being in all of the important ways that might contribute to true social and economic advancement. Lacking a pathway to success and frozen inside crime-infested neighborhoods, this underclass has grown accustomed to inadequate schools, largely inaccessible health care, prison as an alternative lifestyle, single-parent homes, and long-term unemployment.

Equally troubling, America's vaunted middle class, the historic backbone of our economy, the wellspring of social advancement, and the repository of our traditional values, is in serious peril. Literally tens of millions of Americans are now watching uneasily as trends that are beyond their control threaten to dissipate their way of life, while their government leaders too often stand idly by. At the heart of their problem are the twin concerns of illegal immigration and globalization, which affect their collective bargaining rights as well as the overall benefits packages that in the past made our workers the envy of the rest of the world. Today, our workers are at the mercy of cutthroat executives who are vastly overpaid, partly as a consequence of giving their jobs away to other people. Illegal immigration has in some cases eliminated jobs and in others driven wage scales down, while globalization and the internationalization of corporate America have combined to send millions of good jobs overseas.

This is not hyperbolic rhetoric. For several years, corporate profits as a percentage of national wealth have been at all-time highs while the wages and salaries of our workers are at all-time lows. Even as wages and salaries have stagnated, corporate executive compensation has skyrocketed. The stock market performed off the charts, but more than half of the stocks in America are owned by less than 1 percent of the people. Regular, middle-class kids are routinely frozen out of entry into the nation's elite colleges in favor of "legacy" preferences and special-interest admission, while the elite schools have themselves become the breeding ground for an emerging interconnected international aristocracy. Our editorialists and politicians talk about the American dream, and some urge us to bring democracy to the rest of the world. But more than two million Americans are now in prison, by far the highest incarceration rate in the so-called advanced world. Indeed, our system of criminal justice, which is rarely if ever debated in public, is a national shame, a key indicator of how far we have fallen from our traditional self-image as an open, fair society.

As this drift toward societal regression has taken place, America's leadership has largely been paralyzed, unable or unwilling to stop the slide. This is the most confusing aspect of our present state of affairs. A conundrum challenges us with every crisis that goes unsolved. Where are the leaders? Has our political process become so compromised by powerful interest groups and the threat of character assassination that even the best among us will not dare to speak honestly about the solutions that might bring us back to common sense and fundamental fairness?

I believe there are answers. But they cannot be found in the false debates or the emotional detours that currently define American politics. It would be hard to count the number of Americans who have turned off their TVs in utter disgust at one time or another, walking out of the house on their way to work and muttering under their breaths, "What is the matter with our system? Where are the good people, the ones who understand my problems and how the average person really has to live?"

There are certainly thousands of people all around the country who have at one time or another made a speech on Memorial Day, or to the local Kiwanis, and afterward have been greeted by people who were present in the audience, shaking their hands and saying, "Great words. You should run for office! I'd vote for you."

But the truth of modern American politics is that the great speech you just made, or the issue you just talked about, is not very often going to be where your campaign will be fought if you decide to run. Your opponent's media advisers and opposition researchers are going to throw something else—often something manufactured from half-truths, akin to what the Soviet propagandists used to call disinformation—onto the airwaves, night after night, week after week, to remind prospective voters of what a danger you supposedly are to all that America holds dear. If your opponent is an incumbent, particularly an incumbent who has been careful in his or her voting patterns and in the cultivation of powerful interest groups, you will be facing someone with a multimillion-dollar campaign chest who is capable of a massive media assault that will, in the parlance, "define" you as a pretty slimy human being.

With all of this clutter on the political radar screen, the average voter either becomes disgusted or decides to vote for whichever candidate seems capable of doing the least amount of harm. This is how aristocracies, however we may wish to define them, retain their power. And it is also how interest groups thwart meaningful change.

It's pretty safe to say that I am the only person in the history of Virginia to be elected to statewide office with a union card, two Purple Hearts, and three tattoos. But it was no easy ride.

On February 8, 2006, I decided to run for the United States Senate, in an election that would be held nine months later, almost to the day. This announcement did not exactly set the newswires on fire. In fact, the nicest commentary afterward was that I had begun a quixotic effort. "Quixotic," it might be remembered, is defined in *Webster's Dictionary* as "idealistic and utterly impractical," marked by "lofty, romantic ideas that are doomed to fail." "Idealistic" I will admit to. As for those "lofty, romantic ideas," I respectfully demur.

I had never run for political office. In an era where money dominates political campaigns, and where candidates for statewide office typically begin fund-raising two years before an election, I had not yet raised a penny. At a time in our history where candidates often turn to political consultants and media managers to shape their political personas, I had no campaign staff. In a state of more than seven million people, whose demographics and political leanings vary wildly from an activist liberal core in the north to the deepest of conservative red in the far southwest, I had no real constituency in either political party.

In fact, my political credentials were viewed with unease by both sides. On the one hand, I had spent four years as a Republican committee counsel in the House of Representatives and four years in the Reagan Administration, which did not warm the hearts of many Democrats. On the other, I am a longtime union member and a determined supporter of organized labor in a state that is forty-eighth in union participation, and I had helped the United Mine Workers during their landmark 1989 strike against the Pittston Coal Company. I had also been an early and vocal critic of the Bush Administration's Iraq War policy. Neither of these efforts endeared me to the hearts of the Republicans. And although I had written frequently about political issues over the years, I had never attended a political meeting hosted by either the Republicans or the Democrats, other than to lead the Pledge of Allegiance at the opening of the 1980 Republican National Convention. And that was hardly going to help me, since I would be running as a Democrat.

My opponent held all the advantages of incumbency. He had already amassed millions of dollars in his campaign war chest. He had enjoyed a string of electoral successes that dated back more than twenty-five years. His statewide organization was broad and deep, particularly among the moneyed solons of Richmond and Tidewater, and the hardcore Religious Right in a state where both Jerry Falwell and Pat Robertson have kept their headquarters. He had begun his political career in the state legislature, then run successfully for the U.S. House of Representatives, and after that had won two statewide races, serving as governor of Virginia before being elected to the Senate in 2000.

He also was believed to harbor national aspirations. In the early months of my campaign, he traveled frequently to New Hampshire and Iowa. A month after my announcement, he would receive the highest number of votes in a presidential straw poll conducted at the Conservative Political Action Conference's annual gathering in Washington, D.C. His campaign manager had engineered the surprising upset of Senator Tom Daschle in South Dakota two years before, and was frequently referred to as the "next Karl Rove." His longtime chief political consultant had been the driving force behind the hugely financed Swift Boat Veterans for the Truth media blitz, which had permanently damaged John Kerry's presidential run. Swimming in dollars, his campaign had also hired Ed Gillespie, former chairman of the Republican National Committee, and longtime political activist Mary Matalin, who most recently had been a close adviser to Vice President Dick Cheney.

And for those who even bothered to take polls in the weeks after my announcement, on a good day I registered about thirty-three points behind.

I also had another problem. As a former Reagan Administration official, I would have to win the Democratic nomination in a primary against an opponent who had long ties to the state party's leadership and who was willing to put more than a million dollars of his own money into the race. This was no small hurdle. Primaries in Virginia are only one step up from being family affairs. Voter turnout is usually low. Those who do vote are most often from the party's activist base, which understandably had reservations about handing the nomination for the U.S. Senate to someone who had never been actively involved in party politics and whose previous government service had been with the Republicans.

The primary itself would become a bellwether test of the willingness of the Democratic Party to reopen its ranks to those who in previous decades had become, in the parlance, Reagan Democrats. As columnist Joe Klein would write shortly before the primary votes were cast in June, "Republicans look for converts. Democrats look for heretics."

Contemplating the enormity of this quixotic effort, I, Don Quixote, Man of La Mancha, made the most important telephone call of the entire campaign—to my former radio operator in Vietnam. I needed a truth-teller—a Sancho Panza, if you would—someone who could keep me grounded and who would never hesitate to tell me if I was drifting away from my moorings. Mac McGarvey, who had lost his right arm while serving under my command, was working as the night manager at Tootsie's Orchid Lounge, the most famous honky-tonk in Nashville. Mac and I had remained more than friends throughout the decades. We are, literally, blood brothers, both of us having been wounded in a hellhole of frequent combat called the Arizona Valley. I told him what I was going to do. He tried to talk me out of it. After I told him it was too late to change my mind, he quit his job and loaded up his Jeep and headed to Virginia, where he moved into an extra bedroom in my basement and became my driver.

For the next four months, Mac, I, and another former Marine, Phillip Thompson, followed a physically exhausting and emotionally challenging routine, driving tens of thousands of miles throughout the state in my musty old 1998 Jeep Cherokee, making my case to two and sometimes three party gatherings a night. Each meeting followed a similar pattern, the room invariably splitting into two highly charged camps. On one side, interrupting my talks with frequent applause, were those who seemed inspired by my logic when I spoke of the historic, populist roots of the Democratic Party, my long experience in national security affairs, and my concerns about the future of the country. On the other, capable of bitter and accusatory invective, were those who wanted me to apologize for the supposed fallacy of my political journey away from the "new" Democratic Party, a party that in my own view had become too weak on national security issues in the wake of the Vietnam War and too overwhelmed by interest-group politics in reaction to the culture wars here at home.

At every meeting, regardless of the tilt in any audience between these two vastly differing points of view, I laid out the same message. First and foremost, this would be a campaign about the major themes affecting the country's future. These themes emanated from my own years of thought and consideration rather than the slick political positioning that dominates modern politics as a result of focus group "message testing" and overreliance on costly polling. Just as important, the journey was not worth it if I did not retain my independence. I stated clearly that I would not change my views on any issue in order to get a campaign contribution or a specific endorsement. I would tell my audiences as honestly and thoroughly as possible what I believed and what I would try to do about those beliefs.

We won the primary, convincingly. And in the general election, despite the ugliness that has come to define the Karl Rove era, where character assassination and the politics of fear have come to drown out reason, we did not lose our focus.

What we brought to the political arena was a strong belief that it was time for the Reagan Democrats to return to their worker-oriented, Jacksonian roots, and a message that I care deeply about, which we conveyed with relentless discipline. It is a message that I believe should be a continuing part of the national debate, and in fact should become the core message of a revitalized Democratic Party. I've said many times that this nation is going through a sea change in terms of party politics and that the old labels simply don't work anymore. What does it mean to be liberal or conservative, I would ask, when the neo-conservatives, supposedly on the right, are so far to the left that they are spouting Trotskyite nonsense about exporting American ideology at the point of a gun? The political cards are being shuffled all across this country. Good, well-meaning people have watched their government flub things up, from Iraq to the aftermath of Hurricane Katrina. Americans want better leadership. And they want new approaches.

And so, in the campaign I talked about deeper themes rather than mere political issues. We never simply talked about Iraq. Instead, we spoke repeatedly, and in depth, about the need to reorient our nation's national security posture in a way that would allow us not only to withdraw our forces from Iraq but also to restore a measure of stability in that historically volatile region, to increase our ability to fight the war against international terrorism, and to more properly address the wide range of strategic and foreign policy issues that have been dangerously ignored over the past five years.

We did not simply dwell on this bill or that regarding unemployment, lack of medical insurance, and the need to increase the minimum wage. We talked about the larger need for economic fairness and social justice in an era where far too much power and money have been accumulated at the very top, in both economic and governmental terms. I took great pains to outline the dangers in what I have come to call the "three Americas"—a breakdown of our country along class lines, the likes of which Americans have not seen for at least a hundred years. Voters, no matter their own economic circumstances, readily identified with the reality of these three Americas: the huge migration of wealth to the very top of our society; the calcification at the bottom into what could soon become a permanent underclass; and the dangerous atrophy of our shrinking middle class, whose members are increasingly receiving less than a fair share of the fruits of their labor.

And finally, in the wake of such seriously underexamined issues as the NSA wiretapping scandal, the failure of leadership during and after Hurricane Katrina, and the billions of dollars we have wasted in programs designed for reconstructing Iraq, we talked about the need to restore simple accountability to our government, to make sure that the federal system works in the way our forefathers conceived it, and to ensure also that our taxpayers get real value for their investment.

In short, we offered voters context in a time when far too much political energy was being wasted on contrived, emotionally divisive issues such as flag burning, gay marriage, and focus-group-tested phrases such as "cut and run."

We did something else that was a bit different. I was guided by my own sense of values and political instincts rather than by polls and focus groups, and I believe that over time the voters came to understand that. We did our best to keep our message consistent, even when this gave our political advisers serious heartburn. To their frequent consternation, I spoke directly to corporate leaders about corporate responsibility. I became the first statewide candidate in Virginia history to walk a union picket line during a campaign. I spoke openly on *Meet the Press* and during other televised debates about my views that affirmative action was originally a Thirteenth Amendment program, intended to help African Americans remove the badges of slavery, and that its inclusion of every other minority group was rightly perceived to be unfair by poorer whites.

A lot of commentators were saying that I was naive. Others were saying that I was a one-issue candidate, given my lifetime of work on national defense issues and my early opposition to the Iraq War. Still others were saying that my opponent made such serious errors during the campaign that he was responsible for his own defeat. The truth was different. First, one-issue candidates don't beat strong incumbents—this has been axiomatic in politics and was proven once again in the Lieberman-Lamont race in 2006 in Connecticut. And second, while it might have been risky, it was hardly naive to have recognized that our voters have become disgusted with the cynicism of modern-day politics, and to have gambled on the likelihood that people in this country truly desire a clear and unambiguous approach to governing.

A few weeks after I announced my candidacy, my good friend Nelson Jones flew up to Virginia from Houston, where he practiced law, to spend a few days on the campaign with us. Nelson, a former Marine whom I had known since our days together at the Georgetown Law Center, was incredulous that I had decided to run for the Senate after so many years of intellectual and financial independence. He knew the way I lived my life and the things that motivated me. Sometimes I made good money and sometimes I didn't. But I wore no one else's bridle.

Nelson had flown up to stand with me as I met for the first time with the African American members of the Virginia state legislature. The meeting had not gone well, although I would eventually receive more than 90 percent of the African American vote. The group had bitter memories of the Reagan Administration, in which I had proudly served. I had asked them to look at my personal record, which included my six-year pro bono representation of a young black Marine who had wrongly been convicted of murder in Vietnam, and my personal effort to have a black soldier included in the statue at the Vietnam Veterans Memorial. Nelson had spoken on my behalf. They had been polite but not particularly convinced.

We were driving in his rental car, late at night, heading from Richmond back to northern Virginia. He gave me a glance.

"What the hell are you doing this for?"

I told him.

He looked at me again. "You know what's going to happen after the primary, don't you? You know how these people work. They've got millions of dollars, and they're keeping book. You're out there, man. You can't go back."

I told him I knew that.

"Tell me again in November," he said. Then he paused, thinking. "You know what it means to dance with the bear?"

I told him I didn't.

"Well, when you dance with the bear, you can't stop dancing until the bear wants to stop dancing. And you're dancing with the big, big bears."

On June 13, once the primary was finished, I started dancing with the bear.

The conduct of my opponent's campaign was a classic, textbook example of the deterioration of American politics away from notions of leadership and into incessant ad hominem attacks. Armed with what should have been a track record of twenty-five years of accomplishments, including six years in the Senate, he did not engage me directly on any of these themes. Instead, his campaign fell into the predictable hog trough of Karl Rovian negativity. In their ads, in their press statements, in the carefully placed insinuations that floated up from random bloggers so that they might be picked up by major media, my positions were deliberately misrepresented and my character was continually attacked.

Rather than focusing on accomplishments, the major thrust of my opponent's campaign became a misleading, fear-invoking chimera of who I was and what I myself might do.

They claimed that I wanted to betray our troops and "cut and run" from Iraq, even though for more than two years I had been calling for a formula that included robust diplomacy and a careful repositioning of forces. In fact, a version of the approach I had recommended was later adopted by the influential Iraq Study Group, led by former Secretary of State Jim Baker and former Congressman Lee Hamilton. My position in every speech during the campaign had been clearly stated: We went into Iraq recklessly; we needed to get out carefully.

They ran nonstop ads warning that I wanted to raise the taxes of every Virginian by an average of more than $2,000, even though I had said repeatedly, including during televised debates after these ads began, that I would not vote to raise taxes on wages at all. My approach throughout the campaign was to pledge that I would examine lucrative loopholes in corporate tax policies, as well as taxes on passive income such as capital gains.

They claimed that I wanted to give amnesty to all illegal aliens, despite my repeated pronouncements in favor of border security, employer sanctions, and allowing a path toward citizenship only for those who had truly put down roots in their communities. During my fifth month in the Senate, I introduced an amendment to this effect, laying out objective standards to be applied to those who had been in the country for at least four years, in an attempt to put balance into the ill-fated immigration-reform legislation. This legislation, which I opposed, failed because it indeed was going to give amnesty to every person who had entered the country illegally. And it had the full support of the Bush Administration.

A proposed constitutional amendment to ban gay marriage was on Virginia's ballot, which for a variety of strong reasons I opposed—not the least of which is that it was unnecessary, since Virginia law already banned gay marriage. In church handouts and on Christian radio they claimed I was in favor of gay marriage, despite my having repeatedly stated that I am a Christian and that in my faith marriage is between a man and a woman. The question, which still persists, is whether we as Americans should allow religious beliefs to dictate government policies. And in that context I do favor civil unions, which I believe are an appropriate—and fair—function of government.

They warned that I was giving comfort to a basically nonexistent phalanx of left-wing, antiwar hippies who want to burn the American flag, because I believe (along with Medal of Honor winner Senator Daniel Inouye and former Joint Chiefs Chairman Colin Powell) that it is inappropriate to amend the Constitution, our most sacred public document, in order to "fix" a problem that is already covered by statute and that rarely even raises its head.

Those misrepresentations ran repeatedly in television ads, particularly in southwest Virginia, their saturation of the airwaves counteracting the many attempts by our campaign to dispute the inaccuracies through the normal process of press statements and detailed corrections. A press conference can happen once a day. If you're lucky, your rebuttal can find its way into ten seconds of the evening news and in a paragraph or two of the next day's newspaper. A political ad runs as often as your opponent can pay for it, giving him the ability to make the false allegation over and over until it sinks into the public's consciousness like Pavlovian propaganda.

And as it turned out, this was just a warm-up.

On a personal level, I did not allow myself to become distracted by these tactics. I had only a few months to introduce myself as a political figure to prospective voters, to get my message out to them through all the clutter, and to let them hear me speak of where the country truly needed to go. This was my major focus, and after a while it began to take hold. And the more I spoke about the problems that need to be solved, the more our momentum grew. Predictably, as the polling numbers narrowed and eventually showed our race to be a toss-up, my opponent's campaign advisers pulled out all the stops.

The Karl Rove approach to politics is brutally simple and, let me say from personal experience, simply brutal. Damaging an opponent's reputation is more important than contradicting him on the issues. Hit the other candidate where he is perceived to be strong. Cancel out his positives. Sow the seeds of doubt. Create a mind-set among the public that he really does not understand the average American and that he cannot be trusted. Take away his personal credibility. And in the process, "define" him as an out-of-touch, sneaky, dirtbag sleaze.

Looking at the span of my career, my opponent's strategists could quickly see that my greatest strengths have been my independence and my reputation as a writer who is willing to take his readers into worlds they otherwise might never see. From my first days as a Marine in Vietnam, I have always prided myself on a willingness to respectfully and openly confront prevailing orthodoxy, to question current practices, and to come up with different solutions. This mind-set was also a strong reason that I decided to resign my post as Secretary of the Navy in 1988 rather than agree to a reduction in the Navy's shipbuilding program in an era when I believed it would be detrimental to our national strategy. Resigning my post when I could no longer support administration policy was a hard choice, made only after three months of negotiations inside the Pentagon, where I had raised several other options in order to reach congressionally mandated budget cuts.

In my opponent's campaign rhetoric, my willingness to think independently and to take a stand on what I believed became disloyalty and even betrayal. A policy dispute resolved after months of debate, at some personal cost, was portrayed as a character flaw. Their ads warned voters that I could not be trusted. Despite our continued objections, they deliberately and repeatedly stated that I had served in the Reagan Administration for less than a year, when I had in fact served in the administration for four years to the day. Grainy TV ads warned darkly: James Webb cut and ran from the Reagan Administration. He cut and ran from the Republican Party. Now he wants to cut and run from the war in Iraq.

The truly venal character assaults came toward the end of the campaign, with a series of attempts to destroy my reputation as a serious writer and in the process to label me with a laundry list of psychological maladies. Many of my friends and political associates in retrospect make light of this effort, pointing out that it was blatantly desperate, that the average voter could see clearly why it was happening, and that it might even have helped the sales of my books. But with all due respect, those friends and associates have never had the experience of turning on the radio in the morning, or tuning in to a nationally broadcast television show, or opening up such venues as the Drudge Report with its 15 million hits a day, to see and hear yourself labeled as a pornographer, a pedophile, a misogynist, and a plagiarist.

My experience with writing is not that of a politician who has written a few books on the side. For thirty years, writing has been my true profession, no matter what other endeavors I have pursued. A great deal of my life has been spent in frequent solitude and not without frustration, dedicated to building up a body of work to provide insights on our way of life and to pass on these perspectives to future generations. And this body of work in many ways will be one of my lasting legacies.

The novelist Herman Wouk, author of *Winds of War* and other fine historical fiction, once lamented in a conversation with me that the modern American novel is too often simply an interior monologue, a story about a writer trying to write a story about a writer. In the Wouk tradition, I chose instead to write books that might be called "faction": novels based on factual surroundings, and frequently on real events, intermixed with fictional characters that allow the novelist the usual prerogative to shape a plot that fits the best storytelling traditions. In that genre, it is the duty of the novelist to show the world as it exists, not simply as one (particularly a politician) would like it to be, and then to struggle with the human and societal consequences.

In my journalism, in my books, and in the film projects on which I have worked, I have striven hard to do just that. I have interviewed world leaders. I have frequently written about strategic and political concerns, particularly in editorial pieces for such newspapers as the *New York Times,* the *Wall Street Journal,* and the *Washington Post.* But I have also covered wars (in addition to fighting in one), done landmark reporting on Japan's prison system, and been inside some of the rankest slums of Southeast Asia. I was gratified when my television reporting from Beirut in 1983 received a national Emmy Award. My first novel, *Fields of Fire,* recognized by many literary commentators as the classic novel of the Vietnam War, was for years the most-taught piece of American literature across the country in college courses on the Vietnam War. Several of my other books have been taught at the university level. And my nonfiction work *Born Fighting,* a cultural and political history of the Scots-Irish people, was termed "the most brilliant battle flare ever launched by a book" by journalist and novelist Tom Wolfe.

My opponent's campaign took short excerpts from several of my novels, including *Fields of Fire,* pasted them together outside of the narrative that gave them context, and attempted to present my books as pornographic works. One of the books, *Something to Die For,* was especially highlighted for a graphic sex scene that came out of a bar in the infamous Olongapo gate-ghetto near Subic Bay in the Philippines.

Was this book pornography, or was I showing the world as it actually exists so that we might struggle with the true consequences of our acts? In terms of context, novelist Charles McCarry called *Something to Die For* "the most honest, most knowing book about the fateful connection between life in Washington and death on the battlefield ever written." The *Washington Post* reviewer commented: "A century hence, James Webb will be studied for the light he shed on military life and civil-military relations at the climax of the American Century." The reviewer for the *Washington Times* pointed out that "Webb is as much a moral philosopher as a novelist. In a time when fiction seems to find it harder and harder to address moral issues, that makes him a valuable man at the typewriter."

Another vignette, comprising two sentences, was pulled out of my novel *Lost Soldiers*, making the front page of the Drudge Report, accusing me of being a pedophile. In the Klong Toey slum of Bangkok, a father picked up his naked son in front of a hundred other inhabitants and kissed him on the penis, drawing no reaction from those around him. This description came from personal observation while I was visiting that same slum on a journalistic assignment in 1989, along with a Dominican priest. It was totally devoid of sexual content, involving an act that is not uncommon in some Southeast Asian cultures. The priest himself did not even react when it happened. Do I understand this act? Not really. Should I have written about it? As a novelist who believes in rendering the world as it is, so that those who have not seen or experienced this world can comprehend its realities, absolutely.

And what of *Lost Soldiers*? Was this pornographic literature? According to the *Los Angeles Times*, the book is "a strong and unusual novel . . . a war story and a love story. Webb's rendering of Americans in modern Asia is reminiscent of Joseph Conrad's portraits of Westerners in the East a century ago." In the words of the *Asian Reporter*, the book is "a great—perhaps definitive—depiction of the Vietnam that America left behind . . . a pulse-pounder that is filled with wise experience and shrewd observation . . . about honor and betrayal, about loss and hope." *Booklist* found it to be "a compelling, insightful, and beautiful portrait of a fascinating place, as well as a moving saga of revenge, love, loyalty, honor, and, ultimately, redemption." The conservative *Washington Times* called it "the most complete, rich and dynamic portrait in American fiction so far of Vietnam after the last American helicopter departed."

Then, by this point inexorably, came allegations of plagiarism in my novel *The Emperor's General*. The novel, set at the end of World War II and during the first months of the occupation of Japan, addressed, among other themes, a failure of accountability for the rape of Nanking. The story played out in a complicated interaction of General Douglas MacArthur and Emperor Hirohito, which resulted in the hanging of General Tomoyuki Yamashita, Japan's greatest World War II battlefield commander, for supposed war crimes in the Philippines after a shameful kangaroo court in order to deflect attention from the Nanking situation. *Publishers Weekly* called this book "Powerfully compelling and moving . . . historical fiction of a high order. Webb fuses fact and fictional experience through hypnotic storytelling, giving a human face to the victims of war, including . . . the mesmerizing figure of MacArthur, a flawed titan made palpable by Webb."

The supposed plagiarism? In this historical novel, I quoted directly from an official message sent by Japanese General Iwane Matsui, the overall commander of the Nanking operation. Did I footnote the quote? There aren't any footnotes in historical fiction. But I had made sure to actually cite the source of the quote as a part of the narrative. This allegation was more than specious. It was absurd, designed purely to create questions in the minds of those who would only see the bald accusation among the fount of news stories that were now accumulating in the final days before the election.

And so on. And so on.

But I had something special on my side, something that money cannot really buy, a powerful force that political consultants dream of but cannot invent. I had people supporting our campaign who had listened to what I said, who had examined the course of my life, and who believed that I was both capable and serious.

Volunteers were the true backbone of my political campaign, from the very beginning when more than a thousand people signed an online petition pledging (usually small) donations if I would step forward to run. Our campaign was outspent by a margin of at least five to one in the primary, and more than two to one in the general election—with the bulk of that money coming to us in the final two months. But no political campaign in the country had more dedicated volunteers. Early on, I nicknamed these thousands of self-motivated individuals my "ragtag guerrilla band." They worked the net-roots community. They went door-to-door. They put out yard signs, some of them purchasing the signs with their own money. They distributed bumper stickers. They worked the phone banks. They showed up at party gatherings throughout the commonwealth. They inspired me with the depth of their commitment. And, quite frankly, they had something to sell, something for all of us to believe in. Fix our national security. Bring fairness back to the American economic system. Make our national leaders accountable to the people.

By November 7, Election Day, like so many others who have stood for office during this especially vitriolic time, my greatest emotion was one of relief that the daily ordeal of character assassination was finally coming to an end. I had begun this journey nine months before on a quixotic note. I had not wavered from what I believed. Those who supported our campaign knew this, and knew also that if elected I would bring a lifetime of independent thinking to the Senate. But even many political supporters who had not read my works had begun referring to me as "the author of several racy novels." And it was undeniable that many who opposed me and voted against me now viewed me as a flag-burning, tax-raising, gay-marrying, pro-illegal-immigrant, gutless cut-and-runner; a plagiarizing, pedophilic, pornographic misogynist who wanted to bring his depravity to the hallowed grounds of the Capitol.

The election, decided by some 10,000 votes, had to rank as one of the nastiest campaigns in American history. And on November 9, 2006, when I climbed up onto the platform at the Arlington County courthouse square and raised my Marine son's combat boots into the air to declare final victory, a huge relief fell over me. I felt like I was stepping out of a sewer.

A week later, my nerves still raw from the unending months of nastiness, I declined to have my picture taken with President George W. Bush when the new members of the Senate were bused to the White House for a welcoming reception. I have since regained a more proper sense of courtesy. But those who took issue with this decision and editorialized against my reluctance to make instant peace might want to consider the poisonous climate that Karl Rove and his trained successors have deliberately brought to the American political process. In fact, one of the points I had made in my victory speech on November 9 was to call on the President to publicly renounce the tactics created by Mr. Rove, who after all has been Bush's very own political Svengali.

Most important, however, the election was behind us and it was time to do my part in helping to govern. Looking into the future, I was still on my feet when the bell rang at the end of the fifteenth round, and I was still swinging. We had won the fight. I had laid out clearly, without equivocation, the themes on which I would base my term in office. And the time had come to use my best attempts to address the problems that confront the country, without fear or favor. And so the question becomes: Where do we go from here, and what will it take to get there?

Sometimes the times are simply ready for a change. And sometimes it takes smart, tough leaders to change the times. And sometimes, like the present, we need the times and the leaders to coincide. When that happens, it is a time to fight.

CHAPTER THREE

THE UNCLES ON
MY SHOULDER

Most politicians will adamantly maintain, in all honesty, that they follow their consciences not only when they vote but also when they decide on the policy objectives they choose to pursue. And in truth, most of them do follow at least what might be called their political consciences. One's moral conscience reflects the deeply held personal values that an individual holds to be inarguable, so that if he goes against them he is in fact betraying his own sense of self. But it might be said that one's political conscience is just a tad bit different, reflecting instead the firmness of agreed-upon philosophical views, so that if he goes against them he is betraying his political community, and perhaps also the social contract he has made with his political supporters—but not in all cases his personal, moral conscience.

And so, if philosophy shapes political conscience, the true question is this: What are the inputs that feed your philosophy? When, if ever, can they be separated from your personal values? And what other inescapable factors of the American political equation must be addressed before you are able to act, politically, in order to see your philosophy prevail? In other words, to whom or what does your loyalty belong, especially if an issue is bigger or more complex than your basic sense of self? On this last point, former Congressman Ron Dellums, one of the most colorful and controversial members of the House when I was a committee counsel there in the late 1970s and when I was in the Pentagon in the mid-1980s, summarized his views with typical bluntness during a breakfast that he and I shared while I was Secretary of the Navy. "It's not hard for me to figure that out," he shrugged. "I dance with the ones that brought me."

Most politicians do. Different people, different factions, and different interest groups bring different politicians to the table, and vice versa—politicians bring different people to the table. Politics is, as they say, transactional, and make no mistake—money talks. It takes a lot of it to run for office. Individual contributors, public interest groups, lobbyists, political action committees, "bundles" of people gathered around a specific point of view or an overriding issue, all put their money down as a way to place their bets on different candidates. And when those candidates win, their backers generally expect a certain level of loyalty if not fealty, and of performance.

In some cases, this process results in officeholders who have made Faustian bargains in order to obtain the vast sums of money necessary to fund their campaigns. As a result, on the issues where the bargains they made come into play those politicians are akin to mouthpieces for special-interest groups—although in their own views this usually still amounts to answering their carefully defined political consciences. But politics, while transactional, is also subject to negotiation. And the best political leaders gain their financial and organizational backing by telling potential supporters clearly what they believe and what they will do, in the hopes that enough of them will agree, and feel passionately about that prospect, to invest the money and time necessary to give their chosen candidate a chance to prevail. In this sense, the candidates have guaranteed their backers not subjugation but leadership and creative thought, based on an agreed-upon set of philosophical principles.

I have my own way of dealing with these realities. Three factors come into play whenever I analyze a political issue. The first is the set of personal, family, and professional experiences that have shaped my view of justice and fairness. The second is my obligation to consider the unique demographic makeup of our society, since cultural referents play a special role in America. And the third is to consider the ever-evolving nature of our federal system under the parameters set out by the Constitution. On this last point, it is important always to consider the proper balance among the executive, legislative, and judicial branches of the federal government. It is also necessary to consider how strongly, and under what authority, the federal government should assert its jurisdiction on issues that have previously been handled at the state and local levels.

I like to say that in every book I have written, someone—a truth-teller, if you would—was looking over my shoulder, measuring the veracity and integrity of my words, ready to hold me accountable if I have not depicted their world fairly, honestly, and with authenticity. The same is true in analyzing and resolving the issues that confront America today. In every decision I make, I try hard to remain conscious of the struggles of those who have gone before me. Those people are, in a very real sense, my measure of accountability, ready to interpret my conduct under the harsh standards that define my conscience and their history. Their viewpoints, their hopes, their sacrifices, their disappointments, and especially their hard-earned notions of what is fair and what is not inform every proposal I make and every vote I take on the Senate floor.

More than twenty years ago, President Ronald Reagan inspired most of this nation after a period of extraordinary turmoil and self-doubt when he described our country as a shining city on a hill, a beacon that gives hope to the rest of the world. Indeed, in terms of the

American experience writ large, we are, or until the invasion of Iraq at least have always been, the leading example of a nation that proceeds from clear moral principles in our conduct of foreign policy and in the treatment of our own citizens. For all our blemishes, flaws, and scars, America has always had the inner strength to criticize itself and come out stronger.

But that "shining city" was no accident. It did not just happen. Nor was it simply the creation of a group of propertied intellectuals who sat down and wrote a document saying that this is what the country was going to look like and this is what its people were going to do. That shining city was built one brick at a time with human hands and human sacrifice, after a great deal of struggle by farmers, laborers, and soldiers who believed in the validity of our system, and who had to fight against the odds and the elements to get to the top of the hill before they could begin building the city in the first place.

Those of us who have in one way or another reached the apex of the American system would do well to take a moment every morning and reflect on how things look, and have always looked, in the eyes of those others who have been, and still are, struggling to survive, much less succeed. Their only time in the Capitol Building will be as tourists. They will never run a corporation or a film studio. They will never be the host of a talk show. They will never receive a million-dollar bonus. They will never summer in Nantucket or the Hamptons. They will never even set foot on a yacht, much less own one. But there would be no America without them. There would be no Silicon Valley to accommodate and further the careers of high-tech billionaires. There would be no safe city streets so that our Wall Street wonders, Tom Wolfe's famed "Masters of the Universe," could work their trade-leveraging magic. There would be no peaceful sea-lanes on which our importers and exporters could so automatically rely for the bountiful benefits of international commerce.

Here's a reminder for those at the very pinnacle of power, wealth, and influence in our society: Life as we know it in this country is more fragile than we might want to think. Without the people who do the hard work of our society, those who are at the top couldn't even buy their food, or get rid of their trash, or fix the pothole in the road they drive to work on. In other words, *you depend on them and you cannot succeed without them*. And without a true sense of societal fairness, the America we have created would in a short time unravel and disappear.

For the bulk of the rest of America, the great middle class on which our society so utterly depends, life is defined not by the prospect of enormous success but by overcoming struggle, by achieving some level of personal and financial security, by creating families with enough character and education to see us into the next generation, and by allowing for some enjoyment along the way.

My grandmother Georgia Frankie Doyle, who lived with our family from the time I was two until I was eight, epitomized this struggle for me very early in my life, and also gave me the insights to understand it. There is a New Testament passage from Paul's letters to the Romans that I long ago decided was the perfect summary of Granny's view of life. "We rejoice in our sufferings," wrote Paul, "knowing that suffering produces endurance, and endurance produces character, and character produces hope, and hope does not disappoint us, for God's love has been poured into our hearts."

In those early years, my grandmother filled a great void in my life, while my father, an Air Force pilot, was frequently deployed overseas or stationed at military bases where there was no family housing. With her slow, slow drawl and her ironic sense of humor, Granny was a born storyteller, a champion weaver of words, and her words carried with them the power and insights of a life lived hard but also honorably and well. In the Scots-Irish, Southern tradition, every night before we went to bed Granny made our family journey come alive with almost biblical power, giving us the names and dates, turning hardships into parables, defeats into moral lessons, individual travails into a continuum of pride, stubbornness, and ultimately of resilience. And as Paul wrote to the Romans, from resilience came character, and from character came hope. And one thing that Granny and my parents never ceased to preach was hope.

In the dark stillness of the different bedrooms where we lived, which at times included all four of my siblings in one room, the "old days" that went before us came alive. How she and her family traveled in a covered wagon at the turn of the century from western Tennessee just north of Memphis, south into Mississippi for a while, and finally into eastern Arkansas, crossing the Mississippi River on a flatboat barge and then dropping saplings across the swamps, making their own cord-wood roads.

How my mother and her other siblings grew up chopping cotton and picking strawberries, school coming in unpredictable fits and starts, the family sleeping on corn-shuck mattresses and brushing their teeth with twigs. How three of her eight children died of sudden, un-explainable fevers that raged up from nowhere and took them in a matter of days or, in the case of my mother's closest younger sister, Eunice, of typhoid fever itself. How she had left one baby son, who later died, on a blanket in the yard only to look out when she heard him scream-ing to see a hoop snake coiled around his belly, trying to squeeze him to death.

How my grandfather broke his hip in a farming accident, a bone infection becoming so severe that his skin broke permanently open, continually draining, and in the process slowly sapping out his life. How, lacking medical help, she kept two sets of homemade bandages for him, boiling one set every day to disinfect it while he wore the other bandage over the drain holes in his skin. How the world turned even harder after Birch Hays Hodges walked in from tending his truck patch one steaming-hot east Arkansas afternoon, told her he was tired, then lay down in his bed and died. How in her low-down downdest in the months that followed she had no other option but to steal feed corn meant for livestock that was still on the stalk in a nearby field and mix it with lard in order to feed my mother and her younger sister.

How two of Granny's sisters and my mother would take a borrowed pickup truck in the middle of the night, driving surreptitiously onto various absentee farms where they would cut and rick firewood for cookstoves that they would deliver to homes in nearby Searcy and Kensett before first light. *If you don't have a job, make a job.* And my father confirming the wages of those days, pointing out that when he met my mother at age seventeen her shoulders were like a boxer's and her hands were so tough from chopping cotton and cutting wood that they felt like the bark off a tree.

So many stories, years and years of them boiled down to bedtime parables so that all of us might count our blessings, then thank the Good Lord for the food that always was on our table, and for the knowledge that our daddy may not have been at home just then, but he was alive, out there serving our country, and that if he got hurt there would be a doctor nearby to mend him.

And how, not fully logical but powerfully certain in her emotions, Granny knew that Franklin Roosevelt had saved them. The mobilization that preceded World War II brought an ammunition factory to North Little Rock. Granny found a job making artillery shells, donning heavy anti-static work boots to keep from blowing herself up from some random electrical spark and spending long hours packing gunpowder into brass canisters. Every morning before first light a shuttle bus wound its way through the narrow backland roads, picking up my grandmother and others and taking them to the plant, the same bus dropping them off at home in the post-dusk darkness.

Then Granny saving up just enough money for two one-way bus tickets to California, providing her a Sophie's Choice moment as she decided that she could wait no longer, that it was time to take the gamble, bringing her youngest daughter, Carolyn, with her while she left my mother behind. Away they went, heading off into the complete unknown of a place that to her was nothing more than a magical name. After traveling nearly two thousand miles along the parched "Grapes of Wrath Highway" that cut through Arkansas, Oklahoma, Texas, New Mexico, Arizona, and finally across the desert of eastern California, she and my aunt Carolyn, then nine years old, arrived alone and unannounced in Santa Monica. And within weeks my pint-sized, Popeye-armed Granny, then a forty-nine-year-old widow, was working as Rosie the Riveter, crawling into the nose cones of bomber aircraft and inside spaces where few men could maneuver.

Struggle. Persist. Endure. Look back, but not in anger. Never lose hope. And in the end prevail, no matter how others might measure the magnitude of your victory. That was my Granny.

And that was my parents, as well. My mother never let us see the scars of those difficult years, instead referring to them indirectly, now and again, only to push us forward, shaming us with her own favorite homily if we ever started feeling sorry for ourselves.

"I felt so bad 'cause I had no shoes, till I met a man who had no feet."

Count your blessings.

To understand my father, one might begin with Pat Conroy's classic novel *The Great Santini,* a thinly disguised rendition of his own father, who was a Marine Corps fighter pilot, made into a wonderful movie starring Robert Duvall. My father was rough, loud, self-made, frequently drinking too much, and always full of impossible challenges. You could not slow my father down. He was such an optimist that on the weekends he woke up singing, banging on our bedroom doors and demanding that we wake up with him. On Saturday mornings he would inspect our rooms, making us stand before our dresser drawers at parade rest, coming to attention when he walked into the room.

"Dad," I would quietly, tiredly intone.

"Shut up," he would answer. "You're a corporal."

But to fully understand my father, you must consider only this. In those early days when he was back from Alaska, back from England, back from the Berlin Airlift, and back from remote assignments in Texas, he was stationed at Scott Air Force Base in Illinois, and still there was no family housing. Every Friday night when his work was finished, he would climb into his old Kaiser Automatic and drive 380 miles along narrow, two-lane roads so that he could be at our home in St. Joseph, Missouri, to wake us up on Saturday morning. Those were special moments for a young boy who had, through those long years of frequent separation, carried to bed every night a picture of him, standing at attention in his military uniform on a runway in Germany. He would happily and loudly terrorize us all weekend. And on Sundays, after an early dinner, he would give us each a hug, climb into the Kaiser, and head back down to Illinois so that he could be at work on Monday morning.

My father, loud and boisterous and yet rarely intimate in his emotions, never used the word, but that was love. Difficult, demanding, possessed of an exceptional but unrefined intellect, he has always been my greatest hero.

My father's family had pioneered in the mountains of southwest Virginia, eastern Tennessee, and Kentucky from the first days of the frontier settlements, well before the American Revolution, enduring the cultural and economic regression that came from this isolation even as their streak of adamant self-reliance grew stronger. Having migrated into the lush farmlands and thriving towns of Missouri, he became the first known Webb to finish high school. And twenty-six years later, after he had struggled through every conceivable form of part-time and night school courses in between deployments and remote military assignments, the Old Man finished college.

Never once did my father complain about the opportunities he might have had if he had grown up in different circumstances. And on that magical day just after they gave him his diploma, he stepped off the rostrum and walked across the packed gymnasium floor where the University of Omaha graduation ceremony was taking place, and pushed it into my shocked and embarrassed face.

"You can get anything you want in this country," he said, his face lit with fierce emotion. "And don't you ever forget it."

And I never have forgotten either that moment or his words. That was my Great Santini Dad. And it also is, in many ways, America itself.

There were plenty of other struggles to learn from as I was growing up, personal examples to motivate me and also to shape my view of how a society should work. What indeed is the true obligation of a government to its people? Where does self-reliance end, and where should the collective good be brought to bear in helping people solve their problems? We at the pinnacle of power engage in grand debates over such supposedly nonfederal responsibilities as retirement benefits, unemployment compensation, and skyrocketing medical costs, at a time when Social Security is in jeopardy, unions are out of favor, and one out of every seven Americans has no medical insurance whatsoever. For those who are insured, prescription costs are low and medical care is largely covered. But even for them, a huge part of the cost of medical care itself ends up in the hands of the insurance companies, just as the costs of prescription drugs go into the pockets of Big Pharma. And what of those who are not insured at all? Those on the other side avoid this dark reality, warning instead of the drift toward socialized medicine and claiming that government delivery systems would diminish the quality of our medical care.

Who is looking over my shoulder in such debates?

My uncle Ercil, Granny's wildest child, who returned to his hog farm after serving in the Army in World War II only to wrap his truck around a telephone pole one night, severing his spinal cord and leaving him paralyzed. Ercil was the kind of man who could have lived without needs or complaint, not only on his farm but probably even in the wilderness. He could hunt, he could fish. He could grow things and he could raise good hogs. He was a restless, active man and he did not take well to a wheelchair.

When I was a very young boy, I would accompany my mother and father to visit Ercil in the spinal-cord-injury ward at the Veterans Administration hospital in Memphis. The ward was always deathly quiet, the severely disabled veterans lying or sitting in a catatonic numbness in their identical metal-frame beds or wheeling silently along the center aisle in their wheelchairs. Identical large, narrow-necked bottles stood next to every bed, collecting urine that dripped unendingly from their catheters. In an odd way as a young boy, the dripping water bottles reminded me of sand pouring into hourglasses, measuring out the minutes before these somber, forgotten men who had once so willingly served their country would see the end of their lives. This was not a place of hope; it was an elephant's graveyard.

They taught Ercil leather crafts and how to repair a radio, neither of which captured his interest. He learned how to use hand controls, and with his veteran's pension he bought a car. He spent a lot of time driving from place to place, once all the way into Mexico, but usually ending up in a small back room in Granny's house. She rigged a wooden ramp from the yard up to her back door for his wheelchair. Her backyard was fitful and rough, so sometimes he would set up a charcoal grill inside her house and cook his meat there. It smoked up her ceiling, but she understood why he was doing it and did not confront him. He took his own life just after I returned from Vietnam.

Ercil left few possessions behind when he died. She asked, but no one could bring themselves to tell Granny that he had killed himself. I went to see her, and I could not tell her either. In a moment of sad serendipity, she gave me his fly-fishing rod and his Hank Williams record collection. I gave the rod to my mountain-man brother. I still keep the records.

What did Uncle Ercil's life and death teach me? On the one hand, if it had not been for the Veterans Administration hospital system, he would have had nowhere to turn at all. And yet on the other, if there had been a better program—indeed, a better government program— to assist him, he might have found a skill to suit him, and a way to live that did not torture his soul. That's not a hard concept. It just takes focus, and the decision of government leaders to do it.

I learned a simple, guiding concept about life and about leadership from the example of my uncle Tommy, my father's oldest sibling. Tommy was a legend among my father and his friends. Short, powerfully built, and quiet, in his younger days he was famously known for having fought three grown men at the same time and having beaten all three of them to a pulp. Tommy never started a fight, but he never ran from one, either. And he never wasted time with words. If he knew a man was going to attack him, Tommy always threw the first—and frequently the only—punch.

In the mid-1930s, my father's family moved into Elwood, Kansas, a tiny town just across the Missouri River from St. Joseph, Missouri. Elwood was not much of a town. Not long before the Webbs moved in, Elwood, Kansas, had actually been Elwood, Missouri. But one year when the inevitable spring floods receded they found the river had settled into a different course, leaving them on the Kansas side. Legend has it—and the maps prove it—that when the land issues arose between Missouri and Kansas over the river's rerouting, Missouri gladly gave Elwood to Kansas in order to keep the fledgling Rosecrans Airport, also now on Kansas soil, as a part of the state.

Soon after arriving, the four Webb brothers walked the mud streets to the local grocery store, where Bud Colwell, the toughest man in town, was holding court among a gathering of other young men. As the Webbs approached, Colwell eyed them and pointed to a nearby puddle, taunting them as well as the group that stood in front of him.

"You know," said Colwell, "I don't think there's a man in Kansas or Missouri who could put me in that puddle."

Uncle Tommy, who was smaller than Colwell and exactly the same age, did not say a word. He watched Colwell for a few seconds, then walked up and knocked him silly, rolling him into the puddle.

Hello, Elwood. The Webbs have arrived.

Colwell, a seriously tough man in his own right, later became my father's best lifetime friend and a role model whom I would come to call Uncle Bud. Bud was yet another self-made man who had overcome significant hardship, serving overseas for nearly three years during World War II and then building a successful business despite going legally blind. But Uncle Bud still shook his head in wonderment thirty years after that first night in Elwood, remembering Uncle Tommy's fighting skills. "Your uncle Tommy was the only man I've ever actually been afraid of," said Uncle Bud. "He had more nerve than anyone I've ever met."

Tommy was a complicated soul, a whiz at all things mechanical although largely uneducated, fierce and yet almost delicately emotional. One of my father's most vivid teenage memories was of waking up late at night as friends carried Tommy into the house, bleeding profusely from a knife that had been thrust deep into his chest, just missing his heart. Still conscious and still cursing although on the edge of death from loss of blood, Tommy had been ambushed in an alley after an argument over a woman. After moving to California when World War II began, Tommy found work in the Long Beach Naval Shipyard. When my father deployed overseas, my uncle Charlie hand-made a survival knife and worried about how he might get it to him. Ever sentimental, Uncle Tommy left work on a Friday and took a train from Long Beach to Kansas in order to give my father the knife. He stayed long enough to have a cup of coffee with his little brother and then caught the next train back to Long Beach, arriving on Monday morning, not missing a day of work.

After the war, Tommy decided to cash in on a new wave of technology. Trained as an electrician and possessed of an amazing technical mind, he bought himself a television set, put a mirror in front of it, and watched what happened as he took out different tubes and disconnected various wires. Then he hung out a shingle and opened a successful TV-repair business. When air-conditioning came along he did the same thing, and soon he had two businesses.

Tommy had a hard side, but as my father used to put it, he was also the most emotionally driven of the Webb boys. A few years after the war ended, his second daughter, a two-year-old born two months before my own birth, was having a lunchtime picnic on their front porch. A car pulled into the driveway and the driver accidentally hit the accelerator instead of the brake, smashing her to death against the porch steps in her own front yard. Unable to process the tragedy, Tommy was consumed by grief for years. My father repeatedly admonished us never to even discuss the child's death in front of Tommy.

Uncle Tommy was deeply proud when I was accepted to the Naval Academy. At the end of Christmas break during my plebe year, my parents drove me down from Vandenberg Air Force Base to Burbank, where I caught a midnight charter flight back to Annapolis. We walked inside the terminal and there was Uncle Tommy, having decided to drive more than 100 miles round-trip from San Bernardino with two of my cousins, just to shake my hand. It was the only time I ever saw him wearing a tie.

Others who knew Tommy may have come away with different feelings, but to me he was the born leader, the perennial big brother, a man who stood on his own two feet, who did the best with what he had, who would fight ferociously when he had to, but who was not ashamed to wear his heart on his sleeve. And I will pay him the ultimate compliment. Uncle Tommy would have made a hell of a Marine. He was the kind of quiet, sure-footed leader that people would have followed anywhere, because they would have known that in addition to his toughness he truly cared.

I was seventeen years old before I had my first "man-to-man talk" with Uncle Tommy. I had been a boxer for several years by then, and he, having been among other things a "packing house pro" fighter in his youth, showed me a move or two, still powerfully built and agile in his fifties. After a while, I had a chance to ask him what he was proudest of in all the things he had done in his life.

Tommy didn't hesitate, and every time I have faced a crisis of honor in my adult life his words have come back to me:

"I've never kissed the ass of any man."

I also learned from the experiences of my uncle Paul, who watched most of his hand, including his three middle fingers, disappear on the wrong side of a saw when he was working as a "side matcher" at an oak flooring mill just up from Doniphan's Pond in Judsonia, Arkansas. Uncle Paul was a talented carpenter, even away from the mill. Side matchers were skilled tradesmen, responsible for operating the machines that cut tongues and grooves into the flooring. But there were few worker benefits in Arkansas in the 1950s. For the better part of a year, Paul stayed at home, watching the hand mend and learning how to use what was left of it. And then he reported back to work, spending twenty more years at the mill, finally retiring as the senior side matcher in the plant.

During the time Uncle Paul was recovering, my cousin Jerry Paul—a bright, focused boy who was like a big brother to me, and who had even taught me to read—died in a still-unexplained incident while tending trot lines in a nearby pond. As these tragedies enveloped his family my cousin Johnny, the same age as I, took on the demeanor and responsibilities of an adult, beginning at the age of twelve. His maturity and sense of responsibility both motivated and embarrassed me when we would visit Arkansas. I was busy being a kid, struggling with kid-sized problems. Johnny was helping to care for his family, putting in a vegetable garden and a chicken pen to help feed them, and later graduating from high school as his class valedictorian.

Enlisting in the Air Force right after he graduated from high school, Johnny scored so highly on aptitude tests that he was immediately sent a university-level Russian-language program. But soon thereafter his retinas hemorrhaged, as did those of three other cousins, causing him to go legally blind, possibly a genetic condition but also possibly from a virus that chickens were known to carry, which can be transferred to humans in the years following puberty. And so in the space of a few short years Uncle Paul had lost most of his hand, he and my aunt Ima Jean had lost one child to an early, unexplained death, and four of the remaining seven children had lost their sight.

What did I learn from this? An appreciation for tragedy. An understanding that we are sometimes visited with circumstances that we do not deserve. A respect for the resilience and for the quiet courage that Uncle Paul and his family were required to exhibit every day as they pushed forward with their lives. An adamant belief in the reality that strong, independent people sometimes undergo changes that are larger than their ability to handle without outside support. And to count my blessings.

There are other stories, but for now they are best left untold. This is a book about the place of government in our lives, and how our individual lives must sometimes be lived under the constraints, or with the necessary assistance, of our government.

different origins and have simply been sorting things out ever since. Immigrants have come in waves over a period that now spans three centuries. Different cultural groups arrived during different points in the evolution of the American experience, and also at many different geographical regions and locations. As historians frequently comment, our nation began with precious few people, no societal infrastructure, and no economic base. It then grew in two different ways: internally, from the pool of people who had already come to America, and externally, through continuous immigration. Some internal growth created huge advantages; other internal growth, as with the Appalachian Mountain regions and a great portion of the South, resulted in cultural regression. As such, there is a vast difference between having been a pioneer, a settler, or an immigrant. Different arrival times coinciding with vastly dissimilar stages of our country's development created markedly different starting points in terms of how various cultural groups have been able to take advantage of opportunities in America, as well as how America has assimilated their own contributions.

In addition, these widely varying cultural groups had broadly different historical and governmental experiences before they came to America. Some have long traditions of education, dating back thousands of years. Some have little educational tradition at all. Some are descended from generations of entrepreneurial spirit. Some come from cultures that are purely agrarian or have for a variety of reasons never been exposed to the world of business. Some come from countries with rich democratic histories and from the outset of their arrival have elevated our policy debates. Others, particularly our most recent wave of immigrants from Latin America and Asia, come from countries that instead have long experiences with tyranny, autocracy, and corruption, and have little comprehension of the basic notions of governmental fairness, openness, and accountability to the electorate.

Over the course of my life I have lived among, worked alongside, argued with, and come to respect a wide pastiche of the cultures that make up America. Growing up on the move as an Air Force "brat" and then serving in the Marine Corps provided me with an entire young life of what sociologists might want to call "cultural immersion." There is no institution in our society that is more fully representative of America's vast diversity than the military. That reality of the military's internal makeup was reinforced by the external opportunity to live in different communities across the country as our family relocated with every new assignment.

Due to my father's military postings, by the time I reached the age of twenty I had lived in Missouri, Arkansas, Texas, Missouri again, Illinois, England, Missouri one more time, Texas again, Alabama, California, Nebraska, California again, Maryland, and then Virginia. In most of these postings during those transitional years when military "quality of life" programs were in their infancy, there was little on-base housing and my father was forced to find rental homes for the family. This resulted in frequent moves, with all the attendant disruptions, even in between the larger reassignments. In Illinois, once we were allowed to join my father, we lived in three houses in three years. In England, we lived in three houses in two years. In Texas, we moved three times in one year. In our first California assignment, we moved three times in two years. In Nebraska, we lived in three homes during a three-year assignment.

Military moves were tough. But as Granny would have put it, when it comes to understanding the cultural dynamics of our country, I can only count my blessings.

I lived in the oil-rich, cattle-heavy Texas Panhandle for a year while my father was stationed at Amarillo Air Force Base, a place so arid that, as he put it, if you squirted a hose up into the air only half the water came back down. My sixth-grade teacher, Mrs. Pansy Savage, made us practice our handwriting by copying Psalm 1 over and over again, all year, until to this day I can remember most of it by heart. *Blessed is the man who walketh not in the counsel of the ungodly, nor standeth in the way of sinners, nor sitteth in the seat of scoffers . . . But his delight is in the law of the Lord, and in that law doth he meditate, both day and night* . . . One of my classmates was a fifteen-year-old boy just in from the sharecropping fields of east Texas, where he had rarely been to school. Another classmate was his thirteen-year-old brother, who later left the school because he had contracted what they called "the sleeping sickness" in the swamps. My father was a born out-doorsman who taught me to hunt and fish before I could even read. We spent weekends camping in the famous Palo Duro Canyon, which still boasted thin herds of wild buffalo.

I lived in Montgomery, Alabama, during a time of great racial tensions, just after a woman named Rosa Parks fueled the civil rights movement by famously refusing to sit in the "Negro" section at the back of a city bus. I saw the other, socioeconomic side of that painful racial debate as well, going to junior high school with large numbers of white children bused in from outlying farm areas who wore no shoes to school, even on the coldest of days, and who even played football barefoot. Boxing was a favorite pastime in our physical education classes. I developed an unexplainable passion for it. I also watched a seventeen-year-old ninth-grader pick a fistfight with our physical ed-ucation teacher, pounding on him for a good ten minutes. He was thrown out of school and promptly joined the Navy.

I lived for a while in Santa Maria, California, which at that time was the strawberry capital of America, going to school with numerous Mexican-born boys and girls whose families had come north to work in the fields. Some of them were relegated to "special education" classes because they knew very little English and there were no "En-glish as a second language" programs to teach them. Nothing much was taught in "special ed." It was a holding tank until a kid could turn sixteen and leave school permanently.

I lived at Vandenberg Air Force Base during its earliest days, just after it had been converted from an old Army training camp left over from World War II and Korea. The 85,000-acre base was as remote as a ghost town during those days. The outside world was far away. We rarely saw it. Other than our schoolteachers, military people and their families were our only daily contacts. It was a common experience to pick up my .22 rifle or a shotgun, climb over a back fence, and walk through six miles of wilderness to a surging, unswimmable section of beach along the Pacific Ocean, without ever seeing another human being.

I could spring loose a deer or even a lynx from the brush as I walked past rows of eucalyptus trees, through thick hedges of briars and patches of ice plant, and along the dusty ridges. Rabbits were there for the hunting, classified as varmints by game wardens because they carried disease. My brother Gary and I took turns, one with the rifle and the other flushing out rabbits by charging into briars and weed patches as if we ourselves were hunting dogs. Rattlesnakes slithered along the trails. My brother, a dead-eye dinger with nerves of steel, calmly aimed a bow and arrow at a six-footer that had coiled next to one dusty weed patch, ready to strike. Unflinching, Gary shot it through the throat, then brought the rattlesnake home and made a belt out of its skin. Sea lions and cormorants were everywhere along the shoreline. Surprising forms of sea life made their way into and out of the tidal pools. We could camp along the sand dunes, as alone and unbothered as if this were our private wildlife preserve.

I found work as a cleanup boy at the base's only movie theater. I also sold newspapers in the mess halls, learning early to wheedle and cajole young airmen until they would give me a dime and buy a paper just to get rid of me.

"Buy a paper, mister?"

"Go away, kid. I can't read."

"Buy it from me and I'll read it to you!"

"Jeez, give the kid a dime, will you?"

I was thirteen. A couple of the cooks in one of the mess halls adopted me, sneaking me desserts while I made the rounds.

We went to school in an abandoned World War II hospital, its sprawling, creaking old wards converted into classrooms. Everyone was new when they opened up the school, teachers and students alike, causing a surprising form of social and disciplinary chaos when one considers that the school was on a military base. There were few rules, either in the classroom or on the playgrounds. There were a lot of fights. And frankly, there was very little learning.

I spent my last three years of high school among the farms and small towns just outside Omaha, Nebraska. I found this part of Nebraska difficult and prejudiced at first. In contrast to Vandenberg, where there had been no rules, in small-town Nebraska it seemed that everywhere there were rules, usually to protect a social structure that those of us from the outside could not even see. And none of the rules were written down, so they could not be learned. But in time, as with everywhere else, I adjusted.

And always there was the outdoors, which was my youthful passion. A couple of times each summer there would be fishing trips spent in rough cabins on the wooded banks of wild, scarcely populated lakes in central and northern Minnesota. My father's greatest pleasure from his own youth was to be at the nose of an outboard-motor-driven flatboat, stalking a fat largemouth bass or trolling for a northern pike. It was addictive. To this day, my brother and I and both of our sons still talk animatedly of rods and lures and places and methods, not so that we might hire a charter captain who would bring us in a swordfish but in order to work the weed beds and the root-snaggled shoreline of a quiet lake in order to out-think and wrestle home a lunker bass.

In Nebraska, the farmlands were vast and open. Corn was king. Large coveys of fat quail hunkered down in the corn and milo fields, along with an occasional swift, low-flying pheasant. I spent untold hours in those fields, sometimes just to hike and at others hunting without the help of dogs. The birds would run along the rows if you were near them. We would walk the rows toward the open-area drafts between the fields in order to force the birds into the air so that we could shoot them. I loved the high sky and the rolling hills of the farmlands. In the fall, the sky would fill with thousands of geese, heading south, taking guidance from the river below them. I felt free and easy with my shotgun in my hand and usually my brother at my side, with a chew of Red Man in my lower cheek.

I worked after-school jobs all three years, mostly at the Offutt Air Force Base commissary, bagging groceries for tips. Bagging people's groceries was a great learning experience for a boy in his midteens. There was an art to it, or at least a process, chatting with the customer as I packed the bags, making sure the cold things went with the cold things and the cans went at the bottom and the bread and eggs went on top, pushing the cart with the groceries into the parking lot and placing them carefully into the car, then waiting for that magical moment when they would decide how much to pay me for my effort. Working for tips tended to focus my mind on doing the best job possible—good job, reasonable tip; bad job, bad tip. It also helped me learn how to read people, much as being the "new guy" in so many different schools had helped me learn how to read a room. Because sometimes you could do a perfect job and still some self-important jerk would give you no tip at all.

And, intuition being what it is, after a year or so on the job, it became pretty easy to pick out which personalities were which.

I played baseball in the summer, making all-star and pitching a no-hitter when I was fifteen. In the winter I fought—Junior Gloves, Golden Gloves, and in smokers in Nebraska, South Dakota, and Iowa. I learned a lot about fighting, and I learned a lot about people. The Winnebago Indian tribe had a reservation just south of Sioux City. They turned out great young fighters who won championships early and then seemed to burn out by the time they reached the age of twenty, from liquor and the social structure of the reservations. The Winnebagos rarely talked as they waited in the dressing rooms to fight. In fact, they rarely seemed even to warm up. But they would step into the ring and fight like hell.

In South Omaha, a Mexican community that had come to Nebraska to work on the railroad in the early 1900s produced some very fine fighters. In North Omaha, along a well-known section that we all called 24th Street, a large black community not only fed the boxing programs but also turned out a legion of first-rate track stars and football players, including football great Gayle Sayers and his older brother, Roger, one of the finest sprinters in the country.

I made friends across all of these racial and ethnic lines. We also did our best to beat each other's brains out when we were in the ring. Just as important, I had the privilege of being coached by an African American named Harley Cooper, who was not only one of the finest athletes I have ever seen but also was a wise and inspirational role model. Harley, an Air Force sergeant who at the time was nearly thirty years old, won the National Golden Gloves heavyweight championship during my senior year in high school. In 1964, he won a spot on the

Olympic boxing team, only to develop a kidney infection in Tokyo, his backup winning the gold medal. He was smart. He was thoughtful. He had enormous integrity. And he helped me sort out more than one problem that had nothing to do with boxing.

At a time when our country was finally beginning to struggle with the implications of prejudice and discrimination, I knew the truth, from the brutal honesty of what we used to call "fighting under the lights."

Fighting under the lights was more than simply a sport. For a boy with an active mind and a rebellious spirit, it was a small piece of wild-eyed glory. Imagine you are fifteen years old. Your entire world is uncertain, filled with constant change and frequent disappointment. You go to school but you are not really there. You go to work but this is not a place that brings respect. You do not know fully who you are, and you especially do not know where your life is heading. Every day you train in solitude, hitting the heavy bag, running mile after mile, wrapping your hands with cloth strips to protect the knuckles, shadowboxing in front of large mirrors, sparring with people who are older than you, often heavier than you, and frequently better than you, focusing, focusing, when the rest of your life is unfocused. You do not know where you will be in two years but you know that in two weeks you will be in the ring, in front of hundreds if not thousands of people, and that if you are not ready you will be humiliated. You work on your jab, you pivot off your hook, you practice your combinations—jab, jab, cross, hook, cross, uppercut, jab, jab, cross. You get up on your toes, practicing your footwork, bobbing and weaving, shifting into your lateral moves.

Then the night finally comes and when it is your turn you walk slowly from the dressing room along the narrow row between the seats, heading for the ring. You climb into the ring, often as not seeing your opponent for the very first time. The ring is bright, sunlike, on a raised platform above the floor, and all around you it is dark except for the camera flashes and the quick sparks of cigarettes being lit or smoked. In your corner there is a resin box. You do a little dance in the resin box, making sure that the leather soles of your high-top boxing shoes are scratched with it so that you will not slip on the canvas. Your name is announced and the referee brings you to the center of the ring. He gives you and your opponent the basic instructions—fight fair, keep your punches above the belt, no hitting on the break, no hitting after the bell.

You and your opponent touch gloves and you return to your corner. The crowd cheers and applauds. You are fifteen. They are excited, maybe even betting on you, and in any event applauding you for having the courage to step inside the ring to face someone your own size, win or lose. As in a play, your coach dramatically takes your robe off your shoulders. You raise a gloved fist into the air, dancing confidently, staring hotly into your opponent's eyes. Your face and chest are greased with Vaseline so that your opponent's gloves will not tear your skin. You're all glistening and shiny from it, like in a muscle magazine. You are not wearing headgear, and you are wearing eight-ounce gloves, which when they land on you feel like smoothed fists. There are no easy fights. This is going to hurt. Win or lose, for the next week after this fight you will not even be able to hear your teacher talk to you in class, because your popped ears will be ringing too loud.

The bell rings. You dance toward the center of the ring. You are on your own. There is nowhere to run, nowhere to hide, and nobody else to blame. Whatever else may happen, your pride and survival demand that you focus on the job at hand no matter how exhausted you feel and no matter much it hurts. You don't know it yet, but you have already assimilated one of life's preeminent realities: that sometimes pain is an unavoidable prerequisite for respect, even for self-respect.

All of this happens before the fight even starts. And you are fifteen.

These constant military moves also caused a good bit of educational disruption. Between the fifth and tenth grades, I attended nine public schools, in England and all across the country. I saw the entire spectrum, ranging from the good to the bad to the ugly. In England, where the "state school" system allowed individual advancement rather than automatic class promotions at the end of a school term, I had gone through four grades in two years. This caused the school system in Texas to puzzle about what to do with me when I returned as a ten-year-old who had already finished the sixth grade. At the suggestion of my mother they split the difference, putting me in the sixth grade again so that I would be one year ahead of my age group instead of two. In California after a year in Alabama, as I began the eighth grade they tested the entire class and put four of us in a separate room so that we could study at our own pace—an early equivalent of the "gifted/talented" programs.

Four schools later, continually lost in the turmoil of adolescence, the shuffle of new schools, new teachers, and new classmates, I was matriculating into my second tenth-grade school in Nebraska, and the dislocations had taken their toll. I was viewed as a "second track" student, let loose early every afternoon so that I could go to my job as a bag boy at the base commissary. I was taking general science instead of chemistry. I had to repeat second-year algebra due to a dismal performance the first time around. And I was relegated to what we generally referred to as "dummy English."

Two realities saved me from being forever branded by all of this confusion. The first was that I could always do well on standardized tests. At a time when I was blowing second-year algebra, my counselor brought me into her office and told me that I had received the fifth-highest score in our school on the PSAT math test. I also had just received a composite score in the 99th percentile of all students in America on the Iowa Educational Development Tests. The second reality was that I really, earnestly wanted to make something of my life, and although the moves had taken their toll, they also had provided some interesting upsides. Ever the new guy as I began each new school year, I had definitely learned how to read a room. Under the less-than-welcoming scrutiny of thirty new faces, one tends to find friends fast and especially to locate potential problems early. And I knew that my high school counselor, brusque as she was, was a friend.

She asked me what I wanted to do. I told her that my parents, lacking any real educational track, had few referents to use in guiding me, but that I wanted to go to college and I wanted to follow my father into the military. The military was now something of a family business—my brother would later serve in the Marine Corps, and both of my sisters would marry military men. I liked the "git 'er done" attitude of military people. I liked their sense of duty. The frequent moves had been difficult on one level, but the constant motion also had its own seduction. I had lived in more than twenty homes by then, and I was bitten by wanderlust.

But instead of the Air Force, I knew that I wanted to be on the ground. I loved hunting, fishing, and camping. My greatest pleasures in life were when I was in the outdoors, or when I was in a completely new environment and learning to interact with people whom I had not previously known. Like so many in the age group that grew up in the shadows of World War II, I had watched the television documentaries and read about the battles. I told the counselor that I wanted to be a soldier, like the men who landed at D-Day, or maybe a Marine, like those who fought on Iwo Jima.

She worked with me. My test scores, she told me, showed that I could handle any intellectual challenge if I put my mind to it. But looking at my grades, she was frank. They were not good enough to qualify for a military academy out of high school. And then she told me of another option.

The Army had no such programs then, but the Navy had an ROTC scholarship program that allowed a certain percentage to become Marine Corps officers. Luckily for my situation, two factors weighed every bit as heavily as one's grades: The Navy administered its own standardized aptitude test, and if one passed, a lot of consideration was given to personal interviews with two selection officers. Anyone who scored above a certain point on the standardized test could get into the interviews. She wrote a strong letter of recommendation. I took the test, and along with eleven other students from my high school went into Omaha for the interviews. The other eleven included our class valedictorian, our class salutatorian, an all-state basketball player, and an all-district football player.

The first interviewer was a "Mustang" officer who had served as an enlisted sailor and had worked his way up to the rank of commander. As luck would have it, the commander was a boxing fan and had seen me fight. He liked the fact that I had worked all through high school. He asked me what I was going to do if I didn't get the scholarship. I told him that I was going into the military, one way or the other, and that if I didn't get the scholarship he would probably be seeing me next year, same time, same place. Looking over my record, he told me that the naval service was looking for leaders, and that if the leadership and the potential were there, the grades would come. After the interview, he stopped by to see me several times when he was shopping at the base commissary. And I knew I had another friend.

The second interviewer was a Navy captain, an engineer who had graduated from the Naval Academy. During the interview he posed an impossible question, which was a routine procedure designed to test the poise of the interviewee: How do we get the mud out of the Missouri River?

"Captain," I said, my mind working furiously, "I've been thinking about this. You shut down the traffic on the river for twelve hours a day. You run a filtering belt across the river, and on both sides of the river you set up stations that look like car washes, culverts where the hoses flush the mud out of the filters as the belts rotate. After the mud is flushed out of the filters, you have it flow down into drain holes underneath the culverts. Bring trucks to the drain holes and collect the dirt in the truck beds. Then have the trucks drive the dirt back upriver to sell to the farmers. Captain, that's topsoil! The farmers will buy it and the system will pay for itself!"

Actually, I still think the idea has possibilities . . .

Of the twelve of us, I was the only one who received the scholarship. I can still recall the thrill of going to the mailbox on that cold Nebraska Saturday morning and nervously taking out the letter. We had learned the drill—a thin envelope meant a rejection, while a fat envelope filled with additional papers to be filled out meant acceptance. I had a fat envelope. I danced like a demon in the driveway. I thanked the Good Lord. And I vowed that I would never betray the confidence that had been shown in my potential.

This experience created in me a very strong feeling that America needs to remain a nation of second chances for people who somehow get knocked off track. And in retrospect, of course, my "dummy math, dummy English" experience remains no small irony for one who later graduated with an engineering degree and a law degree, and who has made his living largely off the written word.

I left Nebraska three days after graduating from high school, as my family moved to a new posting back at Vandenberg Air Force Base, and I never looked back. I spent a year at the University of Southern California on the NROTC scholarship, standing first in leadership among my peers both semesters. At the suggestion of my supervising officer and with the not-so-quiet urging of my father, I then applied to the Naval Academy, reporting for the rigors of Plebe Summer less than a month after the academic year ended at Southern Cal.

I saw much more of the face of America during my time as a Marine. No system is perfect, and few humans are without some ethnic predispositions, usually involving a fundamental desire to protect one's own. But the military at its best creates a special form of fusion among its members, and the Marine Corps among all the branches of service has throughout its history been able to create a cohesion that lasts for a lifetime once a young man or woman earns the title of Marine. But at the same time, no one checks their cultural history at the door when they put on a Marine Corps uniform. In fact, comparing ethnic backgrounds and discussing life "before the Corps" is an ancient, favorite pastime of all Marines.

Within weeks of taking over as a rifle platoon commander in Vietnam, I had learned and relearned more about hardscrabble, blue-collar America than I could ever have garnered from any book, research grant, or academic career. We were fighting a war under enormously difficult tactical conditions—a war that would eventually produce more than 100,000 killed or wounded for the Marine Corps alone. We in the infantry battalions of the Fifth Marine Regiment lived constantly in the "bush," without tents, cots, hot food, or clean water, without bunkers to fight from or barbed wire around us, and usually without access to roads or any form of motor vehicle. The tropical elements of Vietnam were upon us; we could not escape them. Ringworm, hookworm, pinworm, ulcerous skin sores, shrimp fever, and malaria were common.

The war was everywhere, beginning right outside the perimeter
of foxholes we would dig at every new location, which usually changed
every few days. But inside the perimeter, through the long, scorching-
hot days or underneath the chilling, drenching monsoon rains, when
we were not on patrol or manning the foxholes at night, the talk always
was of home.

Every day, all day, my Marines traded stories. And those stories,
pieced together, offered up an America that few in any other environment could ever compile. About being born in Puerto Rico and growing up in the ethnically mixed neighborhoods of Philadelphia,
dropping out of school in the tenth grade, and washing dishes in hotel
restaurants. About what it was like to do shift work in the automobile
factories in Detroit. About working in the steel mills near Allentown,
Pennsylvania. About being born in Mexico, crossing the border into
Brownsville, Texas, at the age of twelve, then leaving school at sixteen
to find work. About raising horses in middle Tennessee. About working in the lumber mills in western Oregon. About living as a black family and working the tobacco fields of eastern North Carolina. About
dropping out of Vanderbilt and enlisting after a college debate about
the validity of the war effort. About being raised on the wild, drug-in-
fested streets of Harlem. About the small farms and wildcat oil fields
near Grayville, Illinois.

About life as a true, long-haired hippy, selling trinkets in the parks
of San Francisco. About a special Irish American neighborhood called
South Boston, and its longtime Marine Corps traditions. About the
moonshine stills and small family farms of the North Carolina and east
Tennessee mountains. About being a Mexican in love with an Anglo
girl in Chicago, and enlisting in the Marine Corps to prove to her father he was a man. About reform school in New Jersey, and enlisting
in the Marine Corps to avoid a second jail term. About farm work in
small-town Iowa. About a celebratory binge in Massachusetts where
father and son happily took on a bar together and ended up sharing
the same jail cell for a weekend. About growing up as a pacifistic
Seventh-Day Adventist in Kentucky, then becoming an infantry Ma-

rine because, oddly and ironically, although his three brothers all had become medics, he could not stand the sight of blood.

But when the flak jackets and helmets went on, when the bandoliers of ammo were strapped around their bodies, when the grenades were stuffed into their pockets, when the patrols went out or when the fighting holes were manned at night, they were all business. They were in Vietnam, and they were all Marines. They had learned to work together, to take care of each other, and to serve a common good. And no matter what else they would do in their lives, they would always carry with them that one additional word, that identifier that in many ways transcends, and in other ways complements, their ethnic backgrounds: Marine.

And when we are at our very best, that is America as well. We should never abandon or deny the power of our own ethnic heritage. But we must all come together to defend the common good.

I have lived among and seen other aspects of our many cultures since those days. I learned for the first time of the ferocious intellects and highly trained minds of our legal community during my time in law school, and of the strong academic traditions that are emblematic of the Jewish heritage. I have observed many of the other ethnic groups that came to America from the perspective of their nation of origin. I've been able to spend time in dozens of foreign countries as a military officer, a government official, a journalist, a novelist, a screenwriter, and a tourist. And I have interacted on a daily basis with much of the "new" America in the neighborhood where I live, which has become a pulsing center of migration from Latin America, East Asia, and many different parts of the Muslim world.

The high school that three of my children attended in eastern Fairfax County, Virginia, hosts more than 100 different nationalities and was featured in *National Geographic* magazine not long ago as the "most diverse" high school in the country. These were not Embassy kids. At that time, JEB Stuart High School had the highest percentage of school-breakfast and school-lunch programs of any school in the entire Washington, D.C., area, other than two all-black schools in the city itself. Many students were the children of illegal immigrants. Many others were lower-income Muslims who had moved to the area to be near a prominent mosque. My son's football team looked as though it had been formed by a committee at the United Nations: a Palestinian quarterback, a Cambodian running back, a center from El Salvador, a Nicaraguan over here, an Afghani at defensive end, a Greek-born placekicker, an Ethiopian over yonder, a few Irish kids, a few redneck kids, and more than a few black kids. Meanwhile, the Pakistani kids got together and formed a cricket club.

Finally, I have watched the struggles of the immigrant community, and the fresh voice it is giving to many of our challenges, in the experiences of my wife and of her family, who escaped from Vietnam on a boat as the Communists were completing their final conquest in 1975. My wife, Hong Le, came to America as a refugee at the age of seven, unable to speak a word of English. Her father had been a fisherman in Vietnam. One of seven children, she grew up in a household where neither parent spoke English. Among other jobs, she worked in shrimp-processing and crab-processing plants while in her teens. She also was selected for a prestigious magnet high school in her hometown of New Orleans, won academic scholarships to college, worked as a courtroom interpreter for Vietnamese civil and criminal cases during her undergraduate years, and finally graduated from Cornell Law School.

When speaking about this journey recently before a conference of first-generation immigrants, Hong made a few points that I believe embody both the uniqueness of our country and the quality of those who thrive in it.

"I will never lose sight of the reality that it was the American Navy that rescued my family from the open sea," Hong pointed out. "It was the American government that established a system of refugee camps that allowed us to be sponsored and assimilated into communities across this country. And it was the openness of the American system that allowed someone like me, who grew up in a home where neither parent spoke any English, to work hard, to persist, to gain access to the highest quality of America's educational system, and to achieve a professional career—all in the space of less than twenty years."

To me, that truly is America at its best.

Amid all of this happy news, a caveat is in order. With respect to the many cultures that make up America, a special point must be raised. The "badges of slavery" are real. Black America has made many gains during my lifetime, developing a growing middle class and losing much of the stigma that was strongly and undeniably attached to one's African heritage when I was young. But a huge portion of black America is still in crisis. And the rest of America should continue to remember the reasons why this is so. Ours is a rapid-paced nation. We tend to lose patience with ideas that fade from fashion and with people who can't keep up. And yet, almost all of us are still in some way affected by the momentum of events that happened a generation or more ago. And if you haven't had the true opportunity to catch up, you can't keep up.

As we consider the many experiences that make up America, it is important that we not lose sight of the special circumstances that African Americans have faced throughout our history. Their struggle has been unique, not only because of slavery but, just as important, because of what happened after slavery ended. I wrote about this phenomenon in detail in my book *Born Fighting*. I will have more to say about it later in this narrative. But as America becomes ever more ethnically diverse, and as the Hispanic population overtakes African Americans as the dominant minority group, there is an increasing tendency to forget the historical reasons that were used to justify affirmative-action concepts in the first place. And those reasons applied to the special circumstances of African Americans.

Almost every ethnic group, white and minority, can speak of obstacles that they faced upon coming to America or after having settled here. But African Americans are unique in that the barriers they faced were put there through the force and formality of the law. This was true not only during the slave era and the Jim Crow era of a century ago. It remained true well into my own lifetime. It was the government itself that required blacks to attend separate schools, denied them higher public education, made them use separate toilets and separate drinking fountains, mandated that they use separate seat-ing sections on public transportation, caused them to live in separate housing areas, humiliated them, dehumanized them, encouraged their public abuse, and even prevented them from exercising their right to vote.

I make this comment not as a political statement, but as an observation from history, as well as from personal experience. I was fortunate to grow up inside the military, which was the first institution in our society to mandate the removal of racial restrictions. For all the argument and debate about racial fairness in the military, an issue that came to dominate much of the Vietnam era, I saw with my own eyes the differences between the military and the outside world. And as I grew to adulthood, that personal experience made the outside differences even more glaring.

It was not until I was well into grade school that government-directed segregated school systems were declared unconstitutional. It was not until I was in college that discrimination in employment on the basis of race was banned by federal law. I was eighteen years old when poll taxes, a policy designed to keep poor whites and blacks from voting, were finally declared unconstitutional. I was twenty-one years old when the Supreme Court finally overturned the laws of my own state of Virginia that had precluded people of different races from marrying.

One other precatory note is in order. The word "multicultural" seems to have become a lightning rod for blowback among many commentators because of its frequent use during the culture wars of the 1970s. But that usage—and indeed that debate—has nothing to do with the issues raised in this chapter.

The respected columnist Georgie Anne Geyer raised this point in a recent article, lamenting that the "multiculturalism" arguments ginned up in the academic circles of Europe and America, pervading the debates of the seventies, "still doom[s] us today. It sounded so good," Geyer writes. "Not only were all people 'created equal,' as our founding documents had it, but equal opportunity was to be solemnly strived for, and men and women of every stripe and culture were to be guaranteed equal outcome. There was also the underlying (and insulting) idea that those 'others' had no culture or memory or history of their own—they were just like us. They wanted the same things that we did."

The truth is of course the opposite—we are all gloriously different, and those differences energize us. Some people resist the notion, but we are, and always have been, a people of many parts. We can and must insist on a common ground that binds us, a common language, and a common good. We know, as President Andrew Jackson once famously said, that "equality of talents . . . can not be produced by human institutions." We must, as a nation and as a government, struggle with such issues as illegal immigration and the extent that portions of the so-called diversity programs improperly affect fairness and government policy.

But, emphatically, America is a coat of many colors, a nation descended from many nations. This is not only who we are; to a great extent, this is what has made us strong.

government. And it specifies the manner in which the federal government must approach its relationships with state and local governments.

Most Americans tend to take all of these interactions for granted, but in reality the intricate nature of this blueprint and the balance that the Constitution deliberately put into place are uncommonly rare. I like to compare the design of our governmental system to the invention of the game of baseball, commonly accepted as our national pastime. Baseball is perhaps the most intricately designed sport ever created. Whether one enjoys it or not (and I am an unabashed fan), its structure is pure genius. It is an individual sport. It is also a team sport. With every pitch (indeed with every different pitcher), with every count on the batter, and with every new base runner, the strategy of the game can change. Every player has a specific responsibility that puts him in the glare of the spotlights. Every player has the chance to be a star, both in the field and while at bat. But in the end only the team can win, and the team can win only by working together. And on every play the umpire, judge-like, must make a decision before the game can proceed. Baseball's complex rules become a part of the excitement of the game. But the rules never get in the way of the action.

This is pretty much the way our country was designed to operate under the overarching guidance of the Constitution. We are a nation of individuals, but each individual, at least in theory, has a responsibility to the greater good and must play by certain specifically delineated rules. The rules are known, visible, and subject to objective judgment. Our basic freedoms are as common to us as the air that we breathe, and the right to question all forms of authority with impunity is one of the defining characteristics of being an American. But the rules—all subject to constant interpretation—define the playing field.

It is rare in human history to find a system where the opportunity for unbounded wealth and power is adamantly protected by law, and yet where that legal structure just as adamantly protects the right of anyone to question any aspect of the workings of his or her society. No governmental system is error-free. Nor can any government ever mandate complete equality, especially complete equality of the human condition. At the same time, Americans have always adamantly pursued the notion of equal opportunity and of fairness on the playing fields of life. In theory, Americans vigorously reject the notion that social class should define opportunity and privilege, or that family and other personal relationships should in and of themselves trump personal qualifications, as is apparent in so many other countries around the world. And more effectively than any such document ever written, the Constitution seeks to eliminate artificial barriers to success.

In America, this yin and yang of multicultural competitiveness taking place under the protection of our Constitution quietly defines almost everything we do and implicitly guides almost every large-scale debate we have. Creative ideas are welcomed and richly rewarded in America, both in the business world and in academia. The freedom to express one's opinion causes fierce debates, and these debates often cause us to look inward for better solutions.

Our government, the ultimate arbiter of these debates, was deliberately designed through a system of checks and balances, so that the arbiters themselves had their own arbiters. The framers of our Constitution had studied carefully the successes and failures of governments that preceded them. They took a long look at historical models, particularly those of oppressive monarchies that had dominated Europe in the generations that preceded our independence. They took into consideration where the centralization of authority was necessary—for instance, by giving the President the power to be Commander in Chief of the military during wartime. And they also sought to guard against those situations where too much consolidation of power at the top might be dangerous, in the sense of taking away individual freedoms or putting unreasonable restrictions on a free and adversarial press, or by mandating a certain religion as the "state" religion, all of which had been done at one time or another in Europe.

Eternal vigilance is indeed the price of liberty, in terms of both foreign policy and in guarding against the danger of losing our basic freedoms here at home. And the framers of the Constitution clearly had such considerations in mind. They designed a system of continual cross-checks inside our government itself, to prevent abuses against individual citizens and to dissuade tyrannical behavior on the part of our rulers. They created a unique governmental structure where the legislative, executive, and judicial branches would always remain in a state of deliberate tension, equally powerful in terms of the Constitution, literally standing daily watch over one another.

On top of that, they wrote a Bill of Rights into the Constitution, giving every American written, enforceable protection against governmental intrusion into our fundamental freedoms. They recognized that true freedom means the right to live our lives the way we see fit, to speak our minds whenever we want, to worship as we choose, to be free from unnecessary invasions into our privacy, and to be able to assert those and all other rights in open and fair court proceedings before a jury of our peers.

In the context of human history—and in the context of the rest of the world even today—this is an extraordinary set of guarantees.

The Constitution is also a living document, subject to constant interpretation. As our society has evolved and as technology has advanced, competing interpretations of various sections of the Constitution have sometimes resulted in deep divisions among our citizens. Vigorous disagreements, particularly concerning the exact meaning of several sections of the Bill of Rights, have resulted in the most passionate—and in some cases the most unending—debates in American history.

A glaring but almost-forgotten example of the depth of these Constitutional debates is the Civil War itself. Although slavery was undeniably the fundamental political and emotional issue that led to the war, the most vital Constitutional issue—the one that both sides actually went to war in order to resolve—was the applicability of the Tenth Amendment. And perhaps the greatest evidence of that truth is that although President Abraham Lincoln opposed slavery, he never outlawed the practice in the four slave states that remained in the Union.

This was true even in President Lincoln's famed Emancipation Proclamation of January 1863. When I was a junior in high school in Nebraska, my history teacher began one class by announcing that in 1863, Abraham Lincoln had freed all the slaves. I got into a good bit of trouble by informing my teacher that Lincoln actually had not done that. When she accused me of simply being disruptive (which, I must admit, in other circumstances would have been accurate), I asked her if she had actually read the Proclamation rather than the description of it in the class textbook. I had read it; she had not.

My adolescent curiosity had caused me to wonder aloud how Lincoln could possibly have freed the slaves who were in the South, since people in the South did not recognize his authority in 1863, anyway. I had gone to the library the evening before and looked up the Proclamation. To my surprise, I had found that it specifically exempted all the slaves in the Union states, as well as those in the areas of the South that had already been brought back into Union hands. Contrary to what my teacher was saying, the Proclamation did not free any slaves under Lincoln's control at all—only those slaves who would come into Union control in the future. The Proclamation specifically applied only to those areas in the South that were brought back into Union control after the document was signed.

The Confederacy wanted to keep slavery. But in legal terms, they wanted to keep slavery by dissolving their relationship with the Union, according to the powers they believed were retained by them under the Tenth Amendment. That amendment states that "The powers not delegated to the United States by the Constitution, nor prohibited to it by the States, are reserved to the States respectively, or to the people." Those states that left the Union and joined the Confederacy maintained that under this amendment, the Constitutional pact was terminable.

Vernon Louis Parrington, one of America's greatest historians, summed up this argument in his classic book *Main Currents in American Thought*, a tome that was so well regarded in its day that it received a double Pulitzer Prize. Commenting on a fourteen-hundred-page brief filed by Alexander B. Stephens, the vice president of the Confederacy, Parrington found the argument "wholly convincing," summarizing it as follows: "that state government existed prior to the Union, that it was jealously guarded at the making of the Constitution, that it had never been surrendered, and hence was the Constitutional order until destroyed by the Civil War."

Fortunately, the Constitutional arguments that divide us today are not of such virulence that they would sunder the nation and bring hundreds of thousands of our countrymen to die in an internecine struggle. But few issues other than war itself stir up the emotions of Americans as passionately as do our debates over the interpretations of the Bill of Rights, and of the many amendments that have followed those first ten, as well as the arguments over amendments that are frequently proposed regarding hot-button issues of the day. A part of these continuing intellectual brawls reflects the varying religious and cultural referents that come into play in our country when we consider basic rights. Another part is due to a constant concern that the faceless but increasingly powerful federal government might wrongly use its powers to intrude into the privacy and freedoms of ordinary citizens.

The American people are continually caught up in a series of values-based disagreements, and the Constitution ineluctably becomes the focal point of a majority of these discussions. When and where can you say a prayer? When does life begin? When does it end? When can the police justifiably pull you over and search your car, or enter your home and search your house, and when have they abused your reasonable expectations of privacy? When can evidence obtained through inappropriate police conduct be used against you in court? When can the government listen in on your telephone calls, or open your mail, or read your e-mails? What constitutes cruel and unusual punishment? When must a newspaper or television reporter reveal his or her sources? Under what conditions can it fairly be said that the government has actually denied a citizen the equal protection of the law?

We know, for instance, that the First Amendment to the Constitution guarantees that Americans will enjoy freedom of religion. But we debate vigorously how this concept fits into so-called public places in our many-cultured society. Over the past fifty years, members of some non-Christian faiths, as well as agnostics, atheists, and some civil libertarians, have litigated this issue repeatedly, threatened by the open display of predominantly Christian rhetoric and prayers in public places. As a result, this portion of the First Amendment has been interpreted in recent years so that it actually precludes any expression or identification of religion in most public places.

But should freedom of religion mandate freedom from religion?

The phrasing in this portion of the amendment is simple: "Congress shall make no law respecting an establishment of religion, or prohibiting the free exercise thereof." What does this mean in practice, not only as it relates to the intent of the founding fathers but as it affects American society today?

The historical reasons for the amendment went back to colonial days, when different colonial governments would declare a specific religious affiliation to be the "established" religion and would preclude open worship by members of other faiths and even of other Christian affiliations. Members of these "established" religions also held unfair advantages in other areas of society, as a matter of government policy.

For example, my native state of Virginia was founded in the 1600s by the so-called Cavalier aristocracy, who decreed that the English-oriented Anglican Church was the "established" church. As the colony spread westward toward the Appalachian Mountains, fierce confrontations began with the Indian tribes. The frontier needed to be defended. In 1738, Governor William Gooch convinced the warlike, Calvinist Scots-Irish who were then pouring into Pennsylvania from Northern Ireland to settle along the mountains, creating in effect an interlocking string of family and community-based fortresses. The deal he cut with the famously devout and adamantly nonconformist Ulster Scots was that, in exchange for their willingness to provide a bulwark against the Indian tribes, they could practice their religion—a form of Presbyterianism that more closely resembles the Baptist faith of today—in their settlements. But even after these settlements took hold, Virginians who were not of the Anglican faith were precluded from holding public office and were still required to pay an annual "parish levy" for the benefit of the Anglican Church.

This inequitable, direct government sponsorship of a specific branch of one religion was the situation that fair-minded Virginians like Patrick Henry worked hard to remove when they took the lead in advancing the First Amendment to the Constitution. It is a far cry from today's court interpretations, wherein any official mention of religious faith is considered a government taboo. Many government officials, including myself, find it deeply ironic that the courts have interpreted the First Amendment to preclude public schools from starting their day with a prayer, while every session in the Congress begins with one. Indeed, when I am called upon to preside over the Senate, I often find myself staring from my desk toward the doors that mark the main entrance to the Senate chamber. A lone phrase is carved into the marble wall just above those doors: "In God We Trust."

If a minister can lead the Senate in prayer every day before we begin a session, what is so wrong with beginning every day of school with an ecumenical prayer? If we can inscribe a direct mention of God on the wall above the Senate floor, why can't we mention God in a public school or on a government building?

We know that the First Amendment also guarantees freedom of speech and of the press, and that it guarantees "the right of the people peaceably to assemble." But how does this apply in practical terms? When can the press publish harmful information about a private citizen? When can it publish sensitive government information without retaliation? When does a freely expressed opinion in the media about an individual cross the line to the point that it becomes defamation? When does the freedom of an individual to speak turn into an intolerable insult, and when does it transcend all rules of reasonableness and become a virulent and unsupportable attack on another individual? Does the Constitution allow an adult to use foul language in front of my children? How about if it is directed at my children? Do I have any recourse? What if the language is so inflammatory that I can't control my emotions and I strike the person physically? Am I then liable? Can words be just as harmful as physical blows? Can human behavior constitute "free speech" if it is directed at another person? And when does peaceable assembly cross the line into disruptive behavior, even if it involves "mere words" and not physical destruction?

We face these questions in America on a daily basis. We have our ways of resolving them, not always perfectly. But they are always with us, and the search for resolution often ends up in an interpretation of the First Amendment.

We know that the Second Amendment gives Americans "the right to keep and bear arms." But what kind of weapons should we be allowed to keep? And where can they be carried—on our person, in our car, in our office, at our home? If a citizen wants to keep and shoot a machine gun, does the Constitution say that he cannot do so? What about a pistol? What about an artillery piece? And on a more practical level, if the Constitution gives one the right to keep and bear arms, can local governments then pass a law that would prevent a citizen from keeping a personal weapon for self-defense in his own home?

We struggle, frequently and with great emotion, about how to define the beginning and the end of life. Technological advances on both ends of the spectrum make the search for answers far more complex than situations that existed in earlier generations. Many people in our society believe strongly that life begins at conception, and thus that all abortions, even those from pregnancies that are the result of rape or incest, are wrong. Others argue that life begins when a fetus becomes independently sustainable if separated from the womb, and that until that point is reached, a woman must have the power to decide what is taking place inside her own body.

Many people in our society believe that life ends only when every technological capability to prolong it has exhausted its course, even if a person is brain-dead and is being kept alive through external life-support systems. Others believe that it falls upon responsible loved ones or a designated guardian to make the final, painful decision to allow a life to end and to cease prolonging the inevitable. A few years ago the nation watched, in horrible moral paralysis, as members of the United States Congress sought to somehow adjudicate the finality of Terri Schiavo's life. The majority leader of the Senate went so far as to proclaim, after having watched pictures of her on a video, that her mental and physical condition was sustainable. When should the government become directly involved in such decisions? When does that involvement constitute an inappropriate intrusion into a family's or an individual's privacy? And when can the government decide, conclusively, not to be involved?

For answers on such issues we in this country must look beyond our individual faiths and philosophical beliefs to the law. And on complex issues of the law, the ultimate resolution is, again, found in the Constitution. But where, in this exceptional document that erects boundaries around our behavior, do we find a rational approach and a balanced answer?

The answers are often difficult to find, and the places where they are found are not always pleasing to those embroiled in the emotions of the arguments. *Roe v. Wade,* the landmark 1973 case on abortion, was decided not on the issue of where life begins, but instead on a pregnant woman's right of privacy. In supporting early-term abortions, the Supreme Court indicated that this right existed, whether it was "founded in the Fourteenth Amendment's concept of personal liberty and restrictions upon state action, as we feel it is, or, as the District Court determined, in the Ninth Amendment's reservation of rights to the people." Recognizing its existence, the Court decided that this right "is broad enough to encompass a woman's decision whether or not to terminate her pregnancy."

One can agree or disagree with the Court's logic. But these issues and a plethora of others like them are at least resolvable in terms of coming to a legal conclusion that places boundaries on our behavior and on our debates. They are also capable of being further considered under different sets of facts. The country moves forward and society evolves. Technology advances. Theories of criminal justice change. Members of the Supreme Court change, bringing different viewpoints.

In contrast, there are other difficulties that confront our society where the Constitution is vague or silent, and thus where it becomes far more difficult to find some sort of clear-cut resolution. Many of these issues involve serious, philosophically based challenges that demand forward-looking thought on the part of government leaders. Indeed, in today's America it seems that the issues that most divide us in our passions are those where the Constitution is arguable—as with those involving the Bill of Rights—while the issues that most threaten our collective future are those where the Constitution is silent or incapable of clear judicial direction.

For instance, there is nothing in the Constitution that actually demands that there be economic fairness among Americans. The Constitution outlines how commerce will be regulated. It states clearly that no American will be "deprived of life, liberty, or property, without due process of law; nor shall private property be taken for public use, without just compensation." It holds that no state can make or enforce any law that would "abridge the privileges or immunities of citizens of the United States," and that no state can "deny to any person within its jurisdiction the equal protection of the laws."

In other words, when it comes to economic fairness the Constitution is more like a referee in a free-for-all among people of all different sizes, shapes, ages, and backgrounds, charged only with making sure that no one hits below the belt. It doesn't say that people shouldn't be poor, and it doesn't say that people can't get too rich. In fact, the Constitution was written by people who represented the propertied interests of our country—people who largely took for granted that America was and would continue to function in the hands of some form of aristocracy.

Even *Goldberg v. Kelly,* the landmark Supreme Court case that in 1970 established the "right" to welfare benefits to those in "brutal need," did not actually recognize any constitutional right to those benefits at all. Instead, the Court held that the principle of due process of law must apply when denying people welfare benefits. Welfare benefits did not come from the Constitution; they came from the decisions of elected officials who had decided to pass welfare legislation. The court held that "Welfare benefits are a matter of statutory entitlement for persons qualified to receive them and procedural due process is applicable to their termination."

Economic fairness does not come from any specific provision of the Constitution. Instead, to the extent that it exists it comes from a pretty vague phrase in article 1, section 8, which states, among other things, that the Congress shall have the power to provide for the "general Welfare of the United States," coupled with a phrase stating that the Congress is empowered to "make all Laws which shall be necessary and proper for carrying into Execution" these powers. Thus, policies designed to protect economic equity emanate from the judgment and wisdom of those who have been elected to represent the people.

Do we need economic fairness? If people from across the socio-economic spectrum participate in the electoral process, that answer will be a resounding yes. And on this point, it is again interesting to note that it was not until 1964, when I was a freshman in college, that the Twenty-fourth Amendment to the Constitution finally eliminated the poll tax, which in some jurisdictions had prevented many of the poor folk in this country from even being able to vote at all.

Can people get too rich? In America, the philosophical answer to that question is that it all depends on how their gains were won. Most Americans respect achievement; what they dislike is unfairness. Success is commendable. What is deplorable is the artificial manipulation of the government process in order to achieve it, or using undue influence to elude one's responsibility as a full member of the American community. And again, it falls on those elected to office to prevent or curtail such acts by the wealthy and the powerful.

In short, economic fairness is a function of the daily workings of our elected officials, and whether these officials focus on such issues depends, quite obviously, on whom the American people choose to represent them. This reality, simple as it sounds, is often ignored. Only the leaders that we choose to elect can ensure true fairness. On the one hand, they must pass laws that minimize unnecessary government intrusion into an economic system based on free-market theories. On the other, they are charged with ensuring that wealth and power do not bring with them an unfair manipulation of the system, that taxes are fairly assessed, and that all of our citizens have an equal opportunity to succeed.

It wasn't until the presidency of Andrew Jackson that the propertied interests in America saw any sort of serious push-back from elected government representatives. On July 10, 1830, Jackson vetoed legislation that would have renewed the charter of the Second National Bank, an act that Jackson historian Robert Remini termed "the most important veto in American history." Historian Vernon Louis Parrington went even further, calling it "the most courageous act in our political history."

Why was this veto so important? Because the Congress had passed a law creating a bank that threatened to corrupt the state, as the bank would be in the hands of people who were benefiting from personal influence that eluded the average citizen. If the legislation were renewed, Jackson believed, the bank would have perpetuated itself in the hands of a permanent aristocracy, completely insulated from competition and from the oversight of government. Many members of Congress were on the bank's direct payroll, including New England political giant Daniel Webster, who made no secret of the fact that the retainer he received from the bank had become "a dependable source of private revenue."

The bank, as historian Arthur Schlesinger so aptly put it, "served as a repository of the public funds, which it could use for its own banking purposes without payment of interest . . . [It] was not to be taxed by the states and no similar institution was to be chartered by the Congress . . . It enjoyed a virtual monopoly of the currency and practically complete control over credit and the price level . . . [Its President Nicholas] Biddle not only suppressed all internal dissent but insisted flatly that the Bank was not accountable to the government or to the people."

Jackson was vilified by the political establishment and by most of the press for vetoing this legislation. They attempted mightily to prevent his reelection. They did not succeed. In the process, Jackson laid down a marker that applies every bit as much to today's America as it did in 1830. Part of his veto message stated, "In the full enjoyment of the gifts of Heaven and the fruits of superior industry, economy and virtue, every man is entitled to protection by law; but when the laws undertake to add to these natural and just advantages artificial distinctions . . . to make the rich richer and the potent more powerful, the humble members of our society . . . who have neither the time nor the means of securing favors to themselves, have the right to complain of the injustice of their Government."

The Constitution did not prevent the establishment and continuation of the Second National Bank; Andrew Jackson did, acting strongly and alone. America had put the right person in office—at least in the eyes of those who had no special influence along the corridors of power.

Nor is there any wording in the Constitution that gives us firm guidance regarding how our country should approach its foreign relations, beyond certain structural guidelines that divide the formalities of foreign policy between the executive and legislative branches. In these structural realities we can see clearly how the framers of the Constitution wanted to ensure that the branches of government maintained a balance. The President is empowered to make treaties with foreign governments, provided that two-thirds of the Senate concurs. The Congress has the power to declare war, to raise and support armies, to provide and maintain a navy, and to call forth the militia. The President acts as the Commander in Chief of the Army and Navy and of the Militia when called into the "actual service of the United States." The Congress has the sole power to appropriate funds to run the government (and thus the military), subject to the veto of the President.

But what should be the role of the United States in the community of nations? And in a world of constant tension, how far does the President's power as Commander in Chief extend in terms of defining that role? When should the President be empowered to send our military into combat in the absence of a formal declaration of war? And under what constitutional justification do we assert the American tradition of civilian control of the military?

On this last point, many Americans might be surprised to learn that there is no specific mandate in the Constitution regarding what civilian control over the military should actually entail. Nor, by the way, does the Constitution specifically preclude our military from direct involvement in politics. In fact, the Constitution is silent on whether active-duty military members can even run for political office. The reason for this is that our founding fathers had no real conception of a career military force or of standing armies. In the era in which they lived, and in the eras that preceded them, armies were literally "raised" to fight wars, and citizens of all stripes left their ordinary duties to serve until the war or the campaign was finished.

Not so today. The world has become more complicated, and the evolution of technology and modes of transportation has made crises more immediate. The United States itself has evolved from an isolated, transoceanic minor power into the center of world commerce, security, and diplomacy. Wars, or at least extended military actions, are fought without formal declarations of war, sometimes for complicated domestic and international reasons.

Incrementally over the years since World War II, incident by incident and undeclared war by undeclared war, the relationship between the presidency and the Congress has tilted so far toward the executive branch that our system is in serious imbalance. And again, it is up to the country's elected leaders to address such issues.

These disparities should not surprise us, even though they challenge us and frequently frustrate us. The founding fathers had no sure way to accurately predict the evolution and modernization of our society. Nor could they have comprehended the gradual growth of American power that affects our responsibilities in the international community. Nor, indeed, could they have foreseen the changing nature of the federal system itself, as the country moved from a collection of near nation-states into a more centralized, top-down power structure. Our great fortune as Americans is that the document that binds us together was written with such a measure of flexibility and finality that it has withstood the interpretations of the ages, and thus has held the country together at the outside edges despite the frequent turmoil and debate. But our great challenge is to keep a measure of civility where the Constitution is vague, even as we define ourselves more clearly on the issues where it is silent.

But what if there came a time when the country was divided so deeply along class lines that the very notions that we have come to accept as premises for our society were in jeopardy? For instance, what if there came a time when corporate profits and executive compensation were at all-time highs, and yet wages and salaries for America's workers were at all-time lows as a percentage of the national wealth? What if there came a time when a majority of the stocks in the country were owned by only 1 percent of the people? What if those conditions existed and the Congress, just as in Andrew Jackson's time, would not take action to redress the imbalance, but unlike in Andrew Jackson's time, the party of the President was dedicated to continuing the imbalance as well? Where should the people go to find fairness? How could the system be retrieved from the inequality that had overcome it?

And what if the constitutional notion of the President as commander in chief of the military during wartime had been carried to such a dangerous extreme that the President's assumed powers were little different from those of the European monarchs that our founding fathers so deeply despised? What if the President, rather than viewing himself as the executive instrument of a nation's foreign policy, decided that he was its sole creator in economic, military, and diplomatic terms?

What if the President decided that the only check on his authority as commander in chief was the Congress's power of the purse, just as the European kings once viewed themselves as answerable to their parliaments only to the extent that they would raise taxes for the wars the monarchs wished to fight? And what if that power of the purse was an insufficient control, since in order to exercise it the Congress would have to cut off funding for troops that already had been sent into harm's way?

What if the President decided that trade policy was not really the province of the Congress, but rather should be negotiated and articulated by his unelected assistants, to be presented to the Congress for an up-or-down vote as if they were merely a rubber stamp? What if he decided that he could appoint his ambassadors during congressional recesses, so that the Congress could not vote on their qualifications?

The above paragraphs identify the world Americans live in today. It is not the world that we need to live in. Nor is it the world that we must live in. But in order to change it, the American people need to find leaders who are willing to take the action that will be necessary to fix it.

PART TWO

What Went Wrong?

CHAPTER SIX

FROM A SQUARE DEAL TO A RAW DEAL

President Theodore Roosevelt has become something of a cult figure among many American politicians and political commentators from both political parties. A surprising number of offices on Capitol Hill have at least one picture of Teddy on a wall, often alongside framed quotes from one memorable speech or another. Roosevelt had a reputation for physicality, confrontational rhetoric, and intellectual vigor. He was energetic, well born, and well educated. From the time of his boyhood, he was extraordinarily well connected with people from all the power centers around the country. And as President, taking advantage of what he called the "bully pulpit," he had a profound impact in shaping the American psyche for the country's twentieth-century evolution toward the center of the world stage.

Using that pulpit, and coming up with lasting phrases such as "speak softly but carry a big stick," Roosevelt gained a deserved reputation for fairness at home, even as he greatly influenced America's prestige around the world. He also expanded the powers of the presidency. To top it off, in 1906 then-President Roosevelt became the first American to win the Nobel Peace Prize, for his efforts in helping to broker a peace that ended the Russo-Japanese War.

The prevalence of "Teddy Fever" among modern-day politicians is so great that it spilled over—in this writer's view, unthinkingly—into his very brief military career. In 2001, the United States Congress decided to award Roosevelt the Medal of Honor for his part in leading a regiment of Rough Riders up San Juan Hill in 1898, during the Spanish-American War. One hundred and three years after a firefight that made Teddy, in the words of historian Edmund Morris, "the most famous man in America," the Congress decided that Roosevelt had somehow been overlooked for consideration of the nation's highest combat award during that war, and that they should correct the injustice.

From time to time, the Medal of Honor has been awarded after long delays. These retroactive awards usually involve cases where witnessing statements or award recommendations were lost due to the confusion of battle and its aftermath. Some involve reconsiderations of lower awards, particularly where cases could be made that racial discrimination prevented a fair evaluation of one's acts. But the combat awards process, while not perfect, has traditionally remained within the province of the military, and the military itself has provided careful stewardship of how its highest combat awards are measured and awarded.

Service members with long experience in combat never fail to gag when they see politicians meddle in this process. For those who have truly soldiered, slogging out multiyear enlistments including long months and even years in combat, Roosevelt's time in uniform was uncommonly brief, marking him as an avid but nonetheless amateur soldier. He left the Navy Department for military service in the spring of 1898 and by August of that same year was home in New York. He had served a total of 133 days from the start-up of the Rough Riders until its dissolution—about as much time as today's Marine enlistee spends in recruit training alone. He had spent less than two months of this

time in Cuba, where he was involved in two firefights. He stepped off
the brow of the transport ship in August, began campaigning, and by
November he had been elected governor of New York. To top it off,
Roosevelt had lobbied hard to receive the Medal of Honor, beginning
in the days immediately following the battle. This included pressing
the case upon his good friend Senator Henry Cabot Lodge of Massachusetts, to whom he wrote in one letter, "I do wish you would get that
Medal of Honor for me . . ."

Nor had the Army overlooked those soldiers whom it viewed as
having performed at the highest level during the fighting at San Juan
Hill. Indeed, records show that twenty-three soldiers were awarded
the Medal of Honor during one day of combat against fewer than
a thousand Spanish soldiers—in American terms, about a battalion
(Roosevelt would be the twenty-fourth). As a matter of reference, in
the entire Vietnam War the United States Marine Corps awarded only
forty-seven Medals of Honor (thirty-four posthumously), despite five
years of fighting that resulted in hundreds of thousands of enemy dead
and more than 100,000 killed or wounded in the Corps. As of this writing the Marine Corps has awarded only one Medal of Honor in four
years of fighting in Iraq.

But the United States Congress decided that Roosevelt had been
overlooked, despite his voluble lobbying to receive it, despite the fact
that he had been President in the years following it, and despite the
fact that the United States Army had for a full century attempted to ex-
plain to Roosevelt, his family, his supporters, and his modern-day en-
thusiasts that his actions did not equate to the level of performance
that justified the award. It was not until 1998 that members of Congress succeeded in twisting the arm of an official in the Department of
the Army, finally obtaining a letter of support that then was used to
pass special legislation in 2001.

This is the type of activity that the Congress needs to stay out of,
so that it can focus on the kinds of business the country needs to see
fixed. And on the kinds of business the country needs to see fixed, our
national leadership should, emphatically, pay closer attention to the
words and the example of President Theodore Roosevelt.

Principal among the issues facing our society today is the breakdown of our country along class lines. And in this area we all would do well to remember the "bully pulpit" words and the determined actions of this same President. Roosevelt was a well-born New Yorker, but he often praised his mother's Southern, Scots-Irish ancestry and the strong sense of frontier-style democracy that the Scots-Irish brought with them to America. This pioneering culture, steeped in notions of egalitarian fairness, was in historian Vernon Louis Parrington's words "hardy, assertive, individualistic, thrifty, trained in the democracy of the Scottish kirk; they were the material out of which later Jacksonian democracy was to be fashioned."

Despite his lifetime of comfortable association with the elites of American society, and despite his political affiliation with the business-dominated Republican Party, Roosevelt understood the value of properly run trade unions and the dangers to our society when economic power becomes concentrated in the hands of a very few. Those dangers exist today; in fact, they have once again become the greatest issue of domestic policy in the country. And they are not being properly addressed.

For a variety of reasons, the American economic system is more skewed today than it has been since Teddy Roosevelt's time, when he faced down the so-called Robber Barons more than a hundred years ago. The freewheeling internationalization of corporate America in the age of globalization has resulted in the loss of millions of manufacturing jobs to overseas locations, even as the executives of American corporations have been rewarded with historically unprecedented compensation packages. Massive immigration and the weakening of organized labor have combined to lower the ability of the average worker to negotiate his or her own combination of fair and meaningful wages, medical care, and retirement. And, it is painful to say, an uncaring amorality has seized much of America's business community, allowing a separate society to grow that in too many cases has lost a sense of conscience about the well-being of other Americans.

America has been down similar roads before. Andrew Jackson—the first President of Scots-Irish ancestry—found the courage to confront the country's ruling structure and thus to nip in the bud the permanent aristocracy that would have resulted from the continuation of the Second Bank of the United States. And to his lasting credit, Teddy Roosevelt stepped forward as well. He had made much of his political reputation as a "trust buster" after breaking up the monopolies of more than forty corporations. And as President he took to the hustings in an attempt to urge all Americans to put aside any notions of class warfare.

Roosevelt coined the phrase "Square Deal" to describe the necessity for societal fairness. On Labor Day, September 7, 1903, then-President Roosevelt made a speech that marked the beginning of a serious effort to recapture a sense of economic balance in this country. Knowing that the Robber Barons had been accumulating a huge percentage of the national wealth at the expense of their workers, and also fearing widespread social unrest from an increasingly angry workforce, Roosevelt appealed to Americans of all economic classes to understand that they had a common interest. As a guiding precept, Roosevelt mentioned the following:

It has been our profound good fortune as a nation that . . . in the long run, we all of us tend to go up or go down together. If the average of well-being is high, it means that the average wage-worker, the average farmer, and the average business man are all alike well-off. If the average shrinks, there is not one of these classes which will not feel the shrinkage . . . [I]f prosperity comes, all of us tend to share more or less therein, and if adversity comes each of us, to a greater or less extent, feels the tension. . . . It is all-essential to the continuance of our healthy national life that we should recognize this community of interest among our people. The welfare of each of us is dependent fundamentally upon the welfare of all of us. And therefore in public life that man is the best representative of each of us who seeks to do good to each by doing good to all; in other words, whose endeavor it is not to represent any special class and promote merely that class's selfish interests, but to represent all true and honest men of all sections and all classes and to work for their interests by working for our common country.

The take-it-all mentality of corporate America in these early years of the twenty-first century has come to resemble in many ways the uncaring rapacity of a corporate America that Teddy Roosevelt chose to confront a hundred years ago. But answers will be harder to find, because other conditions in the country today bear little resemblance to the America that Roosevelt was speaking to, and about, in 1903. The structure and especially the geographical diversity of today's corporate America are decidedly different from a century ago. In the age of globalization, and because of other domestic factors now at play, the precepts that Roosevelt proposed can no longer be so easily applied.

Why is this so? Because, quite simply, those sitting comfortably at the very top in today's America know that we don't all go up or down together anymore.

Worker incomes in America have been disturbingly and demonstrably declining as a percentage of our national wealth. In August 2007, the Internal Revenue Service reported that average incomes in this country have been lower during every year of the Bush Administration than they were in the year before this presidency began, a phenomenon not seen in modern times till now. Once the Great Depression ended, and particularly in the years following World War II, America has always viewed itself as a land of rising incomes, rising hopes, and rising expectations. According to the *New York Times*, "Total income listed on tax returns grew every year after World War II, with a single one-year exception, until 2001, making the five-year period of lower average incomes and four years of lower total incomes a new experience for the majority of Americans born since 1945." The article went on to point out that "nearly half of Americans reported incomes of less than $30,000, and two-thirds make less than $50,000."

How does this affect us as a nation? Average incomes have been less for five years in a row. Nearly half of the country makes less than

$30,000 a year, and two-thirds make less than $50,000 a year. But at the same time, the stock market has risen to historic highs, and when it comes to personal income at the very top rung of our society, there has indeed been a good bit of growth. According to that same *New York Times* article, growth in total incomes "was concentrated among those making more than $1 million . . . These individuals, who constitute less than a quarter of 1 percent of all taxpayers, reaped almost 47 percent of the total income gains in 2005."

Throughout our history, we have seen cycles where income inequalities have become severe. But over the past twenty-five years, our country has seen an enormous—and perhaps unprecedented—transfer of wealth to the very top of our society. The *New York Times* recently reported that "not since the Roaring Twenties have the rich been so much richer than everyone else. In 2005, the latest year for which figures are available, the top 1 percent of Americans—whose average income was $1.1 million a year—received 21.8 percent of the nation's income, their largest share since 1929. Overall, the top 10 percent of Americans—those making more than about $100,000 a year—collected 48.5 percent, also a share last seen before the Great Depression."

The top 1 percent of our population also owns more than half of our stocks, making the stock market a poor indicator of the overall economic health of our society but a pretty good indicator of how the top 1 percent is doing. What has happened with these stocks? A lot of money is being made by those who are fortunate enough to own them. In 1957, the Dow Jones Industrial Average fluctuated between 450 and 500. By 1982, it was averaging around 900, and it finally broke 1,000 at the end of that year. But by 2007, it had skyrocketed to around 13,000.

And to top it off, the "capital gains" tax rate for making money on stocks is only 15 percent—far lower than the tax rate for most wage earners, some of whom pay more than double that rate for income they have received through the sweat of their labor. This puts many of the wealthiest people in America in the enviable position of not even having to work to make money. In the America of today, it is entirely doable to find a good money manager, let him or her invest your money in exchange for a small percentage of the take, which itself is tax-deductible as a business fee, and then, as billionaire Warren Buffett is reputed to have said, end up paying a lower tax rate than your secretary.

While the average compensation for American workers has actually declined, Reuters recently reported that in 2006 the number of U.S. households with a net worth of more than $5 million, excluding their primary residence, surged 23 percent to surpass one million for the first time. Only ten years ago, according to the Chicago-based Spectrem Group, there were just 250,000 U.S. households in this category. This means that while worker incomes have been declining, the number of "superrich" in America has quadrupled in ten years.

Ours is a country founded on the premise that all of us should have the opportunity to advance as far as our talent and energy can take us. But the question for today's America is a bit more complex than that. It is not whether someone should have the opportunity to make a lot of money. Rather, it becomes whether these hyperbolic incomes reflect a proper share from having generated economic health for all Americans, or whether they are the product of having made money at the expense of other Americans.

Economic theorist and columnist Paul Krugman recently pointed out that "John D. Rockefeller, the richest man in Gilded Age America," made $1.25 million in 1894, "almost 7,000 times the average per capita income in the United States at the time." But, continued Krugman, "That makes him a mere piker by modern standards. Last year, according to Institutional Investor's *Alpha* magazine, James Simons, a hedge fund manager, took home $1.7 billion, more than 38,000 times the average income. Two other hedge fund managers also made more than $1 billion, and the top 25 combined made $14 billion. How much is $14 billion? It's more than it would cost to provide health care for a year to eight million children—the number of children in America who, unlike children in any other advanced country, don't have health insurance."

On the same day Krugman's column ran in the *New York Times*, the *Wall Street Journal* reported that "AT&T Chief Executive Edward Whitacre stands to receive a $158.5 million pension package, one of the country's largest." In addition to his retirement income, the *Journal* pointed out, "When he retires Mr. Whitacre also will have $24,000 in annual automobile benefits, $6,500 in 'home security' each year and access to AT&T's corporate jet for 10 hours a month, according to the telecommunications company's proxy filing with the Securities and Exchange Commission."

As another example, in 2006 the investment banking company Goldman Sachs accumulated the biggest profit in Wall Street history. The company, which according to news reports is Wall Street's leading adviser in corporate mergers and acquisitions, awarded its employees $16.5 billion in salaries, bonuses, and benefits—an average of $662,000 per employee. Goldman's chief executive officer, Lloyd Blankfein, is reported to have been paid $54.3 million for one year of work. And in 2007, he was paid a record $68.5 million. How much is $68.5 million? It is four times as much as the combined salaries of the entire 100 members of the United States Senate. And no, I'm not asking for a pay raise.

Lest Goldman Sachs, Mr. Simons, and Mr. Whitacre feel they have been unfairly singled out, the truth is that they are simply exemplars of a trend that has infected Wall Street and all of corporate America. Wall Street's top earners, who produce not one actual product for the marketplace, are making incomes that defy the common imagination. And among today's larger corporations, the average CEO now makes more than $10 million a year at the same time his or her workforce receives the lowest compensation package, as a percentage of national wealth, in American history. In fact, among Standard & Poor's top 500 companies, the average CEO made $15 million in 2006.

What did these people do to earn these fabulous sums? Did they invent the lightbulb? Did they discover the Internet? Did they provide the world with a vaccine that would eliminate some dread disease? No, they examined trends, analyzed data, made phone calls, and decided where their clients should risk their assets in buying or selling a stake in the international marketplace. They managed people, business structures, or money so that investors, most of whom are already among the wealthiest 1 percent, could increase their wealth, usually paying the lower capital gains tax on their income.

And how did this money become available? In corporate America, it most often comes from profit margins. In the age of globalization, these margins have been increased in part by holding down the domestic costs of business. Costs of business are often held down by reducing wages, either through outsourcing jobs overseas or by in-sourcing cheaper foreign workers, and by closing out American plants altogether. Our current tax laws actually protect American corpora-tions that move operations overseas, deferring taxes on any profits from these overseas operations unless the profits are brought back into the United States. This of course encourages American corporations to in-vest more heavily in additional overseas operations, further reducing opportunities for American workers. Among the buyers and sellers, these sums come from transactional fees, often earned in the busy world of corporate acquisitions, which in and of themselves involve in-flated stock values and the transfer of wealth from corporate capital to the people who arrange the deals.

But it is not always about profit margins. Incredible sums can also accrue even in the face of failure. As journalist extraordinaire Arnaud de Borchgrave recently pointed out, in the aftermath of the "global sub-prime mortgage fiasco, which, in turn, pushed the dollar right off its pedestal, Wall Street's largest banks lost $50 billion, with Citigroup taking the biggest hit at $11 billion. Its deposed Chief Executive Offi-cer Chuck Prince walked away with $100 million in severance benefits. Merrill Lynch, the biggest investment firm, which lost more than $8 billion, fired CEO Stan O'Neal, who had made $160 million over the past five years he had been in charge. His golden parachute added another $160 million."

The turn of events at Morgan Stanley is particularly troubling. In December 2006, the huge investment bank gave its CEO, John Mack, a $40 million bonus. As a reference point for those who have sweated out time-and-a-half overtime for an extra hundred dollars here and there, this bonus on top of his regular salary amounted to about

$110,000 a day. A year later, in December 2007, Morgan Stanley announced a $9.4 billion "write-down" of its assets, giving it an unprecedented fourth-quarter loss of $3.6 billion. Their solution to the problem was to allow the Chinese government—not a Chinese investor, not a Chinese corporation, but the Chinese government—to directly invest $5 billion into Morgan Stanley through a "sovereign wealth fund." As a result, the Chinese government now owns 10 percent of one of America's largest investment banks.

With the Chinese now sitting on more than a trillion dollars as a result of our ill-advised trade strategies, such direct foreign-government investments may increase in the coming years. President Bush has indicated that he sees nothing wrong with this. Corporate executives will not be expected to disagree, since such investments might at least in the short term protect their bottom lines while also ensuring their continued high levels of compensation. But our national security, in both economic and military terms, will indeed be put to the test by the ticklish concept of foreign governments directly investing in our private companies. The United States government does not directly invest in corporations here or elsewhere. To do so would be considered a conflict of interest between the fiduciary roles of government and freedom of the marketplace. But our principal long-term strategic rival now does, as do a number of other countries, including Saudi Arabia and Dubai. The obvious leverage that accompanies this uncomfortable policy has the potential to impact our national interest, both directly and implicitly.

This process, what can only be termed the American business community's lack of a sense of stewardship toward American workers, is tearing apart the fabric of America as we have always defined her. At many levels, it has amounted to what can only be called a wrongful taking from our workforce, which in many cases has lost its ability to negotiate fairly for the value of its services. Nor is the problem confined to blue-collar America. Writer David Sirota provided a clear-eyed and deeply troubling window into the future for the *San Francisco Chronicle* during a recent visit to the headquarters of tech giant Microsoft.

"Business misbehavior was rarely a congressional focus when CEOs were cutting blue-collar wages while padding their own salaries," notes Sirota. "But on a recent trip to the iconic capital of the upper-middle-class professional, [the growing danger] all made perfect sense." During this visit, Microsoft employees "pointed me to company documents published by the worker advocacy group WashTech, proving Microsoft salaries for mid-level full-time employees have been stagnating, even as company revenues rise. They fumed over how the company employs thousands of 'permatemps'—full-time employees technically designated 'temporary' so the company does not have to pay them as well or provide them benefits."

Sirota continues that Microsoft workers "lamented that wages are forced ever lower by Microsoft's use of the H-1B visa program—a program that forces permatemps to compete with temporary, nonresident workers from other countries who are imported here by companies because they will accept low pay (government data shows tech companies pay H-1B workers $13,000 per year less than American workers in the same jobs)." He points out that "pay grades are only part of the ferment—it is also anxiety over job security at a time when 1.1 million American information-sector jobs have been eliminated in the past five years."

Sirota notes that there is "not one Microsoft division that doesn't fear showing up and having their keycards not work because all their jobs were sent to India." He then points out that some workers attempted to unionize, "but those grinning, business-casual Microsoft executives have learned a thing or two about how to bust unions. One example: When a handful of Microsoft workers developing fledgling tax software took an initial step to unionize, the entire project was terminated by management."

Sirota's conclusion is as troubling as it is obvious: "As both the Microsoft story and broader government data show, wage cuts, employment schemes, outsourcing and union-busting are not isolated to blue-collar or entry-level industries: they have become commonplace throughout the economy, an enraging part of the upper middle-class's daily life."

Clearly, Bill Gates did in fact invent a concept almost as important as the Internet, and deserves the rewards of his genius. Not unlike Thomas Edison, hundreds of millions of people have benefited from his intellect. His contributions generate greater economic health for all Americans. The problem is not in rewarding creativity to its fullest measure, but rather with ensuring that the bureaucracy that surrounds such innovation, and often feeds off of it, also takes proper care of those who make it a functioning reality.

Contrary to the bellicosity of the right-wing talk-show mavens, it is not class warfare or envy to point out that economic inequities persist in our society. In fact, the reverse is true: It is class warfare from the top down to pretend that such inequities don't matter. In today's America, vast wealth is being accumulated at the top tier of our society, often at the expense of those with whom this tier should be sharing the rewards of success. In the process, the poor have largely calcified into a seemingly permanent underclass, rife with crime and dependent on government programs. And our vital middle class, which has always carried the economic well-being of this nation on its back, has fallen steadily behind, with wages stagnating at the same time that basic living costs such as education and health care have skyrocketed.

Teddy Roosevelt warned us of the implications of such disparities toward the end of his famous 1903 Labor Day speech. He said this:

In the history of mankind many republics have risen, have flourished for a less or greater time, and then have fallen because their citizens lost the power of governing themselves and thereby of governing their state; and in no way has this loss of power been so often and so clearly shown as in the tendency to turn the government into a government primarily for the benefit of one class instead of a government for the benefit of the people as a whole. Again and again in the republics of ancient Greece, in those of medieval Italy and medieval Flanders, this tendency was shown, and wherever the tendency became a habit it invariably and inevitably proved fatal to the state. In the final result, it mattered not one whit whether the movement was in favor of one class or of another.

> We must act upon the motto of all for each and each for
> all. . . . We must see that each is given a square deal, because he
> is entitled to no more and should receive no less.

In the eyes of those who believe that the fruits of labor should be
more fairly shared, Roosevelt's long-ago warning rings true. But meanwhile, the world in which Roosevelt issued those warnings has vastly
changed.

The principal socioeconomic reality of today is that Americans of
all classes are no longer locked tightly in one another's embrace, as
Roosevelt so optimistically portrayed the country a hundred years ago.
The proof is everywhere that the entire body of our citizens no longer
goes "up and down together" in good times and bad. The historic highs
of the stock market at the same time wages and salaries have stagnated
are undeniable evidence that different forces are in play today, and
that a rising tide does not always lift all the boats. Corporate profits
have steadily been up, executive compensation has been stupendously
up, but wages and salaries are anything but up. The American labor
force of the twenty-first century is sandwiched between the debilitat-
ing realities of globalization and illegal immigration. In the age of globalization, good jobs are too often heading overseas. In an era of
uncontrolled illegal immigration and widely used guest-worker programs, a cheaper, often underground labor pool holds down blue-
collar—and increasingly white-collar—wages and benefits. This mar-
ginally benefits the immigrant worker, since he or she is in America
and has some source of income, however reduced. But it is having devastating effects on the worker who has been displaced.

Another reality is that there is something going on in the American business community that transcends the impact of globalization
and we don't quite know where to push the buttons to fix it. Among all
the "first world" nations, America stands alone in the scale of the rewards its profit makers and corporate leaders are voting for themselves,
at the expense of their workers and even their own shareholders. This
curious and disturbing reality has very complicated roots, which

unfortunately have largely been ignored by the top leadership of both political parties. But it is palpable.

When I graduated from college in 1968, the average corporate CEO made twenty times the salary of his average worker. Today that multiple is more than four hundred. Let's put that into perspective: The average corporate executive officer now makes more in a day than his or her workers do in a year. This vastly increased disparity is not simply a by-product of globalization, for if it were, we would be seeing it in the multiples of chief executive officer compensation in other "first world" nations. By contrast, even the estimates among experts that are most favorable to American CEOs indicate that the average Japanese chief executive makes only ten times the salary of a typical Japanese worker; the German and South Korean chief executives make only eleven times that amount; the French chief executives' multiple is sixteen; for the Italians it is nineteen; for the Canadians it is twenty-one; and British CEOs make twenty-five times the salary of their workers.

Or set the workers aside and compare chief executives among one another. If you compare those multiples, on a ratio basis the average American chief executive officer is paid sixteen times what his British counterpart makes, nineteen times that of his Canadian counterpart, twenty-one times that of his Italian fellow CEO, thirty-six times that of a German or South Korean chief executive, and forty times as much as the average Japanese CEO. And all of them are directing companies that compete with American corporations in the international marketplace.

It is also interesting, and ironic, to note that the most productive countries on this list—Germany, Japan, and South Korea—have the least amount of income disparity between their workers and their CEOs.

We have now reached the point where even American corporate leaders themselves have begun to admit they are overpaid. According to the *Financial Times,* in a study published in October 2007 by the National Association of Corporate Directors, "four out of six chief executives or company presidents . . . said the compensation of top executives was high, relative to their performance . . . Their view was backed up by outside directors, with more than 80 percent of them saying chief executives were overpaid."

The bottom line for our corporate leaders is this: Folks, you're good. But you're not that good.

How did this happen? One might start with the stockholders, who, it can be argued, determine executive compensation through compensation committees on their corporate boards. When more than half the stocks in America are owned by only 1 percent of the people, there are, obviously, fewer checks and balances in terms of corporate governance. Memberships on corporate boards and compensation committees are often inside jobs. The very wealthy are in too many cases busily rewarding one another.

But the problem goes even deeper than that, because our government has in large part turned a blind eye to the forces that have allowed it to occur. Our political leaders, including many of those in the Democratic Party, must share a measure of blame for not having stood up and fought on behalf of America's wage earners. Much as in Andrew Jackson's day, there is very little push-back from government leaders that might stanch this disturbing transfer of wealth to the already wealthy.

And here, the American people have been ill-served by one of the least-reported political phenomena of the past thirty years: the unintended consequences of the Democratic Party's shift in political focus during the so-called culture wars. Over time, the well-intentioned energies that attended the civil rights movement and the legislative focus on the poorest members of our society morphed into an almost unstoppable momentum. This momentum expanded policies and political agendas into a variety of other cultural issues, and also created a plethora of inflexible, litmus-test political positions based on interest groups rather than individuals. This shift in focus took the Democratic Party away from its traditional mission of protecting America's workers. Unintentionally, and alarmingly, it also allowed the economic balance of government power to tilt in favor of corporate America.

How so?

Beginning with the Jacksonian admonition in the 1820s that we should measure the health of our society not at the apex but at its base, the principal focus of the Democratic Party until the 1970s was always the well-being of our working men and women. During the "culture wars," that emphasis shifted beyond the civil rights victories and the poverty programs to a broad pastiche of non-economic issues. In the American political debate, economic fairness often took a back seat to a wide variety of interest-group rights, as well as such hot-button issues as reproductive rights, privacy rights, gun control, and the health of the environment. In key debates, the Democratic Party still stood for the well-being of the poor and dispossessed. But somewhere along the way it lost its historic emphasis on working men and women.

These other issues were all deserving of attention and certainly of debate. But the most important domestic challenge facing America—economic fairness for its workers—was not reaching the venues of government where true, in-depth debate could even be held. And in the 1990s, as globalization kicked into full swing, bringing along with it the internationalization of corporate America and the creation of such international economic bodies as the North American Free Trade Agreement (NAFTA) and World Trade Organization (WTO), the legitimate need for protecting the economic conditions of the American worker fell by the wayside. Indeed, comprehensive worker protection was not even specifically addressed in these landmark agreements.

If the Democratic Party was not going to insist on protecting the economic well-being of our workers, then who would? And if neither party was going to speak principally for working people, then what would become the dividing line when Americans decided to cast a vote? When the Democrats deemphasized the well-being of the American worker, the issues of the culture wars took over the debate. In fact, those issues ended up redefining the divisions between the two dominant political parties. And once these debates went into full swing, a lot of more conservative Americans engaged in predictable and often enraged counterattacks on a variety of these social issues, pushing economic issues even further off the table.

These debates over issues that had no impact on an individual's economic well-being nonetheless stirred the emotions of many of the same people who had traditionally affiliated with the Democratic

Party. In fact, this approach was widely touted as a central strategy of the Bush-era Republican Party. And over time an inattention to the plight of working people who were increasingly caught between special-interest lobbying, globalization, and illegal immigration brought about large-scale defections to the Republican Party among many who had for generations been aligned with the Democrats because of their focus on economic fairness.

The end result was a dominant Republican Party that had created a somewhat unnatural alliance between the very rich, on one hand, and on the other a large segment of our society that had grown tired of what they viewed to be the Democratic Party's extreme views on social issues. The unspoken, unanalyzed, and yet permeating end result of this alliance was that a new era of corporate greed enveloped the country, with precious little comment from political leaders.

One would like to think that today's Democratic Party has learned the lesson of this past approach and that its leadership would be at the vanguard of the movement toward economic fairness. Among some political leaders, that is becoming increasingly true. But at this writing, there are probably as many among the Democratic Party's top leadership who are touting hard-to-grasp themes such as the environment and global warming as the prime political issues of the coming decade as there are leaders who are willing to face the political minefield of economic fairness to our workers.

Issues such as global warming are indeed troubling, but at a time when our national security is in such disarray and our workers are watching their jobs disappear, those themes are not clear enough or strong enough to generate a defining, rock-hard support for any broadly based political platform. To understand this reality, one need only consider basic human nature, according to the hierarchy of needs. First, people want to eat and to be clothed and to procreate. Then they want employment and personal security. Once they have that, they look for meaningful careers and community stability, which also translates into national security. And once all of that is accomplished, they will be able to turn toward global issues such as the suffering on other continents and whether the polar ice cap is melting.

This is no doubt the principal reason that, according to the *Washington Post,* a September 2007 *Washington Post*/ABC News poll showed "less than 1 percent of Americans identified global warming as their top issue for the 2008 presidential campaign, and a January [2007] poll by the Pew Research Center ranked it fourth-lowest out of 23 policy priorities that Americans want the president and Congress to address." Only when Americans feel secure in their careers and in their national defense will they rally around intellectual rather than visceral themes. And only if Americans begin to feel a direct, inseparable nexus between these issues and their daily well-being will they put them at the top of their political concerns. This same hierarchy of needs is also why we have such a difficult time convincing evolving economies such as China and India, who are rapidly becoming the world's greatest polluters, to take a more responsible approach toward carbon dioxide emissions and other forms of widespread pollution.

So why are these other issues still preeminent in much of the debate? Partly because they are legitimate problems that do demand forward-looking leadership. Partly because many at the top of the Democratic Party built their careers during the culture wars, so that their focus and base of support still emanate from such emotional issues as the environment and global warming. And partly because of a hard, unspoken reality: There are huge risks in speaking strongly about the palpable unfairness of our economic system.

To put it bluntly, the realities of modern-day campaign financing give over the reins to the very people who need to be confronted, since the money necessary to compete in political campaigns comes from people who have it to spend and who have reason to spend it. It is estimated that in 2008 the presidential candidates of each major party are going to spend a minimum of $500 million in their election efforts. And combined with other races, as the *Financial Times* recently pointed out, campaign spending on media advertising alone "is expected to reach $3 billion in the 2008 election cycle, according to a PQ media report, creating a potentially insurmountable challenge for candidates who are strapped for cash."

No aristocracy in history has decided to give up any portion of its power willingly. It is true that there are more than a few donors in American politics who have benefited from the fruits of this society and as a result want to see America become a better, fairer place, with wider notions of social justice. But there are limits to this largesse. Former House Majority Leader Tip O'Neill once famously maintained that all politics is local. Let's take it a step further: Human nature dictates that political support usually becomes personal. We should not hold our collective breaths on the possibility that altruism will become the dominant theme in the campaign finance process. Politics is a transactional enterprise. And those who have power, wealth, and influence are rarely interested in losing these advantages.

What these same people will perhaps come to understand is that it is actually in their interest to invest in economic fairness. If we do not rebalance the system and inject greater fairness into it, they will indeed lose, as will all the rest of us. For without balance, we may well go the way of ancient Greece, greed-ridden Rome, medieval Italy, and medieval Flanders, as President Theodore Roosevelt so rightly warned.

No rational government leader wants to upend the American economy or cause American businesses to fail. And no one who believes strongly in the right of every American to reach the level of success that matches his or her talent wants to see that success artificially limited. But at the same time, no business leader who counts himself a truly loyal American should feel comfortable while in charge of an American corporation that is not fairly sharing the rewards of success with its workers, and that is not benefiting either the American workforce or the larger prospects of the American economy.

Thus comes the most complicated challenge for those of us in government, and perhaps our greatest test in terms of how we identify ourselves as Americans. Those who have benefited the most from our unique system, including many who have oddly come to think of themselves as entitled rather than obligated as a result of their good fortune, must understand that without balance there is either decay or chaos. To ensure that they understand this prospect will require something that our political leaders have been hesitant to engage in over the past several decades: an honest but sincere confrontation, a demand that those at the top demonstrate a sense of loyalty to our country, a commitment to community, and a feeling of responsibility for those outside their own peer group.

Tendencies toward self-justification and a desire to push government in the other direction are not new. The eminent historian Will Durant wrote as much nearly forty years ago in his brilliant little book *The Lessons of History,* pointing out that in societies throughout history "the concentration of wealth is natural and inevitable and is periodically alleviated by violent or peaceable partial redistribution." Summarizing this "vast diastole and systole" of the social organism from Greek times to the present, Durant commented on the American experiment and the variations that existed even before this latest disturbing trend. "The relative equality of Americans before 1776 has been overwhelmed by a thousand forms of physical, mental, and economic differentiation, so that the gap between the wealthiest and the poorest is now greater than at any time since Imperial plutocratic Rome."

Ironically, Durant was writing about the America of 1968, the year in which I finished college, when corporate CEOs made on average twenty times what their workers made. In retrospect, that observation seems benign compared to today. One wonders whether even Will Durant was able to foresee what faces the nation in these times—an enormous gap between not only the wealthiest and the poorest, but between the wealthiest and everyone else.

CHAPTER SEVEN

STRATEGY IS NOT A BOARD GAME

S trategy is a much-beleaguered word these days, often used so carelessly that it has lost much of its academic meaning. In very general terms, a strategy is a comprehensive plan of long-term action, while tactics involve the specifics of how that plan is actually implemented. In military terms, a strategy lays out the commanding general's (or admiral's) overriding goals, concept of action, and the end point the military action is designed to achieve. In the American military, such a strategy must begin with the goals and the specific direction of our national political process, which under our Constitution is the precursor for setting military action into motion.

A clearly articulated, agreed-upon national strategy can be difficult to obtain in a democracy. This is particularly true here in the United States, where we rightly value our constitutional system of checks and balances, as well as the open arena of free debate. Presidential administrations come and go, bringing with them new teams of national security advisers and differing economic priorities. The makeup of the Congress constantly changes, not only between political parties but also in its leadership, which puts into play different personalities and sometimes alternative views of America's role around the world. A freewheeling media often forces sensitive deliberations into public debate. Well-financed think tanks bankroll the careers and publications of resident scholars, who inundate the process with adversarial arguments. And just as important, this nation derived from many nations is itself constantly in a state of competitive abrasion when it comes to where our national resources should best be placed.

But without a clear national strategy our system is capable of manipulation, and the result can be the misguided use of military force, in a way that does not advance our national interest.

Historically, the concept of a nation's "grand strategy" has been used to lay out its interests around the world, and to offer a framework with which to both protect those interests and encourage their growth. Grand strategy involves far more than military power. In fact, the investment that a democracy makes in its military is but one small part of a properly constituted grand strategy, something of an insurance policy designed to ensure that a nation's overall well-being is not interrupted by those who wish it ill.

The first requirement of a grand strategy is that a nation's leaders carefully define its economic, cultural, political, and security interests around the world. The second challenge is to examine the threats to those interests, both real and potential, and the threats to the vital interests of other countries with whom a nation has developed alliances. And the final step is to develop a formula that will advance the nation's interests on all fronts. This step includes trade policies and agreements, bilateral security arrangements, membership in international compacts such as the United Nations, NATO, the Association of Southeast Asian Nations Regional Forum (ASEAN), and the World Trade Organization, to name a few, along with a national security program that includes a military system capable of both deterring hostile activities and counteracting them if they do occur.

Over time, different nations have put different weight on each element in the development of national strategy. Some governments place military action at the forefront and seek to expand their influence and export their values through conquest. The Roman Empire and Nazi Germany come to mind, as does the expansionist doctrine embodied in the governing precepts of the former Soviet Union. Others—Switzerland and Japan being the best recent examples—provide for their own self-defense, but in international relations rely almost exclusively on trade, diplomacy, and a quieter set of alliances with friendly nations that do project international military power.

The most important aspect of a properly understood grand strategy is that it imparts a certain amount of predictability into a nation's foreign policy. Friend and foe alike, both internationally and domestically, come to understand the priorities of a nation and thus are able to adjust their own strategies. In this way, sometimes wars are prevented. And when they become necessary, the international community is able to gauge the reasons and to respond accordingly.

America's best national leaders know that they are accountable to history not only for how they fight wars but also for how they prevent them. The greatest strategic victory of our time—bringing an expansionist Soviet Union in from the cold while averting a nuclear holocaust—was accomplished without a direct confrontation between our two massively armed superpowers. We endured decades of intense diplomacy, economic rivalry, and volatile showdowns. We lost blood and treasure in two full-blown "splinter wars" fed by these competing ideologies, as well as numerous minor engagements and continuous military operations. But the major conflagration that could have happened thankfully did not.

Then a different set of circumstances took place, troubling to us because we are still struggling to assimilate their implications. In the wake of the Cold War, the United States fell into something of a strategic vacuum. Once the Iron Curtain fell, the dangerous but somewhat simple bilateral tension between an aggressive, nuclear-armed Soviet Union and the forces of the "free world" dissolved into something far more complex, for a while seemingly less threatening but also more difficult to articulate. And into that vacuum stepped an array of essayists, think-tank intellectuals, and activists with narrow agendas. America, the most powerful nation in the world, with the richest economy, had no clear grand strategy, even though we retained an immensely capable military, and even though there were threats to our interests that were yet to be carefully redefined.

This tension between strategic vagueness and intellectual activism had not been resolved when our country was attacked on 9/11. And in many ways it accounts for the strategic blunder of invading Iraq, which because of its complexity and immediate history deserves a detailed examination later in these pages.

There was a time in my life when all the aspects of war had become my chosen, dedicated profession. In fact, there were several times when this was so—first as a military professional; then as a law student and defense analyst consumed by the notions of military strategy; then as a novelist and journalist covering the military and writing about wars and their societal impact; and finally as a government official who at one time was charged with evaluating our military's ability to meet the requirements of its own war plans.

As with so many others who have chosen the military as their professional calling, at a young age I threw myself into this endeavor with heart and soul, and have continued to broaden and deepen my understanding throughout my life. I have studied how wars start and how they are fought. I have spent a great deal of time reading, thinking, and debating how they might be prevented, how diplomacy and economic policy interact with military deterrence, and how the results of conflict affect a nation's place in the world when they are not prevented.

Often with my son at my side, I have walked a score of battlefields from conflicts in America, Europe, Asia, the Middle East, and Oceania, spanning the Roman and English conflicts in Scotland, the wars of Ireland, the French and Indian War, the Revolutionary War, the War of 1812, the Civil War, World Wars I and II, the French war in Indochina, and the American endeavors in Korea, Vietnam, Lebanon, and Afghanistan.

I have had the good fortune to meet with military planners, defense officials, and government leaders in dozens of countries, discussing the interaction of history, culture, and international alliances, while reaching for common ground and looking for policies that can ensure stability as well as cultural and economic harmony. Thankfully, in terms of intellectual independence, all of this occurred before I reached the United States Senate.

By the time I arrived in Vietnam as a young Marine infantry lieutenant, I had spent four years studying strategy, tactics, and the political manipulations inherent in modern guerrilla warfare. The Gulf of Tonkin incident, which signaled America's direct involvement in Vietnam, took place in August 1964, during my first summer at the Naval Academy. By March of my plebe year the Marines had landed in Da Nang, marking the beginning of a large-scale American involvement. I spent the summer of 1965 serving on two different ships based out of Long Beach, California. While on our second ship, a World War II "straight-deck" aircraft carrier that had been converted into an LPH amphibious assault vessel, we transported a Marine Corps infantry battalion to Hawaii, where it further deployed to combat in Vietnam. And by the end of 1965, the Third Marine Amphibious Force in Vietnam numbered 38,000 Marines.

The war was on. As it heated up it became clear to most of us, particularly those heading into the Marine Corps, that the first assignment of our young military careers would be as combat leaders in Vietnam. The casualty lists began to show names of people who had lived down the hall, or with whom we had played athletics. Those who had fought, and those who were directing the war, started making appearances at the evening lectures in historic Mahan Hall, illuminating the challenges that all of us would soon face. In the daytime classrooms I was studying engineering, however reluctantly, but in truth I was preparing to lead infantry Marines in an enormously difficult and frustrating environment. The Marine sectors of Vietnam offered a combination of conventional and guerrilla warfare with an additional political twist, in that the war was being fought on the heels of a long and ultimately unsuccessful period of colonization by the French.

An engineering degree was mandatory when I attended the Naval Academy, but I make no claims of proficiency in that area. Differential equations class was a nightmare. Fluid dynamics class was a blur. Thermodynamics was worse—entropy, as we used to joke, was alive and living in Argentina. But by the time I graduated I was as prepared as humanly possible for the unpredictable and ever-changing challenges of war. Sometimes in class but often on my own I had read, among others, the works of Sun Tzu, Machiavelli, Clausewitz, Jomini, Alfred Thayer Mahan, Marx and Engels, Liddell Hart, Mao Tsetung, and Vo Nguyen Giap. Since I knew I would be fighting in Vietnam I had studied the French theories of colonial warfare, including the views of the early strategists such as Joseph Simon Gallieni and his brilliant protégé Hubert Lyautey, and also the French Indochina campaigns following World War II, particularly the writings of the legendary Bernard Fall.

As an aspiring Marine, I had also studied in detail the Pacific campaigns against the Japanese in World War II and the campaigns against the North Koreans and the Chinese during the Korean War. And as a prospective rifle platoon commander whose military reach in combat was going to be limited to the narrow battle space of tactical ground combat, I had earnestly followed on a daily basis the battles, tactics, and lessons learned from Vietnam as that war inexorably unfolded before all of our eyes.

This meticulous approach to one's prospective profession was typical of many of my peers. There is nothing particularly noteworthy about it, other than that its breadth and depth have rarely been understood among the pundits, think-tank gurus, and commentators on various talk shows, who tend to regard most low-level military professionals as unschooled in the larger aspects of their calling.

I then spent long months in the "bush" of Vietnam's hotly contested Quang Nam Province, first as a rifle platoon commander and then, at the age of twenty-three, as a rifle company commander. It is not necessary to fight in a war in order to properly assess national security policy, but on the other hand, having had that experience doesn't exactly hurt, either. As in every other area of life, our personal experiences provide us context. Without such context, one risks becoming a prisoner of the advice he or she receives from others who do have it.

Here's an example, randomly chosen for no great reason other than because it is recent. During my 2006 Senate campaign, the Israeli Army moved into Lebanon. Rather than barreling into Beirut, as they had done in a forty-kilometer armored dash in 1982, the Israeli offensive stalled when it hit an extensive Hezbollah bunker complex. The talk shows were rife with American politicians who would often casually toss out the notion that the Israelis simply needed to move more quickly and aggressively against the Hezbollah positions, to get on with the rest of their offensive.

If you've ever had to take out a bunker, it kind of puts that challenge into a different perspective. If you want to move fast, bypass the bunkers. If you can't bypass them, then taking out bunkers is a methodical, time-consuming, high-risk business. It is also, as the planners might put it, pretty manpower-intensive. Taking out interlocking bunker complexes was the reason the United States Marines ended up with nearly 7,000 dead in one month of fighting on the tiny island of Iwo Jima.

On my return from Vietnam, I continued this self-induced professional education. I was running platoons of officer candidates through their rigors, and also teaching weapons and tactics. But in the evenings when I was not on bivouac and during free weekends I studied. I read in detail about the Japanese campaigns in Asia that both preceded and followed our involvement in World War II, including the brutal occupation of China, which in many ways set the stage for the 1949 Communist takeover in that country. I studied World War I in depth, focusing on the repeated failures of diplomacy that led to this catastrophe, whose ramifications are still underappreciated by most Americans. I absorbed, with a new understanding, the implications of the costly trench warfare that brought the British, French, and Germans more than four million dead soldiers. I did some serious thinking about the unintended consequences not only of war, but of how wars are brought to a close, given the reality that the armistice of that war ended up setting the stage for World War II.

I studied all of the campaigns of World War II. Americans, too often self-absorbed when it comes to assimilating the lessons of history, tend to ignore the theaters of that epochal event where our country did not fight. I did reread with fresh interest the best accounts of the North African campaign, the Sicily and Italian campaigns, the D-Day invasion at Normandy, the Battle of the Bulge, the China-Burma-India Theater, and MacArthur's brilliant island campaigns in the Pacific. But I also focused on the brutal and often-neglected warfare between the German and Soviet armies. These campaigns were assuredly the most savage fighting in the history of warfare, accounting for the great majority of casualties in a war where Germany lost 3.7 million combat dead from an army of 12 million soldiers, and the Soviets lost, by conservative estimates, more than 7 million soldiers.

Believing it was my duty as a military professional, I also began studying in depth the political, cultural, economic, and strategic makeup of Asia. Asia was emerging from a political vacuum created by the departure of the European colonial powers and the defeat of Japan, now evolving into the most dynamic region in the world. Northeast Asia was and is the only region where the interests of Russia, China, Japan, and the United States directly intersect. Marines back then had a saying: "We train to fight in Europe, and we die in Asia." The Vietnam War was still grinding on. It was clear that it was not going well, but it was not clear how or when it would end. And once it ended, what would the region look like? What were America's interests, and how should the American military be configured in that vital region after Vietnam? Indeed, how should our national security strategy be shaped in that aftermath?

I began to think harder, in a different way, and I began to write.

During my last year in the Marine Corps, I was assigned to the Secretary of the Navy's immediate staff. During that year, I wrote three major articles for professional journals. One of them pointed out that the Marine Corps, throughout history viewed by the civilian leadership and by the other services simply as an adjunct of the Navy, had no general officer billets of its own on any of the Joint Staffs around the world. In my view, without such billets on staffs where war plans were made and where interservice rivalry was refereed and adjudicated, the Marine Corps would remain a second-class military branch. The article also pointed out the policy danger when the statutory roles and missions of the Marine Corps under the National Security Act were limited to amphibious warfare, while the reality was that the Marine Corps was the nation's preeminent "force in readiness," with amphibious warfare only one of many missions. There had been several attempts to do away with the Marine Corps, most notably just after World War II. What would happen to the Corps in a fickle Congress if the amphibious mission became obsolete?

This article caused a minor firestorm at the top levels of the Marine Corps, with the Commandant of the Marine Corps finally ordering several senior officers to write a rebuttal. But as time progressed, it proved to be a precursor to debates in the Congress more than a decade later, which finally resulted in full recognition of the Marine Corps as an independent military branch, including allowing the Marine Corps full representation on Joint Staffs.

Another article articulated my views regarding a new strategic theory for the United States military in Asia. By 1972, the in-country locations of America's military in Asia were largely the end result of two past wars—World War II and Korea—and one war that was slowly grinding to a painful and inglorious close in Vietnam. In addition to our forces in Vietnam, at that time America kept extensive military bases in Thailand, the Philippines, Taiwan, South Korea, Japan, Okinawa, and Guam. Looking to the future, there was no strategic logic to the positioning of these military forces. I argued that, while political considerations might limit the timing and size of any adjustments, an entire array of diplomatic and strategic realities made it sensible for the United States to withdraw from many of these bases and to consolidate much of its Asian presence in Guam and the Mariana Islands. In so doing, American forces could adopt what classically could be called a strategic "interior position." By consolidating our base structure, we would be making more efficient use of our people, shortening logistical lines of communications, removing our military from the internal political turmoil of various regimes, and still maintaining strong naval forces in the region in order to compensate for the reduction in the bases.

This adjustment could also be made more effective, I argued, by encouraging the Japanese navy to operate alongside the United States Navy in areas such as the Indian Ocean. True, Japan's constitution limited its military to those actions clearly in "self-defense." But what could be a better example of self-defense than defending the sea-lanes through which Japan acquired its oil, especially when Japan had no oil resources of its own? The sea-lanes between the Persian Gulf and Japan were, literally, the main artery of Japan's national survival.

It is gratifying to see, some thirty-five years later, that both of the major conclusions of this strategic view are finally on their way to being adopted by the defense establishment. American military forces are now being relocated from other parts of Pacific Asia to Guam. And the Japanese navy is expanding its role, in cooperation with our own, including deployments in the Indian Ocean.

I was soon on my way to law school, having been medically retired from the Marine Corps due to a secondary infection that had set into the bone of my left leg after I was wounded in Vietnam. The running joke at my retirement ceremony—hosted by then–Secretary of the Navy John Warner, whom I would later join as a fellow senator representing Virginia—was that the Commandant of the Marine Corps had purged me for heresy following my article about Marine Corps roles and missions. I did not want to leave the Marine Corps. But a transformation had taken place in that busy year. The former boxer and infantry officer had learned how to fight with his brain.

Thus began a second, unanticipated career of strategic thought and analysis. While in law school I spent two summers in the Mariana Islands, including one three-month stretch as a consultant to the governor of Guam. One-third of that 208-square-mile island was in military bases or holding areas, some in use and some in weed-choked disrepair. As a part of an assessment of the future land needs of our military on Guam, I wrote an in-depth analysis of every American military facility in Asia, then posited how the United States could modify its strategy in order to restructure and relocate its military presence to the islands of Guam, Tinian, and Saipan, with a strong naval presence operating in the forward areas of the Pacific. I visited Okinawa, examining the extensive base system and training facilities used by the Army and the Marine Corps. I walked or drove nearly every square inch of Guam, Tinian, and Saipan.

To ensure that my recommendations had factual merit, I dug back into the past, finding dog-eared documents and examining the historical records from the American military presence on those islands during World War II. How many troops were stationed there? What did they do? How did their presence affect the vitally important water tables on these relatively small islands?

Political considerations aside, the answers actually made my strategic theory even more plausible. Guam had once housed 202,000 American military personnel, including an entire U.S. Navy fleet at Apra Harbor, which later included a dry dock and a first-rate ship-repair facility. Andersen Air Force Base, from which many B-52 bombing missions were launched into Vietnam, was an underutilized facility. Northwest Field, a spacious area near Andersen Air Force Base that in less than a year would house a tent city for refugees escaping from South Vietnam, was empty. The small, twenty-nine-square-mile island of Tinian had housed 175,000 Americans, most of them belonging to the Army Air Corps. Toward the end of World War II, Tinian had been the largest and busiest airport in the world. The island was now almost unpopulated, and even though nearly thirty years had passed its extensive runway system was still intact.

Back in Washington, the Watergate hearings were in full bloom and Richard Nixon was preparing to resign as President. Elsewhere in Asia, South Vietnam was falling apart, its fledgling attempt at democracy on its way to extinction in a Communist offensive that would become full-blown in a mere eight months. And I was tromping the jungles and ridges of long-ago battlefields, sticking my head inside caves that still held the artifacts of Japanese soldiers, all the while trying to find the formula for reconfiguring America's presence in Asia.

History was everywhere, as were the reminders of the dangers and the costs of war. And sometimes history had a way of playing tricks on your mind.

In the wide, many-hued green lagoon between Saipan's lushly vegetated beaches and the pencil line of coral that made its outer reef, two American tanks jutted like rusted knobs above the perfect skyline. On the anniversary of the American invasion, I stood on top of an old Japanese bunker that had once defended the beach and looked out into the lagoon toward the tanks. I was imagining that I could see all the way to the other side of the distant reef, to where the fleet of landing ships and aircraft carriers had come. The choppy, windblown sea would have been filled with dozens of smoking, swaying warships that had slowly gathered from across the horizon. Naval guns would have been screeching and crashing, working over the beach defenses and the artillery positions in the slate-gray hills behind. Tanks and landing craft would have been crawling down the gates of open-tongued LSTs, nosing over the reef and bouncing into the lagoon, churning up the coral and the sand and heading for the shore.

Troops would have been wading in the lagoon, heading directly into the raking fire of Japanese machine guns. Artillery would have been breaking over them and around them. Their blood would have been pooling and swirling in the clear salt water of the lagoon. They would have come right at the bunker on which I stood. They would have struggled through the waist-deep water with packs on their backs, weapons firing, their bodies lurching tensely but filled with a fierce, unstoppable determination. As they neared I would have seen them, grim-faced and wild-eyed. And soon they would have silenced its guns.

Nearly four thousand Americans died on this little island in the space of twenty-five days of fighting. And the Marines on that very first day had taken two thousand killed or wounded between the far reef and the beach on which I stood.

I was so overwhelmed by emotion, and perhaps by my own memories from a different war, that I found myself choking back tears. It was eerily quiet on this remote island beach, whose visitors were now mainly Japanese tourists. The bunker on which I stood was largely buried now, filled inside with sand and flotsam from three decades of storms and mulchlike tropical rot.

But an emerging thought would not leave me. The tanks had been hit by Japanese artillery. The Marines inside had no doubt been killed. I was not yet born when this happened, but they were fellow Marines. I had commanded troops in combat, many of whom had been killed or wounded after following my orders and listening to my judgment. What could I have said to the Marines wading toward this bunker or in those tanks in order to justify their deaths? What if they and I had known that within a generation of their passing, the island they attacked would become a prominent tourist attraction for the children of the enemy that killed them, while America itself would largely forget that it even existed? What would they have thought if they could have foreseen that this enemy would in a short time become an ally, and the tanks that were their coffins would end up as a conversation piece for the children of that same enemy?

I finally decided that it would have made no difference. Marines fight for one another, and to the accountability of their history. They fight where they are sent. They do not fight for politicians, they fight for their country. And so the question would be better put to the leaders who decide when and where they fight. There was tragedy in their dying, but there was honor, too.

I walked the battlefields carrying a large map of the island on which I had marked the major events of the campaign. History came alive for me. In the tangles of jungle vines I found Death Valley, a place where an Army division's advance stalled as the Marine divisions on either side continued their assaults, opening up the flanks of both divisions to Japanese fire. Yes, here was a battlefield example of the "interior position"—the Japanese, almost by accident, were sitting in the center of a large U and could hammer the Marines on both sides of them and the Army to their front. Amid the vines and thick stands of bamboo-like tangan-tangan I found several old foxholes, rocks piled to their front, some with olive-green K-ration tins still in them, one still sporting the sole from an old military boot whose leather had rotted away. How had that soldier lost his boot? To my right was Purple Heart Ridge, where the Fourth Marine Division's left flank was exposed because of the stalled advance in Death Valley. And to my left were the craggy peaks of Mount Tapochau, which the Second Marine Division had taken, nine hundred meters a day, despite heavy losses.

At the far northern end of the thirty-square-mile island I reached the haunting silence of Suicide Cliffs. From this 800-foot promontory one could see far out into the Pacific. Just offshore was the Marianas Trench, at 38,000 feet the deepest known spot of any ocean in the world. But from this cliff thousands of Japanese civilians, including entire families, had jumped to their deaths rather than surrender to the control of advancing American troops. The Japanese had colonized Saipan and other islands in the Marianas following World War I, turning much of the island into pineapple and sugar plantations. In all, 22,000 Japanese civilians would die during the invasion, two-thirds of the total Japanese civilian population, with a substantial percentage of those by suicide. They had been told that if they were caught, the red-haired Yankee barbarians would rape their women and torture their children.

The island of Tinian, separated from Saipan by a mere three miles of Pacific Ocean, held other historical paradoxes. It was from this now largely empty island, at twenty-nine square miles about the same size as Saipan, that most of the heavy bomber raids on Japan were launched. World War II Quonset huts still huddled along the main road in the island capital of San Jose. Most of the 1,000 or so islanders now lived in them. I stayed at a four-room "hotel," the only lodging on the island. Cockroaches as big as the palm of my hand scurried constantly across the floor, entering and leaving through a large gap in the doorway. The hotel's owners located a fifteen-year-old boy named Benny to drive me around the island in his grandfather's Toyota for ten dollars a day. We rarely needed to follow the rough, narrow roads; we simply took the world-class, empty runways that crisscrossed much of the island.

Benny knew where to drive. He needed to, because most of the island was flat, the weeds were high, there were no landmarks, and the sun was difficult to use for direction. In addition, while the runways were still in near-perfect condition, many of the smaller taxiways were obscured by thick mats of jungle grass that leaned in from both sides, scraping constantly against our car. On the far northwest corner of the island, a sharp cliff fell into a rocky stretch of beach, where just beyond the rocks the deep Pacific surged against the empty shoreline. The thousand or so people who lived on Tinian called this stretch "Dump Coke Beach," because for decades they could climb down onto the rocky shoreline and pick up the leavings of an American military that had been in a hurry to head home after the surrender of Japan. Desks, equipment, foodstuffs—including thousands of unopened bottles of Coca-Cola—had been dumped off the cliff.

One afternoon as Benny carefully drove the Toyota through the jungle grass, the runway opened up into a small clearing. In the middle of the clearing was a pedestal, and on the pedestal was a brass plaque. Intrigued, I asked Benny to stop the car. The plaque stood in a vast emptiness under a brilliant, open sky. I do not remember the exact words, but after more than thirty years I can still approximate them: *From this spot on August 6, 1945, the Enola Gay took off, dropping the first atomic bomb at Nagasaki, Japan, and thereby hastening the end to World War II. We shall always remember the dedication and sacrifice of the brave Americans who made this possible.*

Once, long ago, this had been the busiest airport in the world. Nearly two hundred thousand Americans had swarmed over this remote island like ants at a picnic. And now, all around us there was nothing other than the high grass and the quiet memories that attended the runways themselves.

Stricken with such a quiet emptiness, I could not help but remember the lines of "Ozymandias," the great poem by Percy Bysshe Shelley:

And on the pedestal these words appear:
"My name is Ozymandias, king of kings:

undertook the responsibility of examining whether the plans were realistic, not in terms of questioning the combat plans but by analyzing the actual resources that were being made available to the plans.

Since I was a member of the Defense Resources Board, it fell to me and my staff to examine all of the nontactical aspects of going to war. Were the casualty estimates that the military used realistic in terms of the combat scenarios that were being assumed? If not, the surge of combat medical facilities and personnel being planned to take care of casualties would be deficient, soldiers would die for lack of medical care, and the flow of fresh replacement troops from the training base would be too small. Was there enough strategic airlift to bring troops and equipment into the battle zone, and casualties and family members out? If not, families would be left on the battlefield, causing American civilian casualties and affecting the morale of those in combat, and the assets necessary for continuing any military campaign would not reach the battlefield. Were the readiness indicators of the Guard and reserve units high enough to meet their assigned deployment schedules? If not, our war plans were nothing more than illusory, with "paper" units assigned to do real-world jobs. Could we count on the Individual Ready Reserve, that pool of recently discharged military members who might be vital as replacements in the early days of a war? Could we find these people? Were they physically and mentally capable of being mobilized? If not, then there would be no pipeline of pretrained people available to cover the transitional period between a peacetime military system and one that could function in wartime.

I spent a great deal of time working with military and civilian defense leaders from other countries, particularly our partners in NATO Europe, and with our own military leaders and units deployed overseas. I crossed the English Channel with British forces in their largest mobilization exercise since World War II. I observed several mobilization exercises in the Netherlands. I visited France and Switzerland, observing their military both operationally and at the highest levels of planning. I met with the military leaders of Turkey and Italy. I worked closely with German defense officials and with their army, observing numerous war exercises, mobilization drills, and training regimens.

The Germans were particularly valuable because they were especially serious about the ramifications of a possible Soviet invasion. Having fought the Soviets in the bloodiest campaigns in the history of warfare, the Germans had developed casualty estimates for certain scenarios that were typically four times as high as our own, for the same combat scenarios. This prospect drove every aspect of their mobilization structure, from troop replacement to combat medical care to the need to prepare for the transition of civilian facilities such as school gymnasiums into hospitals. The glaring disparities convinced me that our military needed to rethink its own war models. And as with other occasions when I brought bad news back to Secretary Weinberger, unlike many other government officials throughout our history he took action and ordered that it be done.

In late 1984, I became the first high-level government official to propose, on strategic grounds, that the United States reduce the size of its military commitment to NATO Europe. By the mid-1980s, the United States Army still kept 206,000 soldiers permanently stationed in Germany alone, at a time when the entire British army worldwide consisted of only 145,000 soldiers. Another 88,000 Air Force personnel were in Europe, stationed principally in Germany and the United Kingdom. Most of these soldiers and airmen had brought their families with them, creating a huge and expensive American infrastructure in those countries.

Our military presence in NATO Europe had begun in 1949 as a temporary "surge" in response to an expanded and dangerous Soviet threat. It was supposed to be reduced once Western Europe again found its feet economically. Instead, as with so many American military incursions since World War II, it had grown ever larger. By 1984, there were 55,000 more American troops in NATO Europe than there had been at the end of the Vietnam War, some ten years earlier. Given the economic resurgence of Western Europe, the size of this military presence had also grown less logical. And in terms of true military strategy, it had become even less justifiable. American bases in Europe had become full-blown, independent communities, sporting a huge infrastructure of schools, housing, and recreational and medical facilities. If an invasion were indeed to come, the battlefield plans of our military would become complicated by the logistical and morale problems of having so many American family members in the "area of operations."

The strategic views that I had developed and refined in the Pacific a decade before had not changed. Strategically, the United States was a maritime nation whose interests were best protected through a vigorous seapower presence that would connect us to other nations without unnecessarily involving us directly in their periods of inner turmoil. American ground forces should operate as "maneuver elements" rather than being bogged down in static defensive positions dedicated to the local defense of any one specific country. In November 1984, I wrote a memorandum to the Undersecretary of Defense for Policy, discussing the future use of American military forces. I suggested that over the coming decade the American military should reduce its presence in NATO Europe. Concurrently, I suggested, the overall size of the Army and of the tactical Air Force should be reduced, and the Navy, whose size had been cut in half following the Vietnam War, should continue to grow.

The suggestion did not win any votes on the turf-oriented Joint Chiefs of Staff, nor did it affect short-term national policy. But my strong belief in that strategic formula eventually led me to resign as Secretary of the Navy when a different approach was mandated by Caspar Weinberger's successor as Secretary of Defense. And it did give me some sense of validation when the reconfiguration of our forces in Europe following the first Gulf War, which eventually resulted in a reduction of our German presence to 75,000 American soldiers, closely approximated the recommendations I had brought forward seven years earlier.

Not unlike today, the greatest challenge during my tenure as Secretary of the Navy came from the turmoil in Southwest Asia, and from the desire of some in our government to involve the United States too deeply in the complex, internecine battles of that region.

In the late summer and early fall of 1983, a few months before coming to the Pentagon, I had spent time as a journalist in Beirut, covering the Marine "peacekeeping" force that in October of that year lost more than 240 dead in a suicide bombing at the Beirut airport. The governing structure of Lebanon in the 1980s closely resembled that of Iraq today: a weak central government surrounded by powerful, armed militias engaged in a many-sided civil war, with a stronger nation—in this case Syria rather than Iran—looking menacingly over its shoulder.

On any given day in Beirut, one never knew who was going to shoot at whom, or for what reason. Travelers could not even fly into the Beirut airport in mid-1983. The United States Marines were defending it on the ground, but the Druze militia had pockmarked the airfield with artillery shells and kept it under continuous surveillance from the nearby Chouf Mountains, making the airfield unusable. To reach Beirut our television crew took a flight from Athens to Larnaca, Cyprus, where at midnight we boarded a reeking old steamer that crossed an ocean passage in the darkness, bringing us to the Beirut seaport. The steamer was packed with a mix of Lebanese and international customers, many of them journalists. The old man who operated the small ship was very happy, because the closed airport in Beirut was bringing him a bonanza. We sat all night in his dining area, smoking cigarettes, drinking beer, and eating his homemade sandwiches. It seemed as though he was selling the beer and sandwiches for five of anything—five francs, five dollars, five marks. There was no alternative, and the food in Beirut would be just as random, so we were glad to pay.

In the early morning, we docked at the port of Beirut. Just next to us, a French military ship was unloading fresh troops, weapons, and supplies. A British army unit was also in Beirut, just off a tour in Northern Ireland. An Italian army unit also had joined the four-nation peacekeeping effort. The French, who along with our Marines would suffer a serious suicide bombing attack in October, were all business as their ship unloaded its cargo. A platoon of their soldiers had set up in a hasty perimeter, lying on the dirt-packed berms above the water's edge.

Even though the port activities and the customs house near the harbor seemed to bustle with normalcy, their rifles were pointed in that direction, toward the city.

The city sprawled before us, brightly colored, sand-burnt, many parts of it broken into pieces by years of conflict. From the water's edge inward, Beirut was a place of latent chaos, scarred with memories of violence. The streets leading from the port opened up into the infamous Green Line, a dividing street between different ethnic and religious sects where a once-beautiful part of the city was now obliterated, cratered and ruined. The Green Line was haunting, lifeless and silent. Driving through it, I was reminded of the pictures I had seen of Dresden following the Allied bombings of World War II.

Beirut, once the playground of the Arab world, was now living inside a conundrum, still pulsing with energy and yet powerless to recapture its former stability and charm. Various Sunni, Shia, Christian, and Druze militias and submilitias, and factions and subfactions, were slugging it out with a vicious randomness in a civil war that had begun eight years before. And the Syrians, who have historically considered Lebanon to be a part of Greater Syria, had a habit of rising like armed referees every now and then from over the horizon to join the fray.

In one typical engagement that I covered, a United States Marine outpost was brought under fire by a Druze militia position after the Druze had been shot at by Lebanese army soldiers from a checkpoint on a nearby road. Eventually, a Syrian unit began firing heavy machine guns at both the Marines and the "Lebs" from a position on the far side of a distant string of hills. All the while, in the far distance the Christian Phalange militia was engaged in an artillery duel with another unit that we were unable to identify. Artillery shells hammered into six-story apartment buildings, smacking their outside walls and making sprays of dust. The lights were out inside the buildings. The occupants had already fled, to places only they knew of, to return only if there were to happen, somehow, a cease-fire.

What was the reason for all of this? Borrowing a thought from my frustrating days as an unwilling engineering student, I began to call it cultural entropy. Over time an entire region had fallen into a pattern of destructive behavior, just as all the water in a soon-to-be boiling pot reaches the same temperature no matter where the flame touches the pot. The only way to avoid the heat was to somehow leave the pot, and in fact the brain drain of successful professionals from Lebanon, particularly among its Christian population, was palpable. But for those who stayed, this was simply the reality of the Middle East. Unexplainable violence was the norm.

And so all of that shooting was just another random afternoon in Beirut. As one Marine succinctly put it, "It never pays to get involved in a five-sided argument."

Another Marine was even more precise. The Beirut air was constantly filled with dust, so heavy that the Marines had largely stopped smoking cigarettes. The horizon was filled with destruction—in a city that had not too long before been viewed as one of the crown jewels of the Middle East.

"Sir," he said. "It's time for us to get out of here. This is the armpit of the world."

All right, I'll be honest. He didn't say "armpit."

Journalism has its own flaws, particularly when one comes into a situation with a preconceived political bias. But good journalism, coming from honest, perceptive journalists, has a far better track record with respect to the challenges in the Middle East than do the policies of our political leaders. Sometimes it is easier to comprehend harsh realities when one is able to observe them closely without direct involvement and without having to feel accountable for their end results. And sometimes politicians are so blinded by their policy positions and by the filtering process through which they receive their information that they will never fully understand the true realities of the problems they are trying to fix. In any event, I had come away from this experience with a strong feeling that the United States should tread softly in the Middle East, that it should never give up its military or diplomatic maneuverability by occupying territory in a region so fraught with multilayered conflicts.

And as it was in Beirut, so also is it in the Persian Gulf.

By 1987, the Iran-Iraq War had dragged on for years, a furious bloodletting that Cap Weinberger once dismissed as "a war between the worst regime in the world and the second-worst regime in the world—and you can take your pick as to which is which." But among major allies in the Sunni Arab world, including especially Saudi Arabia, Jordan, Bahrain, and Egypt, concern grew regarding the prospects of an ever-more-powerful theocratic and fundamentalist Iran. Not unlike what one is beginning to hear in some defense circles today, a movement took hold to develop a "pan-Arab" strategy that might over time seal off and contain Iranian expansionist desires. Unfortunately, as part of this strategic shift, the Reagan Administration abandoned American neutrality and tilted toward Iraq.

I have my own theories, but the actual diplomatic journey toward this overt tilt is still historically unclear. Suffice it to say that in February 1987, the Reagan Administration announced a policy whereby Kuwaiti oil tankers would be "reflagged" as American vessels, technically making them American commercial ships under the edicts of international law. This diplomatic fig leaf then obligated the United States Navy to protect the Kuwaiti oil tankers from Iranian attacks as they navigated inside the Persian Gulf and passed through the Iranian-dominated Straits of Hormuz, a vital choke point that led to the open waters of the Arabian Sea.

This was a deliberate and direct provocation of Iran. It was my view then, and it remains my view today, that certain elements in the Reagan Administration decided on this policy as a counterpoint to the revelations of the so-called Iran-Contra debacle, where a renegade element in the White House had, for a complicated set of reasons, provided weapons to Iran. Since our formal policy was to isolate the fundamentalist regime that had taken power in 1979, something needed to be done to convince Saudi Arabia, Bahrain, and other friendly regimes that despite these shipments we had not secretly tilted toward Iran.

And thus began a cavalcade of counterintuitive but nonetheless connected events that resulted, finally, in the strategic paralysis of the United States military trapped inside the unending tribal warfare of Iraq. Is the Middle East byzantine? Is it unpredictable, filled with diplomatic U-turns and clever, vicious ethnic ambushes? Does it make sense for the United States to have directly injected itself into the daily workings of a region where violence is the very emblem of its history and where political loyalties shift like the powdered sand?

Well, yes, yes, and no.

Most Americans remember that Iraq attempted to annex Kuwait in the summer of 1990, which led to our involvement in the first Gulf War. What many forget is that during the Iran-Iraq War, the government of Kuwait was the strongest supporter of Iraq, and that it also happened to be the major friend of the Soviet Union in that region. By reflagging the Kuwaiti tankers and calling them our own, the American government had not only provoked Iran but overtly tilted toward Iraq. This caused Iran to respond by escalating its rhetoric and intensifying its efforts to interfere with Kuwaiti shipping. In May 1987, as these efforts were gaining steam, an Iraqi aircraft attacked and severely damaged an American frigate, the USS *Stark*, killing thirty-seven American sailors. Ostensibly, the Iraqi pilot mistakenly thought that the *Stark* was an Iranian ship. On the other hand, rumor had it that Saddam Hussein rewarded the pilot with a new car when he landed back home in Iraq.

Despite the attack on the *Stark*, and despite the ugliness of both regimes in the Iran-Iraq confrontation, the shift continued. We had chosen sides. Diplomatically, the Iraqis told American officials that they needed better intelligence on American naval operations in order to prevent future miscalculations. A defense official was soon sent to Baghdad to provide the Iraqis with some help. Militarily, wild ideas started sprouting like toadstools in the Pentagon. This was a war—or, well, something like a war—and everybody wanted to play. The region began filling up with special-forces units, minesweepers, CIA helicopters on covert "black" missions, and barges sitting in the middle of the Gulf, to be used as platforms to counteract Iranian Boghammer patrol boats.

From a classical strategic perspective, this new policy made absolutely no sense at all. As Secretary of the Navy, I found myself near enough to observe the circus but, because of the legal and traditional restrictions of my job, too far removed to affect the operational environment. Finally, on August 7, 1987, I wrote a memorandum to Secretary Weinberger laying out my concerns with this approach, consistent with the strategic theories I had advocated in the past and complemented by the on-the-ground realities I had experienced while in Beirut. The memorandum reflected my decision to go on the record regarding the dangers of picking sides in a no-win region, with ramifications for the policies that later resulted in the invasion of Iraq.

 In part I wrote:

Freedom of navigation in the Persian Gulf is beyond doubt a vital national interest. But it is not clear why it became vital to our national interest to re-flag Kuwaiti tankers, thus forcing a freedom of navigation issue that had not existed beforehand . . . In fact, as we learned in Beirut, it could be argued that it was actually against our national interest to become directly involved in a many-sided argument that has been going on for a couple thousand years.

Second, it is difficult for many of our military leaders to see how we can evince a "clear intention of winning" when the nature of our commitment has afforded us no measurement of what it would take to "win." It is dramatically clear that we have offered up a myriad of ways to lose in this endeavor: any time a tanker is hit, any time we fail to be fully successful against an attack on one of our warships, any time a bomb goes off in an airport or a government official is assassinated, we will be perceived as having lost. There is no definitive action that will be accepted as evidence we have won, or when our commitment will be viewed as having been successfully completed.

. . . We have not to this point clearly defined our political and military objectives . . . and as a result we have no way of structuring our missions so that we can claim our military forces have accomplished these objectives. The issue is made more difficult by the political volatility of the region, and by our having lost the tactical initiative when we agreed to re-flag and escort Kuwaiti tankers.

. . . The optimum scenario would be a multinational naval force of reduced size, dedicated to a mission of preserving international waterways for commercial use and committed to using force to defend against the Iranians or anyone else who resumes attacks on shipping. This of course means the Iraqis as well, who as you recall have gained the most in this endeavor . . . Our commitment is to the free transit of all ships . . . and not simply to tilt toward the Iraqis. If our desire had been an Iraqi tilt we should not be doing this at all.

But directly involved we now were, and thus began a mind-boggling roller-coaster ride that has yet to end. I left the Pentagon in February 1988, as the squabbles in the Persian Gulf continued. By that summer, the USS *Vincennes,* from some accounts operating in violation of international law inside Iranian waters and perhaps attempting to draw the Iranian military into a fight, accidentally shot down a commercial Iranian Airbus, killing hundreds of Iranian civilians.

True to the seesaw traditions of the region, by the summer of 1990 Saddam Hussein had invaded Kuwait, announcing his intention to annex his former ally. The United States made yet another return to the region, this time readying to fight the same country that it had tilted toward three years earlier. I initially supported President George H. W. Bush's decision to send troops into the region in order to stand down the Iraqis, but I did so with different premises and a different logic from those who were pushing for an immediate war. This was the third time since 1961 that Iraq had moved on Kuwait. One of those moves had been defused diplomatically by the British, the other by the Soviet Union, a friend of both countries. With the right form of diplomacy it seemed predictable that, as with the other two ventures, a deal would be cut between the two countries and Iraq would soon withdraw.

Instead, the diplomatic rhetoric escalated on a daily basis. Kuwait was heavily invested in the British economy, making their government nervous about the instability the invasion had created. Prime Minister Margaret Thatcher showed up in Washington, urging President Bush to be firm, as she herself had been during the Falklands Islands crisis eight years earlier. Bush, criticized for years as a nonassertive aristocrat, drew his now-famous "line in the sand" against Saddam Hussein. His ratings immediately skyrocketed, and so did the rhetoric. Saddam Hussein became the new Hitler. A chorus of intellectuals, led by the *Wall Street Journal*'s editorial page, began calling for the invasion and occupation of Iraq, and the creation of a "MacArthurian Regency" in Baghdad. The war clouds gathered. Those who doubted its logic became accused in some circles of being unpatriotic, even cowards.

The drums beat ever louder, even though the administration was still talking publicly about a possible settlement—in similar fashion to the months leading up to the invasion of Iraq in 2003. But this deliberate posturing was a relatively fresh technique in 1990. And in October of that year, four months before the Gulf War actually began, I learned from a source in the Pentagon that we were already building permanent bases in Saudi Arabia—bases that in the years following the Gulf War would be attacked by terrorists.

It finally became clear to me that the rhetoric balanced with the supposed willingness to negotiate an Iraqi withdrawal from Kuwait was little more than veneer, a way to spin up the public's emotions and prepare the nation for a war the administration had already decided to fight. And in addition to the permanent bases that were being built in Saudi Arabia, the pressure for taking out Saddam Hussein and occupying Iraq grew louder by the day. My belief that the United States should not be an occupying power in that part of the world had not changed. I began speaking out. As the Congress considered the ramifications of going to war, I testified before the Senate Armed Services Committee, warning of this danger, and also warning that a large-scale war against Iraq brought with it the risk of a significantly empowered Iran.

But the nation had become aroused, caught up in war fever. In many ways, Vietnam had reared its ugly head again, this time as a laughing ghost. Many who had supported the Vietnam War were look-ing for a war to win. Many who had opposed it were looking for a war to support.

Luckily for the United States, National Security Adviser Brent Scowcroft's steady hand fashioned a United Nations resolution that limited our military objectives to driving the Iraqis out of Kuwait, rather than unleashing a further ground offensive on Baghdad. But in a period of less than four years we had demonstrated how the most powerful nation in the world could consistently tie itself into pretzels when faced with the unending backroom dramas of the Middle East. We had assisted Kuwait, a friend of the Soviet Union and the main ally of Iraq in the ugly, no-win Iraq-Iran War, thus tilting toward Iraq and provoking Iran. We had then watched Iraq invade Kuwait, causing us as a consequence to tilt away from Iraq even though we were not in any way seeking to balance our relations with Iran. And finally, we had fought Iraq on the battlefield of its former ally, Kuwait, in the process installing American bases on the ground in the most volatile section of the world.

When the final balance sheet was tallied, we had significantly em-powered Iran, which itself had been strategically reaching out to Rus-sia and especially to China. One might claim that perhaps we did have an agenda here, something of a counterstrategy to contain Iran's ap-proaches to Russia and China. But at this point, just after the fall of the old Soviet Union, we did not have a strategic approach to either of these large countries. We were pumping billions of dollars into Russia to encourage the formation of a capitalist democracy. And we were failing to connect the strategic dots on China's aggressive courting of many Muslim countries, including Pakistan, which would gain a nuclear capability due to Chinese assistance.

The worst was yet to come. Wars do indeed have other unintended consequences. In America, the extremists who had called for contin-uing the war into Iraq and setting up the MacArthurian Regency in Baghdad screamed betrayal when we ended our offensive at the Kuwaiti border. Instead of celebrating a low-cost victory that was al-ready affecting the dangerous balance in the region, these voices began a decade-long push for a full invasion of Iraq. And in Saudi Arabia, a young Islamic fundamentalist from a wealthy family returned from having supported the Afghan rebels in their fight against the Soviet occupation and became enraged that American military bases were occupying the "sacred soil" of his homeland.

His name was Osama bin Laden. Thus was formed Al Qaeda. We would hear from him again.

And the rest, as they say, is history.

CHAPTER NINE

HOW NOT TO FIGHT A WAR

It would be impossible to overstate the impact of our country's having entered the post-9/11 world without a sound national strategy, and thus without a set of clearly articulated priorities that could guide our decision making and define the circumstances under which we would decide to use military force. This lack of a rudder on our national ship of state has affected our relations with many historic friends and allies. Former Defense Secretary Donald Rumsfeld's casual dismissal of the concerns of "old Europe" during the buildup to the Iraq invasion, which meant most of our original NATO allies, comes quickly to mind. It has caused us to become strategically vulnerable to an increasingly powerful China, which has followed a determined national strategy that combines military, diplomatic, and economic policies to increase its influence and leverage around the world. And it has especially affected the manner in which we have approached the actions of a broad spectrum of nations with whom we have some level of disagreement.

The Bush Administration has been characterized by an adoration of the military option on one hand and a lack of adroit diplomacy on the other. In the international arena, its policies toward adversaries, real and potential, has bordered on adolescent behavior, but with grave, adult-world consequences. When it comes to countries with which he disagrees, this President has spent six years blowing things up, or threatening to do so, or attempting to isolate them from the world community when he could have been using the full array of our national assets to bring them into it.

Examples abound. For five years, the Bush Administration largely ignored the Israeli-Palestinian stalemate, abandoning a host of constructive efforts that preceded it. It deliberately worsened the possibility of improving relations with North Korea and Iran by labeling them as members of a Saddam Hussein–centered "axis of evil" at a time when more constructive efforts could have paid dividends for American security. It repeatedly raised the specter of war against Syria and Iran, driving these two unnatural allies closer together when a smart application of all our diplomatic tools could have broken them apart and thus brought greater stability to that turbulent region.

Another useful example of this lamentable state of diplomacy, suitably removed from the heightened emotions of discussing the Middle East, involves the military regime in Burma, or, as its military junta has insisted on calling it in recent years, Myanmar. In the summer of 2001, I visited that country at the invitation of an American businessman who had contacted me after reading a piece I had written in the *Wall Street Journal* about China's steadily increasing influence in Southeast Asia. I spent time in his factories, where Burmese employees were turning out high-quality outdoor furniture that was being shipped all over the world. I watched him mentor and encourage his Burmese employees, several of whom were advancing into management positions under his tutelage. I traveled, often alone and sometimes with my host, throughout Rangoon (Yangon these days) and far into the countryside, interacting freely with Burmese citizens from many different walks of life.

And toward the end of my visit I met with several leaders of the military junta, speaking frankly with them about the need for them to work toward a more open society and to bring Burma more productively into the world community.

These facts were clear from this weeklong visit: That Burma, which in the decade following World War II was thought to be the country with the most promising future in the region, was now ruled by an autocratic, at times ruthless military regime. That the United States was readying an ever-harsher set of economic sanctions against the country to try to pressure the regime to move toward democracy—sanctions severe enough that they were going to require American businesses to leave the country altogether. And that China completely dominated the northern regions of the country and was active elsewhere, including having built a large port facility on the Indian Ocean along its southern border.

In Burma, China was dramatically expanding both its influence and its economic relations. Due to the coming sanctions, American businesses were going to be leaving Burma at the same time that China, along with other nations, would be taking up the slack, enabling the autocratic government to survive while China positioned itself economically, militarily, and diplomatically for the future.

And the results emanating from these facts were predictable. A series of sanctions, especially those put in place from 2003 forward to today, have indeed driven American businesses from the country. Burmese citizens who could have continued to increase their knowledge of free-market practices, other cultures, and other systems of government through their associations with, and under the mentoring of, friendly Americans are now in near-total isolation from the Western world. And, finally, our economic withdrawal from Burma has not hurt the regime so much as it has increased the position of China in that country militarily, diplomatically, and economically. As our trade with Burma has all but evaporated, China's volume of trade, according to the United Nations Statistics Division, has tripled from about $500 million in 1999 to $1.5 billion in 2006. In reality, these numbers very likely understate the true increase in trade volume, since much of the cross-border business between the two countries goes unreported.

Equally predictably, for a few days in September 2007 the Burmese situation flitted briefly across the international consciousness. Protesters, led by a throng of influential Buddhist monks, took to the streets to rail against the ruling regime. They were quickly and brutally suppressed by the government, with precious few international media at the scene to report on either their bravery or the viciousness of the government's response. If westerners had remained in the country, this moment might never have occurred, because it is entirely possible that conditions might have improved rather than deteriorated.

The protest, which was stamped out with unknown numbers of casualties and imprisonments, could have been the catalyst for a full re-examination of our approach to the deplorable situation in Burma. Instead, the response from the American government was characterized by a few days of screaming about the evils of the current regime, including the well-reported recriminations from the President's wife, followed by little more than a hopeless shrug. And the reaction in the Congress was to hold a couple of self-important, didactic hearings and then to propose even tighter sanctions, including a bill to ban the import of products such as teak and jewelry that originated in Burma and were improved in other countries for further export. In the real world of trade, one can only imagine the challenges of trying to determine if the teak furniture you have just imported from, say, Thailand, should be prevented from entering America because it might have come originally from a Burmese tree.

In reality, this predictable cycle of outraged verbal condemnation and "feel good" legislation accomplishes almost nothing. True, it allows American politicians to placate international human rights groups demanding that something be done about a regime's brutal suppression of its people. It also provides a few well-meaning politicians with the illusion that they are taking a hard stand against authoritarianism. But it does little to either eliminate the power or alter the conduct of a regime that can still trade with countries such as China, India, and the Southeast Asian members of ASEAN, all of which are opposed to the approach that we have taken. The greatest impact of these kinds of partial sanctions is simply to take the United States out of the problem-solving end of the formula, like the playground kid who picks up his ball and goes home when the other kids don't let him decide the rules of the game. And while such sanctions are unable to reduce the harm caused by these regimes, they do continue the isolation of the people living under them, who need our assistance and our strong involvement in order to have the kind of future that we claim is our objective in the first place.

It is clearly in our national interest to confront authoritarian regimes around the world and to attempt to change their practices. But refusing to engage them is actually tantamount to ignoring the circumstances that we supposedly condemn. And economic sanctions rarely have the desired impact when other major trading partners decline to participate.

Perhaps the best example of a national policy that enabled us to bring a dangerous regime into the world community is that of China itself, at least in the years preceding the demise of the Soviet Union, when our China policy was anchored in a firm national strategy. In the early 1970s, China was indeed a rogue nation, far more dangerous than the Iran of today. China was already a nuclear power. Its leadership frequently spouted hostile, toxic rhetoric about the United States. It had an American war on its border in Vietnam. And President Richard Nixon had made his political career as a strongly anti-Communist foreign policy leader.

But for a variety of valid strategic reasons, the United States reached out to China, engaging that country diplomatically and economically while never relenting in our military policies, which remained strongly loyal to friendly countries that might feel threatened by resurgent Chinese power. Over time, this approach defused many tensions in the region and increased the economic viability of many countries, not the least of which was China itself. And if the United States is able to recover from its more recent lapses in national strategy while dealing with this important and evolving relationship, an ever-emerging China whose future is interdependent with our own is the healthiest outcome one can hope for, given the interests of both nations.

It must nonetheless be said that such an outcome is in serious jeopardy, given trade policies and the conduct of American foreign policy since the terrorist attacks of September 11, 2001. China, our greatest long-term strategic threat, is now our largest creditor and indeed our banker, even as it expands its influence throughout the world. At the same time, the lack of "grand strategic" focus following the demise of the Soviet Union, along with the national panic following the attacks of September 11, 2001, have brought our nation into a dangerous era where our military is misplaced, our economy is seriously weakened, our alliances are in question, and our national goals are no longer clearly defined.

How did this happen?

I have rarely visited the Pentagon since my resignation as Secretary of the Navy in February 1988. And thus it was unusual that I was in The Building, as it is so frequently referred to, on the morning of September 11, 2001.

This does not mean that I in any way abandoned my interest in national security, which in fact continued to grow. But I have largely stayed away from the Pentagon, for two reasons. The first is that I decided while serving in the Defense Department that I did not want to be seen as trading on my experiences by entering the "military-industrial complex" when I left. This thought process can raise a few quizzical eyebrows in today's Washington, but I had decided upon it after long thought about the unfettered role I have always sought as a writer.

Winston Churchill was something of a role model on this point, even though the British and American governmental systems are not completely analogous when thinking of this concept. Having served as First Lord of the Admiralty at the outset of World War I, and as Prime Minister during Great Britain's most difficult but finest hours, Churchill was in my view a leader of historic proportions. But he also was a truly memorable writer, having won the Nobel Prize not for peace but for literature. Churchill made a good bit of money writing, even while he was a sitting Member of Parliament. But in so doing, he was marketing the value of his insights to the public at large, not simply trading on personal contacts that might help sell a product. People wanted to read Churchill's unvarnished opinions and to gain insights from his wisdom. This was entirely different than if he had sought to profit from his services as First Lord of the Admiralty by attempting to sell guns and ships to the Ministry of Defence.

I valued my philosophical and political independence, and I did not want to trade away the credibility of any controversial position I might hold by having opponents claim that I was merely trying to sell a product or to advance a client's point of view. For this reason, although I have given much advice on a pro bono basis over the years, and although I have argued in different forums for a variety of defense programs and policies, I have never taken money for doing so. Even in the mid-1990s, when I was bringing American companies into Vietnam, I declined to do any work that related to defense industries or with companies that had ties to national security.

The second reason is that on the political landscape, I had become controversial. People sometimes forget that at its highest levels the Pentagon is a political and not a military place. The Pentagon is the epicenter of the entire concept of political control over the United States military. It is the headquarters of the Department of Defense, with the emphasis on "Department," meaning a part of the President's cabinet, just as there is a Department of Justice, a Department of Transportation, and a Department of State. The Pentagon is a political arm of the executive branch, directed and overseen from its E-Ring offices by whichever presidential administration happens to be in power at the moment.

This makes the people at the top, from the Secretary of Defense on down, first and foremost political figures, answerable to their President. It also makes them the sometimes nervous overlords of their temporary domain. When a former Secretary of the Navy shows up inside the Pentagon, whether it is at the office of a political appointee or a high-ranking military leader, questions might arise and problems might occur—not for him, but for the people he is visiting. And this is particularly so when the former Navy Secretary is viewed to be a political "renegade," as one former Secretary of Defense put it when mentioning my name.

I had resigned as Secretary of the Navy during the Reagan Administration, continuing to speak and write about my concerns over American policies in the Persian Gulf and about America's strategic positioning around the world. I had then warned loudly, both during and after the first Gulf War, about the dangers of America's becoming an occupying force in the Middle East, which did not endear me to the first Bush Administration. Things didn't get any better during the Clinton Administration. Like many who had served in Vietnam, I had strong feelings about Bill Clinton's youthful criticism of the military and of those who had served. I also wrote about the Clinton Administration's treatment of some active-duty military officers. I was particularly concerned about its unwillingness to stand up to an emerging China when we were beginning a dangerous drift, selling off important military technology and failing to confront China when it enabled Pakistan to become a nuclear power.

Suffice it to say that over the years my views gave me a reputation among many current and former defense officials as being both unpredictable and impossible to persuade on purely political grounds.

In the E-Ring corridor outside the Secretary of the Navy's office, there is a long hallway filled with the portraits of former Navy Secretaries. The position of my portrait on the wall became something of a running commentary among my many friends and colleagues who still worked in, or with, the Pentagon. When it was moved closer to the Secretary of the Navy's office door, they would call me and joke that I was surreptitiously being listened to. When it was moved farther away, they would remark that I was reentering my own form of Churchill's "wilderness years." And by the time President George W. Bush was elected, my portrait was all the way down a far corridor, on the other side of a fire door.

At the same time, my relations with much of the active-duty military remained broadly based. My writings have always had a strong following inside the military. My feature film *Rules of Engagement*, a courtroom drama that deals with the perplexing question of when our military can use deadly force in the complex diplomatic situations into which we now send troops, was the number-one movie in the country during April 2000. And most important, the personal relationships that I have carried from the time I was seventeen years old have held fast. Many of my longtime friends were getting promoted. And their loyalties rarely were affected by the politics of any particular administration.

On September 7, 2001, my novel *Lost Soldiers*, a story that took place mostly in modern-day Vietnam, was published. As with my other books, my publisher expected strong sales among military audiences and had scheduled an autograph session at the Pentagon bookstore for the morning of September 11. Learning that I would be in the Pentagon, my friend Jim Jones, who was then serving as Commandant of the Marine Corps, invited me to breakfast in his private dining room. Jones, an officer of exceptional talent who later became the first Marine to command the allied forces in NATO, employed an embracive leadership style that was in direct contradiction to the near-paranoid hierarchy that had overtaken Donald Rumsfeld's Pentagon. A veteran of heavy combat in Vietnam who was awarded the Silver Star for gallantry, Jones speaks fluent French, knows the Congress intimately from a seven-year stretch as a Marine Corps legislative aide in the Senate, and is highly regarded for his wide grasp of international affairs.

General Jones had been on the go for several hours by the time we met in his office at eight o'clock and then proceeded to his private dining room for breakfast. We took our time as we attended to our plates of scrambled eggs and bacon and drank our coffee. Having known each other for years, we talked openly and frankly, working our way around the Corps and indeed around the world, sharing thoughts about policy, politics, old friends, and new leadership challenges.

And then, just before nine o'clock, the world changed.

The door to his dining room opened and one of the General's aides stepped quickly inside.

"Sir," the sergeant said. "It looks like a missile just hit one of the towers at the World Trade Center."

We left the dining room, stunned into near-silence as we walked a series of corridors back toward the General's office. As we neared his office entrance, Jones turned to me, gesturing inside.

"Do you want to come in and watch it on CNN?"

"No," I answered, knowing that the Commandant would soon be inundated with fresh responsibilities. "I think I'll just go back to my own office."

I walked down a set of stairs and then outside, into the parking lot of the Pentagon's Mall Entrance. By the time I reached my car and turned on the radio, the news was reporting that it had not been a missile but a passenger aircraft and that a second aircraft had now slammed into the south tower of the World Trade Center and exploded. Hysterical firsthand reports dominated the airwaves. I reached the building where I keep my writing office, parking in the underground garage and taking the elevator to the eighth floor. Following the long hallway to my office, I unlocked the door and walked down the stairs that led to its main room.

The phone rang. As I answered it and began talking, I heard an odd, metallic thunk, almost like the tinny sound of outgoing artillery. Still talking on the phone, I walked to the balcony and looked toward the familiar sight of the Pentagon. In my direct line of sight I saw an American Airlines passenger liner nosed against the building, most of the broken aircraft covering the lawn area near the helipad. Ugly plumes of smoke and flame were curling into the brittle-clear late-summer sky. From this balcony I would watch the Pentagon smolder and burn for the next three days.

We had abruptly entered a world of stultifying unknowns, facing a crisis that nonetheless required firm, immediate action. Just as disturbingly, we were entering it without a clear, agreed-upon national strategy. And over the next several months our foreign policy was hijacked by a small group of intellectuals who did indeed have a strategy—unfortunately, the wrong strategy. Among the top figures in the Bush Administration, and particularly in the Rumsfeld Pentagon, were several of the loudest voices who had called for an invasion of Iraq during the first Gulf War. And they wasted no time in furthering their agenda: that the proper response to the Al Qaeda suicide bomb-ings of the Twin Towers and the Pentagon was to decapitate the regime of Saddam Hussein in Iraq.

This same celerity was evident in major "neoconservative" media outlets such as the *Wall Street Journal*. As irony would have it, an ed-itor of the *Journal's* opinion page called me during the afternoon of 9/11 and asked me to write an article for them on how the nation should respond to the attacks. Amid the chaos of that day, I put to-gether a piece titled "Where Do We Go from Here?" which outlined my views on a national strategy for combating international terrorism. The essay advocated a program of aggressive military action against in-ternational terrorist targets, including against their logistical suppliers and training elements. But it also urged that basic strategic and histor-ical lessons be applied to fighting this menace. The terrorist movement was working the "seams" of international law, carefully defining itself as not aligned with any particular nation-state. It would behoove us to fight them under those same conceptual terms, using our maneuver-ability as a key military approach.

This article remains the only editorial I have ever been asked to write for the *Journal* that they did not publish. And I immediately sensed the reason why. What was it? A portion of my essay gave the following warnings:

> Those who are aligned with the terrorist movement, whether lo-gistically or in a training environment or operationally, should be considered legitimate targets and should not be spared. But ran-dom bombings and the deliberate destruction of populated areas without such a connection should be avoided. Over the long term this approach would deny terrorist armies not only their support base, but also their present justification that the United States and its allies are conducting a broad war against the Muslim people.
>
> <u>Do not occupy territory</u>.
>
> The terrorist armies make no claim to be members of any nation-state. Similarly, it would be militarily and politically dangerous for our military to operate from permanent or semi-

permanent bases, or to declare that we are defending specific pieces of terrain in the regions where the terrorist armies live and train. We already have terrain to defend—the United States and our outposts overseas—and we cannot afford to expand this territory in a manner that would simply give the enemy more targets.

There was a bit of kabuki going on here. The country had entered unknown waters. Knowing of the *Journal's* previous positions, I was writing about Iraq without using the word, and after years of working with editors at that paper it seemed clear to me that they knew it. They were beginning to push again for an invasion of Iraq without yet saying the word, and after they declined to run the article I knew it. In those hectic days immediately after the attacks, public opinion was being shaped in a hurry. This was clearly not the message that some on the editorial page of the newspaper that had been advocating a "MacArthurian Regency in Baghdad" during and since the first Gulf War wanted to print.

Thus, on September 12, 2001, I had no doubt that the neoconservatives were again intent on going after Baghdad. I posted the article on my personal Web page, where it has since remained.

The morphing of the war against international terrorism into the invasion and occupation of Iraq began in earnest in those first days after the 9/11 attacks. The well-placed advocates in the Bush Administration and in the media moved quickly to justify not a general response against Al Qaeda but an all-out invasion of Iraq, possibly followed by invasions in Iran and Syria. This pursuit of a war policy against Iraq was not just a strategic error; it was also a profound and costly diplomatic mistake. Just after the 9/11 attacks, the sympathies of almost the entire world were with us. Newspapers and television stations across the globe expressed their support. Flowers and notes were placed in front of American embassies. Our tragedy was palpable, and our emotions were shared. But as the weeks went by, the Bush Administration and its media allies squandered an historic opportunity to rally the world to our side in the effort to defeat the forces of international terrorism.

While their stated logic was that an Iraq invasion would make the world a safer place, proper strategic thinking actually argued in the opposite direction. If terrorism was principally a Mideast phenomenon prior to 9/11, after that date it was clearly a global dilemma. This made it imperative that smarter minds in America resist the notion of taking over one country in one region, potentially for decades, when the threat now extended across several continents and into the communities of a large percentage of the world's 1.3 billion Muslims.

On October 3, 2001, three weeks after the attacks on the Twin Towers and the Pentagon, I made an extemporaneous presentation to the Naval Institute Conference in Virginia Beach, discussing the strategic and policy implications that the nation was then facing. An estimated 1,000 military professionals, historians, and citizens concerned with national security policy filled the auditorium. For more than an hour I spoke to, and with, the assembled audience. The mood was somber, reflective, and interactive, like a large family gathering to sort out an unexpected crisis. We did not know where or if another terrorist attack might take place. I spoke strongly about the need for aggressive military action against terrorist training cells, and the need for the United States to take advantage of its unparalleled military maneuverability. A much-shortened version of this talk was later printed in the *Naval Institute Proceedings* under the title "Go After Them and Eliminate Them."

During the discussion, a prominent naval historian asked my view about invading Iraq. While recognizing that the war drums for occupying Baghdad were again beating in the usual circles, I cautioned against such an effort on purely strategic grounds. My position was that to fully understand the long-term strategic implications of the 9/11 attacks, it was vital that in terms of nation-states we focus not on Iraq but primarily on China and Iran. Saddam Hussein's regime was not a major threat in this new strategic situation. In fact, if we handled the larger question of international terrorism properly, in time Hussein's regime would become strategically irrelevant. My conclusion was that it was far more important to watch China, to watch Iran, and to watch China with Iran. Each country had different cards to play, individually and possibly together, but both of these countries needed our careful strategic attention. Their separate powers, and the strategic axis between them, had been developing for many years.

It has been a major frustration, and dangerous to our country's national security, that the strategic nexus between Iran and China has been largely overlooked as we have become obsessed with Iraq. And for those of us who have spent decades following strategic trends, it was no surprise when in November 2007—six years after that discussion in Virginia Beach—the *Washington Post* commented that "the rapidly growing relationship between Iran and China has begun to undermine international efforts to ensure that Iran cannot convert a peaceful energy program to develop a nuclear arsenal." The article commented further that "China now gets at least 14 percent of its imported oil from Iran, making it China's largest supplier," and that "Tehran in turn gets major arms systems from Beijing, including ballistic and cruise missiles and technical assistance for Tehran's indigenous missile program." Later on, the article mentioned, tellingly, that "the new Tehran-Beijing relationship is likely to further delay or dilute international diplomacy, because the two powers share a strategic vision, experts say."

All true. But despite the wording of the article, this strategic interplay between China and Iran—and indeed between China and several other Muslim powers—is hardly new. It was in full bloom more than twenty years ago, when I was serving as Secretary of the Navy. The challenge in those intervening years was to convince many business-minded Americans that it existed and to warn of the national security ramifications if we ignored it.

In 2001, we were indeed ignoring it. And the strategic mousetrap that the United States was about to spring upon itself in Iraq would only strengthen both China and Iran. Over the past several years, as the United States has attempted to isolate Iran with trade sanctions due to the possibility of its developing a nuclear program, China has become Iran's principal trading partner, surpassing Japan in 2006. In fact, this volume of trade has quintupled since 2001. As the *Financial Times* recently observed, "the US pressure has had no impact on Iran's big-ticket exports to China, such as oil, petrochemicals and minerals." And during this same period, the Chinese and Iranians have jointly developed the largest land-based oil-production facility on Iranian soil.

All of this was predictable—and predicted.

Weeks went by. The debates progressed. The invasion of Iraq grew ineluctably closer. For several months, I appeared as a guest on different radio and television shows, discussing the policy implications of our national response. It was a curious process. So-called military experts of widely varying levels of talent and experience were flooding the airwaves, interacting with hosts of, shall we say, widely varying levels of knowledge, under an umbrella of an intensely displayed, almost self-conscious patriotism. It seemed that every lapel now sported an American flag pin, as if this conscious display were mandatory to ward off accusations of disloyalty. And few discussions involved any true evaluation of the nation's grand strategy or the implications of the quagmire that awaited a long-term occupation in the Middle East.

As the weeks fell into months, the airwaves were filled with chatter that moved the public focus further and further away from the larger issue of international terrorism, until virtually all that was being discussed was Saddam Hussein and Iraq. The process itself became futile and frustrating. And all the while, the Bush Administration was consciously manipulating American public opinion regarding the situation that our country faced.

On what issues did they mislead the American public and media? First, that invading Iraq was somehow linked directly to the war against international terrorism. Second, that Saddam Hussein had direct ties to Al Qaeda. Third, that Saddam Hussein possessed an active capability to deliver weapons of mass destruction on international targets— and here it should be emphasized that these were specific and definite allegations by government officials of either weapons or delivery systems that could be in place in a matter of hours, rather than amorphous "development" programs. Finally—and extremely important at this point—that it would not take a sizable military presence to run the occupation of Iraq.

It would be naive to write off the administration's error on this last point as simple negligence, as many now claim. Given the level of knowledge easily available to the President, it could only have involved a conscious deception regarding the true price that would have to be paid after the initial military incursion. The only real question for historians is to whom the blame should ultimately fall for allowing the deception to take place. Many of the top civilian leaders in the Pentagon came to the administration with a prejudgment that a war in Iraq should take place. They, as well as their top military advisers, were given solid, consistent military advice that militated against such an action, warning them of the predictable long-term consequences. Good people with long experience were predicting that it would take hundreds of thousands of American troops to stabilize a post-invasion Iraq. That advice was deliberately, and some would say willfully, ignored.

With many key people in this administration wanting a war from the outset, and soon convincing the President himself of the validity of their views, there were few tools to be used from outside the process to stop them. The great failure of our endeavor in Iraq—other than that it should never have taken place at all—was that the debate occurred in the absence of a declared strategic vision. The national transition away from Cold War thinking was partially to blame, but a greater aspect of that failure was deliberate. Absent an agreed-upon strategy, the intellectual advocates for war in Iraq were able to push a long-held agenda into the vacuum. Tellingly, as the movement toward war gained momentum, the President and his administration never clearly defined the strategic objectives that were calling for war, and never outlined a firm set of benchmarks that, once obtained, would bring an end to the fighting, including a withdrawal of our military from Iraq.

In other words, we were moving cavalierly toward a war that could change our entire geopolitical focus, without a clearly articulated worldview, without specific, long-term guidance from which the military could properly define a war strategy, and with no clear referent from which the American political process could garner a sense of predictability about the war's outcome. In the congressional hearings that led us into war, the President's witnesses, particularly among the political appointees at the Department of Defense, were repeatedly asked how long we would be in Iraq if we invaded. They repeatedly answered, in an arrogant, prerehearsed litany, that we would be in Iraq "as long as is necessary, and not one day more."

For the average soldier, this meant three months. For the average neoconservative, this meant fifty years or perhaps forever.

Like many loyal but skeptical Americans, I had become torn as the months passed by. On the one hand, having lived through the ugly, painful final years of the Vietnam era when our veterans became the scapegoats for the war itself, I did not want to undercut the morale or the efforts of our military. Further, I did not have access to current intelligence information, which weakened any arguments I might make against administration officials who could claim that my views were based on inaccurate or dated assumptions. But on the other hand, as the months went by it was becoming ever clearer that something was amiss. The books were being cooked. They were too smug in their refusals to directly answer the very basic questions that needed to be addressed before a nation went to war. And they were not mentioning at all the long-term implications of an Iraq invasion.

And what was the hurry? The Iraq invasion would be, pure and simple, a war of choice. Saddam Hussein's regime, for all its despicable behavior, posed no direct threat to any vital interests of the United States. Iraq had not harbored Al Qaeda's terrorists. In fact, Osama bin Laden was widely reported to have welcomed the prospect of our invasion. Whether he personally did so or not, it was beyond cavil that the invasion of Iraq would help his cause not only through recruitment of new members, but also because he counted the Iraqi regime as an enemy of Al Qaeda's long-held goals due to its secular rather than religious makeup.

Contrary to the situation of a decade before, United Nations inspectors were on the ground in Iraq, looking for evidence of weapons of mass destruction with the cooperation of the Iraqi government. Numerous American intelligence analysts were warning that an invasion would be followed by an enormously difficult occupation, which would increase the influence of both Iran and Al Qaeda. Retired military experts with long experience in the region, including two former commanders in chief of the Central Command, whose responsibilities included Iraq, were opposed to an invasion, as was retired General

Brent Scowcroft, who had served as National Security Adviser under the first President Bush.

All the while, the administration was hyping the nature of the threat from Saddam Hussein, downplaying the difficulty of a post-invasion occupation, predicting a "cakewalk" of an invasion, and offering no clearly articulated vision of what our national goals would be once the occupation began. This was not negligence. It was political calculation.

I finally decided that it was my duty to clearly lay out my concerns. In September 2002, six months before the invasion, I wrote a piece for the *Washington Post*. Its title was "Heading for Trouble: Do We Really Want to Occupy Iraq for the Next Thirty Years?" Part of that article read as follows:

> With respect to the situation in Iraq, two realities seem to have been lost in the narrow debate about Saddam Hussein himself. The first reality is that wars often have unintended consequences—ask the Germans, who in World War I were convinced that they would defeat the French in exactly 42 days. The second is that a long-term occupation of Iraq would beyond doubt require an adjustment of force levels elsewhere, and could eventually diminish American influence in other parts of the world. Other than the flippant criticisms of our "failure" to take Baghdad during the Persian Gulf War, one sees little discussion of an occupation of Iraq, but it is the key element of the current debate. The issue before us is not simply whether the United States should end the regime of Saddam Hussein, but whether we as a nation are prepared to physically occupy territory in the Middle East for the next 30 to 50 years. Those who are pushing for a unilateral war in Iraq know full well that there is no exit strategy if we invade and stay . . .
>
>   Nations such as China can only view the prospect of an American military consumed for the next generation by the turmoil of the Middle East as a glorious windfall. Indeed, if one gives the Chinese credit for having a long-term strategy—and those who love to quote Sun Tzu might consider his nationality—it

lends credence to their insistent cultivation of the Muslim world. One should not take lightly the fact that China previously supported Libya, that Pakistan developed its nuclear capability with China's unrelenting assistance and that the Chinese sponsored a coup attempt in Indonesia in 1965. An "American war" with the Muslims, occupying the very seat of their civilization, would allow the Chinese to isolate the United States diplomatically as they furthered their own ambitions in South and Southeast Asia.

The afternoon that my article was published, I received an e-mail from Marine Corps Lieutenant General Greg Newbold, who was serving as the director of operations on the Joint Chiefs of Staff. Newbold was one of the most highly regarded officers in the Marine Corps. Many military insiders believed that he had been assigned to the Joint Chiefs billet in order to prepare him to replace General Jim Jones as Commandant of the Marine Corps. Unbeknownst to me, he and a few others had been quietly attempting to confront the civilian leadership about the looming war.

Greg Newbold is a taciturn guy. His e-mail was to the point. *You are not only right*, he said. *You may not even know how right you really are.*

We met for a beer. It turned into a several-hour discussion. Despite all the political rhetoric from the President claiming that we would go to war only as a last resort, the wheels were turning and it seemed certain that there was going to be an invasion. And after the invasion, from the perspective of Newbold and several other officers, the occupation of Iraq was going to be a mess. Toward the end of our conversation, Newbold mentioned *Dereliction of Duty*, one of the most closely read books to come out of the Vietnam War, in which H. R. McMaster, a West Point graduate, painted a damning portrait of the high-ranking military officers in the Pentagon who had not stood up to the feckless manipulations of Defense Secretary Robert McNamara.

"Someday somebody is going to write the *Dereliction of Duty* of the Iraq War," predicted Newbold. "And it's going to be a whole lot worse."

Few could have foreseen that reality in September 2002 or even nine months later, after the lightning strike toward Baghdad. But few can deny it today.

Those who brought us into Iraq gambled that a quick battlefield success would erase the questions that led to the war itself. They were certain that American "boots on the ground" would change the public perception, because as soon as our forces were in harm's way the American public would rally around them. And rally around them the American people did, at least until the conventional fighting was over and the tedious occupation began.

The only actual strategy put into place by the Bush Administration leading up to the Iraq invasion (or since, for that matter) was the worrisome doctrine of preventive war. This heretofore unprecedented concept is premised on the notion that the United States has the right to begin a war unilaterally whenever the President decides that the national interest is, or even *may be*, at risk. In other words, the preemptive-war doctrine is based on the notion that the United States—or, to be more specific, the President of the United States—has the right under international law to take out another governmental system and to occupy a country merely on the basis that the country is behaving in a troublesome manner.

Preemptive wars are much different in concept from the historically accepted doctrine of preemptive attacks, where the President, acting as commander in chief, has the constitutional power to conduct rescue missions and to protect specific American interests that are directly being threatened. Examples of recent preemptive attacks include the 1983 rescue of American students in Grenada and the 1989 incursion into Panama to take Manuel Noriega into custody. Examples of preventive wars include—well, they include the disaster of Iraq.

A unilateral war—a war in which a country attacks another when it has not itself been attacked—must be undertaken only when the country's national survival is clearly at stake, or under circumstances where the international community is so threatened that a strong power such as the United States must save it from an enormous menace. Iraq clearly did not meet either of those tests. The goal of those who pushed for a war in Iraq was to achieve their own long-term objective of having American troops on the ground in that part of the world for the indefinite future, for a variety of political and strategic reasons that are part and parcel of the think-tank discussions but were never articulated by political leaders who were making the case for the war. And the results of their deceptions have proven to be gravely serious, with consequences that will reverberate for decades.

Those who wished for a "MacArthurian Regency" in Baghdad that would reign for fifty years forgot one important historical fact: After World War II, General Douglas MacArthur did not even set foot on Japanese soil until the Emperor had officially announced Japan's surrender. MacArthur then carefully preserved the structure of the Japanese system and governed through it. By contrast, the government of Iraq was decapitated without a government to replace it, and its main political party was eliminated. Our occupying troops in Japan immediately became the friends of the Japanese people. In Iraq they immediately became terrorist targets on a daily basis, the most visible symbols of an unfinished violence brought upon Iraq from the outside. From the first months after our invasion, insurgents from a variety of ethnic groups, all of which resented an American occupation, worked hard to kill them. Japan is an island nation, insulated from outside forces. By contrast, Iraq is smack-dab in the middle of an overwhelmingly volatile region. Foreign jihadists, guerrillas and suicide bombers alike, flocked quickly to Iraq, seeing American forces as targets of opportunity.

Just as important, Japan is ethnically homogeneous, but once the Saddam Hussein government had been decapitated the various ethnic and subethnic factions in Iraq declared war on each other, even as the countries around Iraq were thrown into greater instability after our invasion. Much of the cream of Iraqi society began fleeing their own country, leaving behind battle-pocked neighborhoods and citizens in need of medical assistance, education, and stability. As millions fled the country, other millions became internal refugees, dislocated from their own communities. In an eerily reminiscent replay of Lebanon's tribulations twenty years earlier, a weak central government passed meaningless edicts as the traditional tribal structures retained true power outside of the heavily fortified Green Zone. And the region continues to ferment, with Iran, Saudi Arabia, Turkey, Jordan, and Syria growing ever more uneasy.

All of this tragedy has occurred under the umbrella of an increasing resentment of the United States around the world, which has already translated into further terrorist recruiting. And here at home, this situation has brought our own country a swath of critical long-term problems. Our military, particularly its ground forces, is physically worn down and its equipment is in need of a multibillion-dollar, bottom-to-top replenishment. Economically, it is now estimated that over time the bill for the Iraq War will be at least a trillion dollars, and probably much higher. Domestically, all across the country our national infrastructure is deteriorating and underfunded, leaving bridges, highways, railways, and seaports in serious need of modernization and repair.

Commentators and politicians keep talking about the continuing war in Iraq, but the war, in military terms, was quickly over after our invasion. What followed was an occupation that took on an ugly life of its own.

The military approach inside Iraq might classically be termed a holding action, designed for the very purpose of allowing political solutions to move forward. This is totally different from the aggressive role a military force plays during an invasion or a campaign. It is far past time that this holding action be brought to a skillful close, and that the Iraqis proceed forward with their own resolution of the ethnic and sectarian strife that still scars their country. This is not abandonment; it is the logical conclusion of our involvement, and a realization of the limitations of our ability to affect conditions that have been ongoing for a millennium. The alternative, which was an unspoken objective of those who brought us the invasion in the first place, is for the United States to remain in Iraq for at least the next fifty years as a supposed guarantor of stability in the region. This argument is self-defeating. In a region that has resisted every foreign occupation for at least the past one thousand years, there can be no greater guarantee of long-term instability than for the Americans to remain in Iraq.

At the tactical level, our military has done everything that was asked of it, and they have done it well. What our military could not do was re-shape the historic ethnic and political landscape of Mesopotamia. Nor should it ever have been asked to occupy territory in the most volatile region in the world.

And what of the role that Congress played in this debacle? Many well-intentioned senators and congressmen worked hard to avert this invasion, with all of its predictable consequences, from the beginning. But as an institution, the Congress failed the country.

From the days just after the 9/11 attacks, the world's greatest deliberative body was manipulated by the administration in a blatant power grab, the effects of which are still with us today, and not only with respect to Iraq. Congress failed to insist on clear, careful answers from the Bush Administration to questions that should have been viewed as inalterable prerequisites to voting in favor of war. It failed to conduct proper oversight over rogue activities inside the administration that were cooking up deliberately flawed, "cherry-picked" intelligence reports that differed from the estimates of our traditional intelligence agencies. It failed to give proper weight to the statements of people such as General Shinseki, General Zinni, General Hoar, and General Scowcroft to the effect that an invasion of Iraq would be a misadventure.

In a vote conveniently scheduled in October 2002, just before the midterm elections, the Congress allowed the country to descend into a disaster created almost exclusively by a handful of well-placed administration officials and media mavens. In the House of Representatives, the vote was 296 to 133 in favor of giving the Bush Administration the authority to invade Iraq. In the Senate, the vote was 77 to 23.

Once the war resolution was passed, the Congress lost its chance to avert a strategic blunder of historic proportions. The President had the authority he needed, and he would not be back to ask for more. The invasion took place. The Middle East, indeed the world in which all of us live, had changed.

A war begun recklessly could not and will not be turned around without great care. The eventual goals of the United States must be a complete removal of our combat military forces from Iraq; the creation of a strong diplomatic structure among the countries in the region that will provide it a measure of stability; a renewed emphasis on eliminating the military, cultural, and economic forces that together form the basis for international terrorist activities; and an emphasis on America's larger strategic posture throughout the world. Inside our constitutional process, the Congress is ill-equipped to drive this train, especially in the aftermath of the military action that it authorized. But it must continue to use the tools at its disposal, for these goals are eminently attainable.

And what of the top leadership of our military? How do its actions, and inactions, fit into this equation?

CHAPTER TEN

MACARTHUR GO HOME

The character and extent of civilian control over our military is another of those areas, like economic fairness, where our Constitution guides us only at the far edges of any debate. As a consequence, the parameters of this relationship are determined largely by tradition, the nature of our global involvements, the input of Congress, and finally the interplay of strong personalities, both inside government and in academia. Since the dark days after the Korean War began, and particularly since Vietnam, the pendulum has swung widely toward the political side of this equation. From that point forward, the views offered by military leaders as they relate to grand strategy and sensitive international commitments are most often characterized as being beyond the realm of their responsibilities and even of their authority.

More than twenty years ago, I bumped into a Marine three-star general in the corridor of the Pentagon after he had left a meeting with

a Reagan Administration appointee known for his arrogance toward
the uniformed military. The general, a veteran of combat in two wars,
was livid, having been cut off from making a policy observation during
the meeting.

The general had begun by saying, "Mr. Secretary, I think—"

And the civilian appointee had immediately interrupted him:
"General, we don't pay you to think."

Some military leaders have been given good play in recent years
for their views on operational matters. General Colin Powell enunci-
ated a concept regarding the use of overwhelming force that closely
resembled Secretary of Defense Caspar Weinberger's policy of a few
years before, a set of principles that came to be called "the Powell
Doctrine." General David Petraeus has devised an operational policy
to implement what came to be called "the surge" of military force in
Iraq. But any senior military officer who advocates a wide-ranging shift
in strategic philosophy or current operational policy is likely to be
shouted down as having crossed the line into the realm where civilians
hold both judgment and control. And, as with the cases of Generals
Eric Shinseki and Greg Newbold, he is also likely to be asked to leave
"the team."

In early 2006, General Newbold broke his public silence and wrote
an editorial for *Time* magazine as part of what has come to be called a
"revolt of the Generals," several of whom had become concerned not
only about the situation in Iraq, but also with the possibility that it
might be repeated with an ill-advised attack on Iran. Citing his time on
the Joint Chiefs of Staff, his attempt to stand up to the officers and political officials above him, and his retrospective summation of their
failed policies, in part General Newbold wrote:

> The commitment of our forces to this fight was done with a ca-
> sualness and swagger that are the special province of those who
> have never had to execute these missions—or bury the results.
> Flaws in our civilians are one thing; the failure of the Pentagon's
> military leaders is quite another. Those are men who know the
> hard consequences of war but, with few exceptions, acted timidly

when their voices urgently needed to be heard. When they knew the plan was flawed, saw intelligence distorted to justify a rationale for war, or witnessed arrogant micromanagement that at times crippled the military's effectiveness, many leaders who wore the uniform chose inaction . . . The consequence of the military's quiescence was that a fundamentally flawed plan was executed for an invented war, while pursuing the real enemy, al-Qaeda, became a secondary effort.

The warning shot fired by General Newbold and his fellow officers did have some national impact, especially on the willingness of civilians inside the political process and also responsible media commentators to ask harder questions about the direction of the Iraq War. But it also subjected these officers to retaliations from defense intellectuals and other senior retired military officials. In their eyes, Newbold and his allies were disloyal to the troops in the field and to the President, their commander in chief. They were supposedly bitter. They did not know their place. And they ostensibly did not recognize that there are limits to the advice that military officers can give and the impact they can have on a political process that decides when, where, and ultimately how to go to war.

The debates on this point become volatile because in truth there are no firm answers, for there is no clear demarcation point from which to measure the propriety of a military leader's public comments. If an active-duty leader speaks too loudly, he stands to lose his position and thus his ability to influence a better result. If he speaks too softly, he has failed to utter the truth and must accept accountability for the policy that does move forward. But in far too many cases, as General Newbold intimated, senior military leaders simply choose to focus on the implementation of a policy rather than its larger merits. Thus, on the crucial issues of whether and where, rather than how, military force should be used, key military leaders sometimes end up rationalizing that the articulation of grand strategy and political policy is "above their pay grades," and thus beyond their senses of personal and professional obligation.

Other issues hover in the background of this ethical ebb and flow: the changing nature of the American military, the intricately complicated diplomatic world in which our country has been required to operate since World War II, and—hugely but ironically—the legacy of General of the Armies Douglas MacArthur, whose bitter standoff with President Harry Truman set in motion many of the unresolved tensions between the military leaders and policy makers of today.

How so? Several issues come into play. They most clearly came into focus in Vietnam, but the true turning point emanated from the bleak hills of the Frozen Chosin Reservoir, in the farthest reaches of North Korea.

We are continually reminded by historians and political commentators that the Vietnam War ended disastrously for the United States and that the condition of our military at the war's end was, at best, lamentable. But the army whose final contingents limped out of Vietnam in early 1973 was not the army that had marched into battle nearly eight years before, any more than the tumultuous, often-angry America of 1973 was the self-confident, somewhat reflective America of 1965. In truth, unit for unit and leader for leader the United States military at the beginning of the Vietnam War was the finest military our country has ever sent onto a battlefield. And for several years it fought a complicated mix of political, guerrilla, and conventional wars all at the same time, with extraordinary competence and devastating effect.

This is not a self-serving evaluation. I was not a part of the military that first went into Vietnam, although I did grow up in it, and although my early years at the Naval Academy overlapped with it. My Marine Corps service, of which I remain deeply proud, began just after the 1968 Tet Offensive, which is largely viewed as the demarcation point when the American military—and American society writ large—started to show its wear and tear. And it is important to understand that journey.

In terms of their grasp of traditional strategic concepts, their battlefield experience, their technological know-how, their can-do leadership, and the assets that were made available to them to carry out the tasks they were called upon to do, the military leadership of that era was unparalleled. One could expect no less of those members of what has come to be called "the Greatest Generation." They had been mentored by many of the historically recognized giants, leaders such as MacArthur and Marshall and Eisenhower, Halsey and Nimitz and Vandegrift, who understood history and, in some cases, had made it. Many of them had spent long months in the brutal campaigns of World War II and Korea. As young officers, they had made the landings at North Africa, Anzio, Sicily, Normandy, Guadalcanal, Tarawa, and Iwo Jima. They had fought the sea and air battles in the Atlantic, in the Pacific, and over Germany and Japan. They had flown in the Berlin Airlift. They had landed at Inchon. They had fought in the Frozen Chosin Reservoir and along the Imjin River. They had been told to build a missile program from scratch after the Soviets put Sputnik into space in October 1957, and within five years a fleet of Atlas ICBMs were on the launching pads at Vandenberg, ready to be launched if necessary during the Cuban missile crisis.

It would be wrong to imply, as many do, that these leaders did not understand the battlefields of Vietnam. Indeed, the Hanoi government's official acknowledgment in 1995, on the twentieth anniversary of the Communists' final takeover of the South, is a definitive response to that assumption. After decades in which American journalists, historians, and antiwar academicians had ridiculed our military's estimates of enemy "body counts," the Hanoi government admitted that its "elusive guerrilla force" had lost 1.4 million soldiers in combat, as against 58,000 American and 245,000 South Vietnamese dead.

Our military had more than done the job that was asked of it on the vicious and unforgiving battlefields of Vietnam. What had changed was the overarching diplomatic environment in which America's wars were now being fought. America's place as the preeminent nation in the world community after World War II had created a new national concern: the potential for smaller, regional military confrontations to have far-reaching global reverberations. This concern brought with it an equal reverberation on the battlefield, since global political considerations often resulted in operational limitations that flew in the face of all traditional military logic. And thus an entirely new set of diplomatic and military complexities evolved when America was required to use military force. Over time, these new realities brought about a more nuanced relationship between our military leaders and the national political leadership. An inverse formula had unavoidably evolved: Never before had our regional military objectives been so limited by global concerns, and never before had global diplomacy been so threatened by the implications of regional conflict.

This process of politicizing the battlefield, and as an unintended consequence bringing military confusion to it, actually began before Vietnam, with the diplomatic complexities of limited warfare in Korea. It continued to evolve afterward. It is still evolving today. And the domination of political considerations in circumstances where American military personnel are fighting for their lives is part of a many-faceted set of changes that have brought about a much different relationship between America's military and the political leadership that governs its policies.

The dedication and quality of our military men and women are beyond question. Their respect among our populace has rarely been higher. The technology that serves them is the best in the world. But over the past fifty years, America's military culture has slowly transformed into a system that would have both surprised and perplexed our founding fathers. This is not a question of individual or unit performance, but rather of the military's relationship with the whole of our society. Of special note—and concern—is the environment in which the military's top leadership now functions, both during and after their military service.

Three different societal forces have come together in the years since World War II in a way that has changed the complexion of the military's place in our society, as well as its relationship with our national leadership. The first regards the impact of limited wars, and how this has affected civil-military relations on the battlefield and in the councils of government. The second involves the evolution of the military-industrial complex, intertwined with the perpetuation of a large standing army. And the third relates to the more overt politicization of the career military, combined with a growing separation between the military and society as a whole.

The first societal force devolved from new concepts of limited warfare in the aftermath of World War II. These concepts accompanied not only the advent of the nuclear era but also America's more dominant role in global diplomacy. In this environment, political considerations far away from the battlefield of one arena might now dramatically limit the options of a military commander who otherwise could be pursuing traditional strategy and tactics to address the challenges that immediately confront him. The key event in defining civil-military relations in this new era was President Harry Truman's firing of General of the Armies Douglas MacArthur during the worst fighting of the Korean War. This event, often celebrated as an act of presidential firmness in the face of an arrogant and potentially renegade field commander, is rarely examined in terms of the new international—and interpersonal—environment in which MacArthur's actions were taking place.

To a true student of military history, it is no small irony that General Douglas MacArthur's combat leadership during the Korean War is so often considered a failure because of his having been relieved of command by President Harry Truman at the height of the war's worst fighting. This is hardly the case. In fact, in purely military terms, Douglas MacArthur was never better than in his days as the commanding general of our forces in Korea.

MacArthur, a vainglorious and utterly conflicted genius about whom I wrote extensively in my novel *The Emperor's General,* had graduated from West Point at the top of his class, fought with distinction in World War I, and had been one of the youngest officers ever to serve as Army Chief of Staff. After his service as Chief of Staff, in 1936 MacArthur became Field Marshal of the Philippines, a post that gave him command of American and Filipino military forces in what was then an American colony. In this highly ceremonial and somewhat hybrid position, for which he famously designed his own elaborate uniform, MacArthur reported not only to Washington but also to the President of the Philippines. Indulging his passion for Asia but serving in what many believed to be a military backwater, over the ensuing years MacArthur lost a step or two. Consequently, he began World War II with an ignominious defeat at the hands of the Japanese.

MacArthur was not at his best in those early days. A fleet of Japanese bombers destroyed much of his own air force as the planes sat idly on the runway at Clark Field, several hours after he and the world had learned of the attacks on Pearl Harbor. A Japanese ground invasion followed, during which MacArthur equivocated regarding the movement of his forces, resulting in considerable loss of supplies and manpower before he retreated and consolidated his forces on the Bataan Peninsula. Cut off from reinforcements and logistical help, his situation from the outset was desperate. But his defeat, which led to the infamous Bataan Death March, could well have been prevented or at least mitigated if MacArthur had been more decisive in his early responses to the Japanese, and if he had listened to his field generals and made better tactical adjustments as the campaign unfolded.

Bottled up on the Bataan Peninsula and on the small island of Corregidor just offshore, MacArthur finally fled the Philippines in a small naval craft and headed for Australia. As his PT boat churned southward his beleaguered army steadily collapsed behind him and was then marched off to prisoner-of-war camps. Thousands would perish before the war's end, both during the march and in the camps. At the insistence of General George C. Marshall, MacArthur was awarded the Medal of Honor for his actions in escaping Japanese captivity. But many believed that this award was politically motivated, designed to counter enemy propaganda that claimed MacArthur had committed a cowardly act when he abandoned his troops on the battlefield.

Stung by the reality that he had indeed left his soldiers behind, and humiliated by this early military failure, MacArthur then caught his breath and devised a brilliant strategy to retake the Philippines from the Japanese. Combining sea, air, and land power in a succession of amphibious attacks as he moved northward from Australia through Borneo and other islands, MacArthur bypassed enemy strongpoints rather than attacking them head-on, leaving major Japanese bases "withering on the vine," unable to be repositioned or resupplied. Leapfrogging the American Army along the island coastlines, controlling the air with the Air Corps, dominating the sea-lanes with the Navy, he eventually made his world-renowned "return" to the Philippines.

This strategy was devastating to the Japanese. It also saved countless American lives and was replete with a slew of new tactical doctrines that were decades ahead of their time. One memorable adjustment involved a way of using cargo and other small aircraft along with amphibious forces in a concept that he termed "triphibious warfare," an innovation that presaged modern versions of "vertical envelopment." In the years following the war's end, MacArthur showed formidable diplomatic skills with his visionary reign as the proconsul of Japan, which earned him the usually respectful moniker "The American Caesar."

For those reasons, Douglas MacArthur undeniably deserves a place at the table when one considers America's greatest military leaders. And this, ironically, is no less so for his actions in Korea, which in military terms showed a strategic grasp and personal boldness of a scale even greater than in the campaigns of World War II. MacArthur's downfall came because at the age of seventy his famous arrogance toward political leaders had ripened into hubris, and also because the intellectual largeness of his desired response to the Chinese entry into that war did not fit into the post–World War II diplomatic environment. This state of affairs had tilted the conduct of American warfare away from battlefield generals and toward those responsible for international diplomacy. The extent of this tilt was so great that military leaders with the scope and political audacity of MacArthur would no longer be considered appropriate in the new era of limited wars.

And it's also fair to say that MacArthur saw it coming.

In the waning days of June 1950, the North Korean army suddenly burst across the 38th Parallel, along which Korea had been divided between Communist and non-Communist forces following World

War II. Within weeks the North Koreans had pushed American and South Korean forces all the way to Korea's southeastern tip, where they were huddled in defensive positions inside what was being called the Pusan Perimeter. Not surprisingly, the nation turned to MacArthur, who was then commanding the occupation forces in Japan as well as overseeing that country's postwar government. In addition to the title of Supreme Commander, Allied Forces, Pacific (SCAP), he was given the new, additional title of Commander in Chief, Far East (CINCFE), in charge of American and United Nations forces in Korea.

Stepping into this new role with his usual vigor and famous self-importance, from the very beginning of the war MacArthur was leery of, and hostile to, the civilian leaders in the Truman Administration. But despite his difficult personality, MacArthur's reservations about the judgment of the nation's civilian leadership were not only justified but eerily prescient. As William Manchester wrote in his classic work *American Caesar*, MacArthur "believed that they understood 'little about the Pacific and practically nothing about Korea,' and that they were certain to blunder because errors were 'inescapable when the diplomat attempts to exercise military judgment.'"

These observations were not simply the grumblings of a militarist who disliked the notion of civilian control. For starters, in the years preceding the North Korean invasion of South Korea the Truman Administration had dramatically cut back the American military, especially those forces responsible for the security of Asia. Only a year before the war began, Defense Secretary Louis Johnson, widely characterized as unqualified for his post, had faced a famous "revolt of the Admirals" when he tried to kill the Navy's vital aircraft carrier program. This attempt was so potentially damaging to the future of our naval forces that it prompted Secretary of the Navy John L. Sullivan to resign in protest. At another point, the administration had attempted to do away with the Marine Corps. Eventually viewed as culpable for the military's woeful condition at the outbreak of the Korean War, Secretary Johnson himself was fired by Truman just after the war began.

Even more relevant to MacArthur's reservations, the administration's diplomatic bungling had arguably caused the war in the first place. In June 1949, at a time when American forces in Korea were being cut back in the face of a North Korean military buildup near the 38th Parallel, Truman's Secretary of State, Dean Acheson, had testified before the House Foreign Affairs Committee that the South Koreans "will be able to defend themselves against any attack from the northern half of the country." Then, during a speech at the National Press Club in January 1950, Acheson omitted South Korea when he discussed America's line of defense in the Pacific in the aftermath of the tumultuous 1949 Communist takeover of China. In Acheson's view, if either Taiwan (then referred to as Formosa) or South Korea was attacked, they would have to prove they were "resolute fighters" and then appeal to the United Nations for help. One cannot imagine a clearer invitation to North Korea to begin a war.

Nor was MacArthur alone in his views on the Truman Administration's diplomatic and military misfeasance. In 1952, General of the Armies Dwight Eisenhower, who had been courted by both major political parties to run for President, would castigate the conduct of the war—significantly, in light of today's debates, while it was still ongoing. Citing the folly of refusing to commit to the defense of Taiwan and South Korea after the Communist takeover in China, as well as the withdrawal of American troops from Korea at the same time the North Koreans were clearly preparing for war, Eisenhower stated, "The responsibility for this record cannot be dodged or evaded. . . . [T]he responsibility for the fateful political decisions would still rest wholly with the men charged with making those decisions in the Department of State and in the White House. They cannot escape that responsibility now or ever . . . The old Administration cannot be expected to repair what it failed to prevent."

But unlike MacArthur, Eisenhower was not commanding troops in Korea when he made his condemning remarks. And in fact, he had already taken off his military uniform.

The full-scale conventional war that had begun in Korea was from the outset being micromanaged from the White House and the State Department, as a result of its worry over the turmoil in China and the emerging superpower tensions with the Soviet Union. And MacArthur, from the beginning, resisted this interference. In retrospect, although it would take several months before President Harry Truman relieved him, MacArthur had unknowingly predicted the terms of his own professional demise. The diplomats who were now deciding that international politics should rule over military judgments were actively working against his strategic judgments and undercutting his combat efforts.

Perhaps the fairest thing to say is that MacArthur had decided to fight a 1940s-style war when American diplomacy had entered the 1950s. Years later, in his memoir *Reminiscences*, he would lament that he had assumed that "the full power and means of our nation would be mobilized and dedicated to fight for victory—not for stalemate or compromise. And I set out to chart the strategic course that would make that victory possible. Not by the wildest stretch of imagination did I dream that this tradition might be broken."

In purely military terms, MacArthur was never better. At seventy years of age, the General could still out-think not only his enemies but also his more cautious and less experienced contemporaries on the Joint Chiefs of Staff. With American and South Korean forces surrounded in the Pusan Perimeter, he made a breathtakingly bold decision to land the First Marine Division 150 miles to the north along the piers and seawalls of Inchon, a place with no beaches and burdened with swiftly changing, heavy tides. As William Manchester noted, the Joint Chiefs adamantly resisted his decision to make this landing, the Chief of Staff of the Army terming the Inchon operation an "impossibility." Just to be sure, the Chiefs sent him a cable a week before the landing occurred, requiring that he accept personal responsibility if it failed.

Inchon did not fail. Instead it was a masterpiece, one of the most brilliant battlefield maneuvers in American history. On September 15, less than three months after the North Korean invasion, the Marines stormed ashore, pushing eastward, and cut off the North Korean logistical lines. Within a few days, they had defeated an estimated 40,000 enemy soldiers at the cost of 536 dead, 2,550 wounded, and 65 missing. The North Korean hold on the Pusan Perimeter was immediately lifted, followed by a breakout of American and South Korean army units, who quickly assaulted northward. As Manchester wrote, "After nearly three months of defeat and besiegement, MacArthur had freed all of South Korea of Communist domination in fifteen days."

MacArthur then proceeded farther northward, and there his political troubles began anew. On the one hand, the Truman Administration was leery of provoking China or the Soviet Union. On the other, they had supported a resolution from the United Nations Security Council calling for "the complete independence and unification of Korea." Again according to Manchester, with his administration torn by internal bickering, Truman carefully authorized MacArthur to head across the 38th Parallel "if there was 'no indication or threat' of intervention by Peking or Moscow," and to "make plans for the occupation of North Korea." As Manchester put it, "Washington backed MacArthur as long as he was winning, but he was never told exactly what he was expected to do . . . He wanted a firmer mandate, and . . . the new secretary of defense George Marshall gave it to him in an 'eyes only' cable: 'We want you to feel unhampered tactically and strategically to proceed north of the 38th parallel.'" To seal the deal, on October 7, the United Nations General Assembly "endorsed a U.S. proposal drafted in the State Department declaring that the UN objective was the establishment of 'a unified, independent and democratic government' of all Korea."

But as MacArthur's forces pushed north, their logistical lines became ever more vulnerable. At the same time, the Chinese army began moving into Korea and along its border. In late October, it was reported that 200,000 Chinese were already in Korea and another 250,000 were massed on the border. At this perilous moment, torn by indecision and internal debate, the administration grew even more cautious. On November 6, the Joint Chiefs ordered MacArthur not to strike targets within five miles of the Manchurian border, even denying his request to take out bridges across which large numbers of Chinese troops were now moving into Korea. MacArthur strongly objected, claiming that "every hour that this is postponed will be paid for dearly in American and other United Nations blood . . . [and] may well result in a calamity of major proportion."

This exchange of messages set off a chain of virulent disagreements between MacArthur and the Truman Administration that would continue for five more months. The restrictions against offensive operations continued, even as the United Nations forces under MacArthur's command became ever more exposed. In a series of instructions that eerily presaged the Vietnam War, Chinese power plants in the Yalu River were to be spared and forces retreating into Chinese territory were not to be attacked. In a moment of strategic surrealism, when the authorization to take out bridges finally came through, MacArthur was told that his aircraft were to destroy only the sections of the bridges that were on the Korean half of the Yalu River, and that in so doing, the aircraft were not to enter Chinese airspace.

And then, on November 27, an estimated 300,000 Chinese soldiers attacked the Army, Marine, and South Korean forces that had stalled near the Chinese border, decimating many units and changing the face of a war that would not end for another two and a half years.

What MacArthur sometimes suspected but did not know was that the Soviets and the Chinese were reading Harry Truman's mail. As MacArthur had proceeded north toward the Chinese border, Truman was passing a high volume of sensitive message traffic to the British government, which had troops fighting in Korea and which also was nervous about further Chinese actions in locations such as Hong Kong, a vital British possession that remained out of Communist control. Some of these messages were copies of communications between MacArthur and the Pentagon. Others included Truman's assurances that the war would not be allowed to expand across the Chinese border.

In a costly historical twist, three top Communist agents had penetrated the British diplomatic service at its highest levels. Kim Philby was then serving as first secretary of the British Embassy in Washington; Guy Burgess was second secretary; and Donald Maclean headed the American Department in London. Working together, they were feeding Truman's message traffic to the Soviets, who were then sharing the information with the Chinese. As a result, the Soviets and Chinese had full knowledge of both the intentions and the limitations of MacArthur's advance.

As Russian historian Roy Medvedev wrote after extensive interviews with Maclean, who defected to the Soviet Union in 1951, by the autumn of 1950 "the days of the Korean People's Republic were numbered when Stalin insisted on Chinese interference. Mao hesitated, afraid that the Americans might move the war onto Chinese territory and even use the atom bomb on Chinese troops and industrial centers . . . Donald Maclean, head of the American desk of the Foreign Office . . . managed to get a copy of an order from Truman to Gen. MacArthur not to cross the Chinese border under any circumstances and not to use atomic weapons . . . Stalin immediately passed on the information to Mao Tse-tung, and the Chinese reluctance came to an end. On Oct. 25 a vast army of 'Chinese people's volunteers' crossed the Korean border and attacked American and South Korean troops. The bloody war entered a new stage and ended three years later."

MacArthur would later point out in his memoir *Reminiscences* that General Lin Piao, the Chinese commander in Korea, wrote after the war, "I would never have made the attack and risked my men and military reputation if I had not been assured that Washington would restrain General MacArthur from taking adequate retaliatory measures."

In the months that followed, MacArthur grew ever more adamant that the Chinese entry into the war was a defining moment for the free world in terms of global strategy, and that the United Nations forces should counter the Chinese aggressively and thoroughly, including entering Chinese territory. Many have argued that his views clearly entered the political realm beyond which military leaders did not travel. But his warnings were also infused with the reality of a battlefield commander with vast experience in Asia who was facing an enemy whose mentality he believed he understood and whom he had been ordered to defeat.

On March 20, 1951, MacArthur crossed the final, irreversible political line. In a letter to Congressman Joe Martin, the House Minority Leader, he stated: "It seems strangely difficult for someone to realize that here in Asia is where the Communist conspirators have elected to make their play for global conquest, and that we have joined the issue thus raised on the battlefield; that here we fight Europe's war with arms while the diplomats there still fight it with words; that if we lose this war to Communism in Asia the fall of Europe is inevitable; win it and Europe most probably would avoid war and yet preserve freedom. As you point out we must win. There is no substitute for victory."

President Truman, the "someone" referred to in MacArthur's letter, countered this slap in the face by relieving the General of command. On April 10, Truman issued a statement that read in part: "I have concluded that General of the Army Douglas MacArthur is unable to give his wholehearted support to the policies of the United States Government and of the United Nations in matters pertaining to his official duties. In view of the specific responsibilities imposed upon me by the Constitution of the United States and the added responsibilities entrusted to me by the United Nations, I have decided that I must make a change of command in the Far East."

Defense Secretary George C. Marshall, a career military officer who had mastered Washington politics better than MacArthur although having seen far fewer foreign battlefields than the General, agreed with Truman's decision. Marshall, who had found it necessary to balance MacArthur's brilliance against his difficult personality since their days together in World War I, found himself once again in the middle and spent seven days defending the President in testimony to the Congress. MacArthur's firing, he testified, was the result of "the wholly unprecedented position of a local theater commander publicly expressing his displeasure at and his disagreement with the foreign and military policy of the United States."

These stinging words would reverberate with a special impact through every military command in America. Notwithstanding his enormous ego, MacArthur understood grand strategy and its application to the battlefield as well as any American then alive. He also understood Asia better than anyone in a position of true power in the Truman Administration. And now the great, innovative strategist of World War II, the American Caesar who more than any other figure was responsible for the success of modern-day Japan, saw his views and actions characterized—and diminished—as simply those of a "local theater commander."

Truman did, undeniably, have the legal authority to remove MacArthur from his position. As such, there was no room for the General to dispute or even to substantively reply to the President's findings. If there had been, he could have begun by stating that his duties in Korea encompassed another "wholly unprecedented position," that of a theater commander whose responsibilities were hardly local, extending as they did throughout the Far East and all across the Pacific, and that he was being required to fight an enemy that he knew full well his commander in chief had no intention of actually defeating. But the Truman Administration had fired him at a critical juncture in the war, where the battlefield had abruptly changed as a result of its own misfeasance, ridding itself of MacArthur largely because they were powerless to address the very issues he had raised. The end result was that MacArthur was largely blamed both for failing to anticipate the Chinese entry into the Korean War and then for insisting on military responses that might indeed have aggressively countered and even preempted much of the Chinese effort.

The impact of this controversy between MacArthur and Truman, and its final conclusion, is still felt in today's civil-military relations. His relief from command was in many ways the old passing into the new, the crossing of a threshold into a completely different relationship between the political and the military, at a time when the United States itself was moving forward into its new and often uncomfortable role as the leading nation in the world community. After MacArthur famously "faded away," there followed the inevitable promotions of generals and admirals who must now, by the very nature of America's delicate international role, accept limitations on the use of force that may even bring harm to their own people, not simply by the nature of their enemy but because of strategic "ripple effects" that transcend their own battlefield. And those generals and admirals who are rising to the very top must also accept a more restrictive and subordinated relationship with their political leaders, even when it comes to the day-to-day activities within their own areas of responsibility.

Such restrictions tend to work against the career aspirations of those with strong egos, sweeping intellectual vision, and firmly held geopolitical viewpoints.

It is not true, as was so often whispered during the Vietnam War and in the decades hence, that the American military is incapable of producing another MacArthur. What is true is that the American political system is no longer capable of tolerating another MacArthur.

CHAPTER ELEVEN

DON'T BREAK MY RICE BOWL

The second trend that has profoundly altered the military's place in our society since World War II is the evolution of what has come to be called the military-industrial complex, coupled with the establishment of a sizable and permanent standing army. These phenomena are largely taken for granted in today's America, but neither existed at all before World War II. When considered together they have had a dramatic, and some would say permanent, effect on both the nation and the highest levels of the military. Their impact has been even greater because of the changing nature of long-standing career patterns in American society as a whole, particularly as they relate to traditional retirement age, which has affected the "follow-on" second careers of many military officers.

As the wartime relationships between military commanders and America's political leadership were changing during and after the Korean War, so also were the structure of the American military around the world and the very nature of the country's industrial base. With the advent of the nuclear era, and with the rise of America as the pre-eminent national power confronting Soviet expansionism, our military entered a permanent wartime footing. When this happened our industrial base followed, for the first time in our history focusing a substantial portion of its research, productivity, and marketing on advanced weaponry and defense-related technology.

Prior to World War II, our country had no tradition of a large standing military force. At the beginning of the Civil War, the entire United States Army consisted of only 14,000 soldiers, even though millions would eventually serve during that war and more than 600,000 Americans would die in it. This tradition continued in the aftermath of World War I, when America dramatically reduced the size of its peacetime military despite the fact that we had for the first time entered the world stage as a major power. By the mid-1930s, as the Japanese invaded Manchuria and Hitler began to consolidate the power of the Nazi Party in Germany, the United States was fielding only the sixteenth-largest army in the world. We had no overseas bases, other than small outposts on such American possessions as Guam and the Philippines. Indeed, when General Douglas MacArthur was Army Chief of Staff he was widely credited with preserving the Army's size at only 132,000 soldiers by convincing President Franklin D. Roosevelt to allow the Army to administer the Civilian Conservation Corps, whose responsibilities included such arcane functions as planting trees along highways and clearing rural mountain ranges to prevent forest fires. During that same period the Marine Corps, which less than a decade later would suffer 90,000 casualties in World War II, had only 14,000 members serving on active duty.

The Constitution itself argued against a large standing army. The framers were acutely mindful of a European history where mischievous monarchs had too often waged unnecessary wars. To preclude this possibility, they inserted two key provisions in the Constitution in order to deprive the Chief Executive of any unilateral authority as it related to making war. First, while giving the President the power to oversee wartime operations as "commander in chief," the Congress retained the power to declare war. This allowed the legislative branch, not the President, to decide whether and when wars would actually be commenced and under what circumstances they would be fought, except in narrow tactical situations such as directly repelling attacks on American forces or conducting rescue operations. Second, while authorizing the Congress to "provide and maintain a Navy," with respect to ground forces they decided that the Congress should "raise and support Armies, but no Appropriation of Money to that Use [shall] be for a longer Term than two Years."

In other words, the framers of the Constitution were acutely mindful that if you gave a king an army, he would want go to war, often out of personal pique or for grandiose reasons that did not always relate to the national good. Thus, they made it clear that a navy was necessary to be "provided for" even in peacetime in order to connect America with the rest of the world and to protect its interests, including the sea-lanes along which our international commerce moved. But they also determined that armies were to be raised and supported on a provisional basis, only in circumstances where the case had been made to take the nation to war, and that such a determination would be revisited at least every two years.

It was not until the aftermath of World War II that this perception of the use of the American military changed. The nuclear era had arrived and the Cold War with the Soviet Union had begun. The economic and military exhaustion of our European allies, who had been bled dry in two successive world wars within one generation, necessitated a much larger U.S. military presence on that continent. Few Americans remember that we actually withdrew most of our military forces from Europe after World War II, and that a second, supposedly temporary infusion of American troops became necessary in 1949 with the creation of the North Atlantic Treaty Organization following the 1947 crisis in Greece, and in reaction to blatant expansionist pressures from the Soviet Union.

In Asia, a succession of undeniable realities demanded our continued military presence. The entire region was dramatically destabilized by a power vacuum that encompassed the southern and eastern countries of Asia following World War II. Japan was forced to retreat from the territories it had conquered, leaving behind massive instability. The European powers had been weakened militarily and economically by the two costly world wars and had dismantled most of their Asian colonial structures. The 1949 Communist takeover in China increased both the anxiety and the turmoil of the region. And finally, the explosion of violence on the Korean Peninsula in 1950 signaled a greater, long-term commitment of the United States to the region, as northeast Asia became the only place in the world where the interests of China, Japan, the Soviet Union, and the United States directly intersected.

With the world's most robust economy, and having suffered less, proportionally, in terms of casualties on World War II's battlefields, Americans rather surprisingly found themselves occupying a ring of military bases across the globe. And the responsibilities that were thrust upon us as the sole member of the "free world" still fully on its feet after World War II created a momentum that changed the very character of our country. Not the least of these changes involved our defense industries and, over time, our military itself, particularly among our military's top leadership.

President Dwight D. Eisenhower warned of this tectonic shift in his 1961 farewell address to the nation. Eisenhower, it will be recalled, was the most experienced military person ever to hold the presidency and the only general officer to serve in our nation's highest office in the twentieth century. A West Point graduate who attained the rare rank of five-star general while commanding the Allied forces in Europe during World War II, he had retired after more than forty years in uniform and almost immediately ran for President. Historically undervalued, this master of military policy assumed the mantle of the presidency during the Korean War and then quickly ended that war, bringing a period of relative calm in our international affairs. The eras that preceded him and that followed his presidency lacked that calm. It is worth remembering that our military buildup in Vietnam began within months after Eisenhower left office, culminating three years later in the large-scale combat presence that followed the 1964 Gulf of Tonkin incident.

No one could question Eisenhower's understanding of, or intrinsic loyalty to, the military in which he had so honorably served. But there is little doubt that Eisenhower would be shaking his head with disbelief if he were alive to see the changes that mark today's military-industrial relations.

At the end of his eight-year presidency, Eisenhower provided a somber—and truly prescient—warning to the country. "Our military organization today bears little relation to that known by any of my predecessors in peacetime, or indeed by the fighting men of World War II or Korea," he noted. "Until the latest of our world conflicts, the United States had no armaments industry . . . But now we have been compelled to create a permanent armaments industry of vast proportions. Added to this, three and a half million men and women are directly engaged in the defense establishment. We annually spend on military security more than the net income of all United States corporations. This conjunction of an immense military establishment and a large arms industry is new in the American experience . . . The total influence—economic, political, even spiritual—is felt in every city, every State house, every office of the Federal government. . . . Yet we must not fail to comprehend its grave implications. . . . In the councils of government, we must guard against the acquisition of unwarranted influence, whether sought or unsought, by the military-industrial complex. The potential for the disastrous rise of misplaced power exists and will persist."

Eisenhower was not only speaking about politics. He was hinting at another cultural issue, rarely addressed by public officials today: the symbiotic interplay between high-level military leaders and the gargantuan defense industry. And his warnings have played out in spades.

Unlike their historical predecessors, today's top military leaders rarely fade into the sunset when they take their retirement pay and move on. Retired generals and admirals are heavily represented in the management and on the boards of corporations that do billions of dollars' worth of business with the Defense Department. On one hand, the relationships between these retired "flags" and their former subordinates who are now occupying the highest levels of the active-duty military remain strong—and persuasive. On the other, many active-duty officers who are preparing to retire from the military have no greater professional desire than to join the ranks of their predecessors in corporate America.

It is no secret that in subtle ways, many of these top leaders begin positioning themselves for their second-career employment during their final military assignments. The end result of these two realities is a seamless interplay that threatens the integrity of defense procurement, of controversial personnel issues such as the huge "quasi-military" structure that has evolved in Iraq and Afghanistan, and inevitably of the balance within our national security process itself.

The day-to-day influence felt by this melding of the highest levels of the military with our behemoth defense industry is indeed, as Eisenhower warned, "economic, political, even spiritual . . . felt in every city, every State house, every office of the Federal government." As one would logically expect, retired military officers are represented at every level in an industry that receives hundreds of billions of taxpayer dollars every year. Particularly among the officer corps, this is not your grandfather's military, which gave good service and then took its pensions and headed south to fish and play golf in Florida. The modern defense industry represents a career continuum, the next logical step for applying talent and expertise learned on active duty during a military career that can end as early as one's mid-forties.

Where the requirements of national security are proven, there are many positive aspects to this career continuum. Military leaders are on the whole good managers, and also bring a vast wealth of knowledge to defense programs run by civilians but benefiting the military. In many ways, such a continuum benefits the country, since it also allows expertise gained while on active duty to be amortized throughout the career cycle of retired military professionals. But things get complicated when one's past military service becomes a factor in choosing which defense programs should be funded, or when former military people now working for defense corporations are sent forward to justify their employers' business objectives based on narrow versions of strategic needs and national goals.

Eisenhower was right to warn of the "disastrous rise of misplaced power" that attended the creation of the military-industrial complex. The mammoth defense industry, like any other, wants to stay in business, to sell a product, and to make a profit. And it goes without saying that career military people who have transitioned into the defense industry want to keep their jobs. In addition, their former subordinates and associates who remain on active duty often hold the power to shape defense priorities and thus to influence which defense programs should be approved and, to an extent, which companies should get the contracts.

Human nature is at play here, and a hard truth falls from these realities. At a policy level, the strategic direction of any presidential administration will rarely if ever draw an expression of concern from those who make their livings and their profits off of the national security industry. As an obvious example, the so-called Global War on Terror and the Iraq War specifically have provided thousands upon thousands of jobs for retired military officers and others who have worn the uniform. These jobs range from in-theater contractors to tactical and technological consultants, all the way to developing and selling new products that cover the entire military gamut, from super-secret weapons systems to caffeinated chewing gum.

We might hear a thousand short-term suggestions that go to the implementation of policy—for instance, about how to improve body armor, or which new vehicle might better absorb an IED blast, or which unmanned drone provides the best surveillance, or which new food product should be included in the latest cycle of ready-to-eat combat meals. But few of those who make their living from the military-industrial complex tend to question the wisdom of a particular program or a larger strategic policy when it provides them their way of life. Their reaction, much like the military itself, is simple: We don't make wars, we help fight them. It would be rare indeed for anyone questioning a defense program or calling for a strategic drawdown of our forces to receive support or encouragement from those involved in the military-industrial complex.

Those in this industry have long used a phrase for this phenomenon: *Don't Break My Rice Bowl*.

The symbiosis between military careers and the rewards that follow in the defense industry is particularly strong among the most senior military officials. At these higher levels, the benefits that a top-ranking general or admiral might receive after he retires can be enormous. It is not unusual for four-star generals and admirals to receive incomes that approach and even exceed seven figures when they retire, much of it from the same corporations that only a few years before were trying to sell them their products, ranging all the way from beer to satellite technology. In some cases, these corporations are buying technical expertise, but in many others they are buying access to, and inside-baseball knowledge of, the military personalities now in power.

In the Defense Department this kind of access is unusually useful, because the military career path is unique. The military more than any other institution in our society is a vertical structure that promotes only from within, and the relationships both up and down the chain of command are its defining characteristic. These are lifetime relationships, formed over many years through the bonds of personal loyalty. Few high-ranking officers would violate their sense of ethics when being visited by a former superior who wants to discuss a product or a program. But virtually all of them would take such a meeting, for it would be a personal insult to refuse.

These "many-hatted" second careers are capable of creating a broad range of ethical challenges and possible conflicts of interest among former military officers, as well as confusion among the American public when key policy questions are being debated. It has not been uncommon for retired four-star generals testifying before the Congress regarding the situation in Iraq to have listed on their official biographies that they were serving on the boards of corporations that have extensive dealings with the Department of Defense, including doing business in Iraq, teaching at our service academies, and appearing as paid consultants to major television networks.

None of these responsibilities are wrong or unethical, but all of them can affect one's willingness to unequivocally address policy issues. Keeping each of these varying constituencies properly compartmentalized can be a daunting challenge when someone is wearing so many different hats. Should a retired military officer, and particularly a former general or admiral, be able to use his access to internal Pentagon briefings to assist companies that are doing business with the Pentagon and in Iraq? If not, should he be required to terminate a life-time of permanent relations that extend deep into Pentagon policy areas? Since he realistically would be incapable of terminating such relationships, knowing that so many of them also form the basis of his social network, is it even possible that he can separate this information out when making recommendations to the companies that employ him? Since it is not possible in a real world, isn't this the very defini-tion of special access?

In the same vein, should he be able to use this kind of information to inform his television analysis? If he does, is it not possible that an im-plicit cooperation tends to develop between him and the Pentagon, so that if he were to criticize policy too strongly he would lose access to inside information that allows him to remain valuable as a commenta-tor or as a business consultant? To be more specific, if he were to speak directly and strongly against a controversial policy, would it harm his business relations, or embarrass a former military subordinate who now is in a top-level command, or cut off his ability to continue to receive inside information from the Pentagon?

Some generals handle these kinds of challenges better than others. One thinks immediately of former CENTCOM commander General Tony Zinni, whose insights on Iraq and other issues have been invalu-able. Others have not. More than a few have done little more than ad-vance the Bush Administration's political agenda during a time when the nation needed principled, unvarnished advice. And in all cases, logic and propriety demand that potentially conflicting endeavors be directly discussed when former military officers are testifying before the Congress, and when they are being offered to the viewing public as analysts capable of objective comment on matters of policy.

Here's a thought, or at least a ground rule: Truth in advertising should prevail. Any "defense expert" testifying before the Congress or providing commentary in a public or media forum should be required,

at the outset, to list corporate or other relations that might cause a conflict of interest. That little scroll underneath one's face on CNN or Fox
News should not only give one's former government title. It should
also indicate one's present involvement in any area that could in some
way prejudice or distort his or her observations. And those involvements should become a part of the discussion.

An additional complication is that some of these defense-related
companies thrive on providing mercenary soldiers to the battlefield—
mercenaries who overwhelmingly once wore the uniform of the
United States military. I write these words with the full knowledge that
many of those who are employed by civilian contractors have served
honorably and well in our armed forces. Some of them spent long careers until reaching mandatory retirement age, and desire simply to
"follow the sound of the guns" in order to continue to pursue their life's
calling. I would be the first to say not only that I cannot fault them,
but also that I can empathize with them. A similar motivation has been
behind a great deal of the journalism I have done over the years.

But it must be emphasized that they are no longer in our military,
any more than I have been when covering the military as a journalist.
It is one thing if our government wanted to call military retirees back
to active duty. It is quite another if a military retiree signs up to work
with a civilian contractor that is making a profit from our government.
In so doing they, like the rest of this vast "almost army" from nations
as disparate as Uganda and Peru that has descended on America's foreign battlefields, have become soldiers for hire. And while this phenomenon reflects more on the government that has created it than it
does on the men and women who follow in its wake, it does not alter
the nature of that employment.

What does it say about the United States of America, which was
proudly founded on the notion of citizen-soldiery, that it now must rely
on mercenaries to fill out its ranks when it fights its wars?

Nowhere is the immense growth of the military-industrial complex more troublesome, both in practical terms and in our national self-

image, than in this use of "defense contractors" in today's operational environment, and particularly in the vast quasi-military force that has grown up in the shadow of our regular military. This trend, which existed before the invasions of Afghanistan and Iraq, expanded exponentially in their aftermath. Part of it has been fed by congressional limitations on the size of the Army and Marine Corps, which forced Defense planners to rely on outside "contractors" to perform functions that historically have been carried out by the military. Another part of this costly trend is political in nature, designed to meet the requirements of America's involvement in places like Iraq and Afghanistan without having to create vast political dissent by invoking the draft.

And yet another part is economic. In the age when "contracting out" government functions to private industry has become all the rage among Republican lawmakers, providing private contractors and mercenary soldiers to the battlefield is seriously big business. As financier Felix Rohatyn wrote approvingly in a 2004 article in the *Financial Times* titled "The Profit Motive Goes to War," a silent revolution has occurred in America's national defense. "In the first Gulf war," wrote Rohatyn, "the ratio of American troops on the ground to private contractors was 50:1. In the 2003 Iraq war, that ratio was 10:1." More disturbingly, by 2007 the ratio had completely reversed. In Iraq, even with the much-debated "surge" that increased American troop military levels by 30,000, the ratio had become less than 1:1. Private contractors actually outnumbered military personnel by a margin of 180,000 to 160,000.

The wars that America is now fighting have become civilianized, in many ways to the detriment of our military people and also of those who are paying the taxes that fund the programs. And war profiteering has become the order of the day.

These private contractors have been hired under the auspices of such corporate leviathans as Halliburton, whose CEO was once Vice President Richard Cheney, and its many subsidiaries, who have made tens of billions of dollars by providing a wide range of services in Iraq, Afghanistan, and elsewhere. A sizable percentage of their services has been the result of "sole source" or undercompeted contracts under terms that, to put it mildly, seem irresponsibly arrived at. Most of their work involves duties that in other wars were performed by the uniformed military at a fraction of the cost.

Independent contractors now do the laundry. They slop food in the military's mess halls. They drive convoys. They guard many American military installations. And at last count, more than 30,000 of them were directly involved in armed security missions, carrying weapons and militarily engaging the "enemy," however it might be defined at any particular moment.

I did not fully appreciate the extent of this civilianization until 2004. While covering our military operations in Afghanistan as an embedded journalist, I was amazed at the extent of the contractor services. A lifetime in and around the military, including four years as a defense executive in the Pentagon, had not prepared me for this new and expensive reality. Sitting in a mess hall at the huge American military base at Bagram, I marveled at the hundreds of civilians who had served our food, done our laundry, loaded and driven supply trucks, and operated the kind of feel-good facilities that in the past one might have found in a Kurt Vonnegut novel. I turned to my son, who was then on assignment with me as my photographer.

"The mothers of Middle Tennessee are lonely tonight," I joked. "Their sons and daughters are over here fighting our wars. And their husbands are driving trucks and hashing meals for Halliburton."

Blackwater, which in recent months has become the most visible of the companies providing quasi-military services in Iraq and elsewhere, is also a case in point as to the dangers of mixing politics with the other vagaries of the military-industrial complex. According to an October 1, 2007, memorandum prepared by the House Committee on Oversight and Government Relations, Blackwater is owned by Erik Prince, a former Navy SEAL who operates the business through a separate holding company. The House memo states that Prince was a White House intern in the late 1980s under President George H. W. Bush. After his father died, his mother sold the family's automobile-parts company for $1.3 billion, and Prince moved to Virginia Beach, where at the age of twenty-seven he personally financed the formation of Blackwater USA. The memorandum points out that Prince's father was a prominent contributor to conservative causes, his sister is a former chairwoman of the Michigan Republican Party who earned the title of "Pioneer" by arranging at least $100,000 in donations for the 2004 Bush presidential campaign, and her husband was the 2006 Republican nominee for governor of Michigan. Prince is described as a frequent political contributor, including more than $160,000 to the Republican National Committee and the National Republican Congressional Committee.

The memo continues, pointing out that "Blackwater went from having government contracts worth less than a million dollars in 2001 to contracts worth more than half a billion dollars in 2006 . . . In total, Blackwater has received over a billion dollars from the federal government during fiscal years 2001 to 2006. Of this amount, $523,649,287 (51%) was awarded without full and open competition."

Certainly, the needs of the war in Iraq were a driving factor in these contracts, but it is legitimate to wonder how so many of them ended up with Blackwater, including the half a billion dollars awarded without full and open competition. And when one consider the services rendered by Blackwater's mercenary forces, the amount of these contracts boggles the mind, given the fact that our taxpayer dollars were paying for tasks that traditionally have been performed by regular soldiers. Again from the House Committee memorandum: "Blackwater bills the United States government $1,222 per day for one individual Protective Security Specialist. On an annual basis, this amounts to $445,891 per contractor."

This means that the American taxpayer has been paying nearly half a million dollars a year for one ordinary mercenary soldier. To put it into context, this is more than double the pay of the Army's top general in Iraq, and six to nine times the total compensation of a married Army sergeant, including salary, a housing allowance for his family back home, and subsistence pay.

Journalist Jeremy Scahill has spent years examining independent-contractor activities in Iraq. In a comprehensive 2007 article he wrote, "House Oversight and Government Reform Committee Chairman

Rep. Henry Waxman estimates that $4 billion in taxpayer money has so far been spent in Iraq on these armed 'security' companies like Blackwater—with tens of billions more going to other war companies like KBR and Fluor for 'logistical' support. Rep. Jan Schakowsky of the House Intelligence Committee believes that up to 40 cents of every dollar spent on the occupation has gone to war contractors."

These practices are widespread. At the same time, they have been virtually uncontrolled by the American government. An October 2007 federal audit of DynCorp, another large company whose management and corporate board are heavily represented by former military officers, was so riddled with misinformation that the State Department maintained it "does not know specifically what it received for most of the $1.2 billion in expenditures under its DynCorp contract." This particular contract was for the Iraqi Police Training Program, although DynCorp is also one of two companies besides Blackwater that have been used for personal-security contracts in Iraq.

As an October 2007 article by Aram Roston of MSNBC put it, in this specific case "DynCorp's contract was part of the U.S. strategy to arm and train a new Iraqi police force in the wake of the 2003 invasion. Training the police was a key part of the Bush administration's efforts in Iraq. The training was considered crucial because police are often unable to withstand insurgent attacks, and are considered penetrated by various militias." The training provided by this civilian company was of the sort that has historically been conducted by America's uniformed military and other government employees. "DynCorp's contract, issued in February 2004, entailed broad responsibilities, including equipping, housing and security for police training. It was overseen by the State Department's Bureau of International Narcotics and Law Enforcement Affairs, or INL, which also assigned the company to handle police training in Afghanistan."

And accountability, even for such mundane practices, is almost nonexistent. As Roston pointed out, "The federal watchdogs, with the Special Inspector General for Iraq Reconstruction, or SIGIR, said that they even had to suspend their audit because there wasn't enough data to check the books, which were in disarray . . . The State Department admits that it was unable to reconcile the books for the entire period of February 2004 to October 2006."

The operations of these security companies, and many others, raise vital questions about who we are as a country and how we present ourselves on foreign battlefields. Many of these highly paid mercenaries have their own sophisticated weapons systems, their own helicopters, and even their own rules of engagement, administered loosely under the jurisdiction of the American leadership in Iraq. But they have to date answered under the law to no one. American government policy has put them on the streets of Iraq without a disciplinary structure to monitor them and hold them accountable for their behavior.

Despite hundreds of shooting incidents, many involving the deaths of Iraqi civilians, to date not one American civilian contractor in Iraq has been held criminally accountable for wrongful behavior related to such incidents. The United States government has refused to allow their prosecution in Iraqi courts. The United States military has no true jurisdiction over them under the Uniform Code of Military Justice, since they are not military personnel. Indeed, it was not until October 2007 that it was finally decided that private contractors in Iraq would be subject to some form of federal law, and the extent of their accountability remains vague.

As one who has spent five years in the Pentagon, the first year as an active-duty Marine and the last four as a Defense Department executive, I can only observe that the failure to plan for this kind of legal accountability falls somewhere between incompetence and actionable negligence. For four years as Assistant Secretary of Defense and Secretary of the Navy I had the pleasure, and the informative experience, of sitting in on daily staff meetings with the Secretary of Defense, as well as on such high-level policy groups as the Armed Forces Policy Council and the Defense Resources Board. Given that backdrop, I can say without hesitation that the parameters of legal accountability for civilian contractors would have been the first issue raised by more than one member of Cap Weinberger's staff upon learning that civilians might be wearing uniforms, carrying weapons, and engaging in military confrontations inside a war zone.

*What are we going to do when some careless, irresponsible, scared,
stupid, or crazy civilian contractor decides to blow away a few Iraqi
civilians, or even if he's acting responsibly but has a moment of care-
lessness and runs over somebody with his truck? You can't turn them
over to the Iraqis; there isn't a real government. They don't belong
under the UCMJ; they're not really military. You can't fail to take any
action at all; it affects military morale and it also encourages further
misconduct. Is there a plan?*

The question, which is not complex, apparently was never asked in
the Pentagon of the Bush Administration. Or if it was, like so many
other career-ending observations about the strategy of the Iraq War
itself, it was buried and then ignored.

If this alarming shift away from the uniformed military and toward
civilian surrogates continues, we are in danger of losing permanently
our traditional notions of citizen-soldiery and becoming an American
version of the British who hired Hessian mercenaries to fight our
determined soldiers during the Revolutionary War. And we have been
shifting in this direction without a conscious discussion about what
such a change really means, not only in the context of its ramifications
for the American military but also for the definition of American
society itself.

It would have concerned the framers of our Constitution if they
had known that the United States would eventually decide to keep a
large standing army, even though the global circumstances that caused
this shift were not foreseeable at that early point in our history. Nor
could they have predicted that we would become a nation with such a
globally committed standing army at the same time we abandoned the
notions of citizen service. But it would have been beyond their collective imaginations to think that we might follow in the steps of our
British forebears and allow a large mercenary force to take to the battlefield in the name of our national honor, doing much of the work of
that standing army as we fought a string of confusing foreign wars.

CHAPTER TWELVE

"SO WHO DOESN'T LIKE SOLDIERS NOW?"

T he third set of circumstances that have affected the military's relationship with the rest of our society relates to the politicization of its career force along party lines, and to a similar trend that has evolved among the overall veterans' population. Despite having prided itself on its apolitical posture throughout most of American history, in recent decades the career force of the military, as well as its large and influential retired community, has overwhelmingly identified with the Republican Party.

Two profound experiences brought about this historically unprecedented sea change. The first was the virulence of the Vietnam-era antiwar movement, which was centered in the Democratic Party and which despite modern-day denials specifically targeted the military. And the second was the creation of the all-volunteer force toward the end of the Vietnam War, which has skewed the military's demographic makeup while also separating it as an institution from much of the rest of the country.

The political tilt inside today's active-duty military is profound and undeniable. According to a recent article in the *Washington Post Magazine,* a study conducted in the late 1990s by the North Carolina–based Triangle Institute for Security Studies showed that inside the military, Republican officers outnumbered Democrats by a ratio of 8 to 1. The article further pointed out that in 2006 only 16 percent of the active-duty respondents in a comprehensive *Army Times* poll identified themselves as members of the Democratic Party. This split also carries over into the veteran population, particularly among those who are politically active. Our nation's two largest veterans' organizations, the American Legion and the Veterans of Foreign Wars, are aligned with the Republican Party on a host of political fronts, ranging from their unquestioning support of the Iraq War to such symbolic issues as the push for a constitutional amendment forbidding the burning of the American flag.

It was not always thus. At the dinner table in the house in which I grew up, my career-military father was a fount of political, intellectual, and philosophical discussion. In fact, as one might expect from a Great Santini dad, there was no problem on earth that he did not believe could be solved if only "those guys" would listen to his remedies for saving the world. But to this day, I cannot say with certainty which candidate my father voted for in any given election. When asked, from the earliest days of my childhood he would adamantly demur, explaining that it was his duty as a military officer to remain silent about such specifically political matters. And in the military of my younger life, my father was the norm.

General Samuel B. Griffith II, a Marine who was awarded the Navy Cross for extraordinary heroism in World War II and afterward enjoyed a career as a respected intellectual, was one of the foremost warrior-scholars of his generation. Griffith stated the traditional view of military-civil relations most succinctly in 1961, in an introduction to a book on Mao Tse-tung's view of guerrilla warfare, which he himself had translated from the Chinese. He famously wrote: "In the United

States we go to considerable trouble to keep soldiers out of politics, and even more to keep politics out of soldiers."

The Vietnam War changed a good bit of that, not so much because the career military wanted to change it, but because the military profession itself was so vilified that they were forced to pick political sides in order to defend the integrity of their service. The effects of that embittering experience are still deeply felt today, both among the veterans who fought that war and inside the uniformed military, which carries within its culture a long and complicated legacy of the war's many-faceted travails. The bitterness about the way the military was treated during the Vietnam War is deeply ingrained. It goes much further than the typical dismissals in the media and among historical commentators insinuating that such feelings are merely sour grapes, part of the debate over whether it was the media, the antiwar movement, or the military that contributed most to the failure of the war.

The unfounded calumnies directed toward our profession of arms during the Vietnam War put those who had served into an almost impossible conundrum. On one hand, our military people understood and largely accepted that in America the military is the servant of the political process, and as such that they were duty-bound to fight our country's battles. On the other, it was no secret that people with overtly hostile agendas were misrepresenting the context of military service during a horrendously difficult war in order to demean America's national goals and thus to end the war itself. And so the nature of their service became the focal point of an ugly debate designed to discredit the war; at the same time, they could do little to defend themselves against the calculated attacks. This paralysis was especially difficult to endure because the insults, when they came, were often not only institutional but also deeply personal, directed at the very notions of honor and integrity that are the principal motivating factors for good people to choose the profession of arms.

A generation removed, the slogans and the vicious insinuations still sting: "Baby killers." "Drug addicts." "Military justice is to justice as military music is to music." "Define a contradiction in terms: military intelligence." "Ho, Ho, Ho Chi Minh, the N-L-F [Viet Cong] is gonna

win." "Join the military. Travel to exotic places. Meet interesting
people. And kill them."

The denigration of the military during that era still resonates
among those serving in today's military, for two strong reasons. The
first reason is that the military culture emphatically views itself as part
of an historical continuum. For example, the heroism and sacrifice in
such battles as World War I's Belleau Wood, World War II's Iwo Jima,
and the Korean War's Chosin Reservoir Breakout still inform the dignity of Marine Corps service today. In the same vein, the remembrance
of the unfounded attacks on those who fought in Vietnam has become
a part of the emotional makeup of those who now serve. In short, the
wrongful treatment of our Vietnam veterans has become a part of
the American military's DNA.

The second reason is that the creation of the all-volunteer military
has narrowed the demographic base among those who serve, particularly in the combat arms, and thus has accentuated these feelings. Contrary to our historical tradition of fielding a citizen-soldier military, a
very small part of American society has been carrying the national security burden since Vietnam. Not surprisingly, a sizable percentage of
new recruits come from the most conservative geographic areas of the
country. Others, as with my own family, are following generations-old
traditions of service, still honoring the citizen-soldier concept even as
the country has largely given up on it. Indeed, statistics show that in
any given year, nearly half of those enlisting in the Army are following
in the footsteps of a close relative. This sense of family continuity colors even further the treatment of those who fought in Vietnam, since
it was happening to fathers, uncles, and even grandfathers.

And so, when one reflects on the conduct of American society during the Vietnam War and its impact on today's politics, an irony is at
work. In the media, academia, and among America's elites, Richard
Nixon is remembered with a special vitriol for ostensibly prolonging
the war after his election and for the incursions he ordered into Laos
and Cambodia. But among a large percentage of those who served during Vietnam, and in the military generation that has followed, the enduring villain of that era was and remains the Democratic Party.

Most of the Democratic Party's top leadership still does not understand that this is true, or even why it might be so. But it is, emphatically, the case.

If you ask those who served in Vietnam to look back at that war and its legacy, a surprising number will quickly remind you that it was the Democratic Party that put Robert McNamara in the Pentagon and bungled the war's strategy; the Democratic Party that later on became the epicenter of an antiwar movement that wrongly labeled those who were fighting the war as the scapegoats for its failure; the Democratic Party that nominated George McGovern, who promised to go on his knees to Hanoi to end the war if he was elected President; the Democratic Party that pulled the funding plug on South Vietnam with the first vote of the so-called Watergate Congress in early 1975, thus precipitating the fall of Saigon; and Democratic President Jimmy Carter who immediately upon assuming office issued the first blanket pardon of draft evaders in our entire history, elevating every person who broke the law and evaded military service to the status of moral purist.

Curiously, these feelings transcend individual beliefs about whether the war was winnable and whether it should have been fought at all. As I wrote in an editorial for the *Washington Post* in 1976, by the end of the war in Vietnam "the same people who once called upon us to bleed were now whispering that we should be ashamed of our scars."

And just as curiously, most leading Democrats, especially those whose careers began during and immediately after the Vietnam era, remain tone-deaf to the lingering emotional depths of this resentment—a resentment that defines the way many of our military and our veterans view the Democratic Party of today.

To this day, many national leaders in the Democratic Party look back with fondness and a sense of vindication to the time when the antiwar movement successfully cut off funding for the Vietnam War. Some of them persist in using that experience as a proposed template for ending the war in Iraq. What they do not fully appreciate is that many who fought in Vietnam remember the cutoff of funds as an act of national betrayal, a signal that gave a green light to the final Communist invasion that toppled the South Vietnamese government, sending a million of our South Vietnamese allies into reeducation camps and causing two million Vietnamese to flee their homeland. This feeling persists even among many who had concluded at the time that the war was not winnable, but who believed that after twenty years of fighting, those South Vietnamese who had been loyal to us and to the principles of democracy deserved a chance to properly negotiate a less disastrous political conclusion.

In short, Democratic Party leaders reject out of hand what so many of our military and our veterans still believe strongly: that in the tenor of the times, the national goals in Vietnam were commendable, even though the policies that evolved to carry them out had become acutely flawed. The Republicans, including a long list of "chicken hawk" leaders who chose not even to serve in Vietnam, have always comprehended this distinction, as well as its visceral power among a vast percentage of Americans.

Their intense involvement in the antiwar movement is such an ingrained part of many Democratic Party leaders that they tend to reject out of hand the notion that the American public might feel differently about the end of the Vietnam War. But the American public has never agreed with the antiwar movement on this point. In August 1972, eight years after the Gulf of Tonkin incident and long after the American public had lost its faith in the overall conduct of the war, Americans still agreed in a Harris Poll by a margin of 74 to 11 percent that "it is important that South Vietnam not fall into the control of the communists."

On another key point, while many Democrats to this day refer to those who served in Vietnam as reluctant draftees or as victims, it is beyond question that most of those who fought in Vietnam remain deeply proud of their service, regardless of their politics and regardless of the end result of the war itself. Two-thirds of those who served during the Vietnam era were volunteers, not draftees, and 73 percent of those who died in Vietnam were volunteers. In the most thorough survey ever done about the attitudes of Vietnam veterans, a Harris Poll taken in late 1979 and early 1980, when their service was still being widely demeaned, found that 91 percent of those who fought in Vietnam indicated they were glad they had served their country, 74 percent agreed that they had enjoyed their time in the military, and nearly two-thirds said they would go again, even knowing the end result of the war.

And thus there is a deep but often quiet divide between the Democratic Party and the American military not only as it relates to history, but also in the way that past human conduct affects attitudes in modern-day crises such as Iraq and Afghanistan. The Democrats who came of age during the Vietnam era, and many others who have grown up under their tutelage, have erred greatly for many years in not understanding the positive aspects of military service. And in so doing, in the eyes of those who have served, the Democrats became not simply the antiwar party but also the antimilitary party.

I lived through this uncomfortable journey, my own feelings finally becoming so strong that they caused me to move away from the Democratic Party for nearly thirty years. I did not fully understand it at the time, but my father lived through it also, in a simpler but more profound way. Assigned to the Pentagon in 1965 after being deep-selected for colonel—usually a sure signal that an officer was on his way to becoming a general—my father then worked for two years in the Air Force's Office of Legislative Affairs, assisting Air Force leaders in their relations with the Congress. Within months of reporting to the Pentagon, he had developed a startling dislike of Defense Secretary McNamara and his handpicked civilian minions, a coterie of usually young, nonveteran intellectuals that had been termed the "Whiz Kids." To my surprise, by the time I was commissioned in the Marine Corps in 1968 he had begun to openly question the political direction of the war in which I would soon fight. His own feelings about the mismanagement of the war and its impact on those who were fighting it were so strong that when I received my orders to go to Vietnam my father retired from active duty, telling me that he "couldn't bear to watch it" while still wearing the uniform.

My father was not alone among his World War II veteran peers, who had reached similar conclusions about the Democratic Party through a journey completely different from mine and that of my fellow Vietnam veterans. But we all agreed on one thing: The Democrats had abandoned us. My father and many of his contemporaries felt betrayed by the Democrats because of the naive yet arrogant way that McNamara and his Whiz Kids ignored military advice as they conducted the war in Vietnam. My generation of Vietnam veterans grew disgusted with the Democratic Party because of the antimilitary methods they and their supporters were using to end the war.

This legacy is still with the Democratic Party today. Like a boil that must be lanced, it needs to be examined before it can be overcome.

Despite current rhetoric to the contrary, during Vietnam the core leadership of the antiwar movement emphatically did not separate the warriors from the war. In fact, in 1967 the major strategists of that movement consciously decided to make the military rather than the Congress the focus of their dissent. This strategy was unveiled while the Mobilization Committee to End the War, at the forefront of the antiwar leadership, prepared for a large-scale march on the Pentagon in October of that year. The march on the Pentagon was memorialized in Norman Mailer's Pulitzer Prize–winning book *The Armies of the Night*.

Throughout the Vietnam War but especially from that point forward, a generation was set against itself. Among the elites of our society, including many media commentators, student protesters were lionized at the expense of the hapless soldiers who were frequently required to face down their confrontational antics. In the process, those who had fought on Vietnam's brutal battlefields were ridiculed, humiliated, and dehumanized by many of the more advantaged members of their own age group. To have served in one of the most vicious wars in American history—a war that for the Marine Corps produced more total killed and wounded than even World War II—often brought venomous attacks from others who comfortably claimed a higher level of morality by simply deciding not to serve.

In our entire legacy, there are few stronger examples of the denigration of one set of Americans by another on the basis of class and privilege.

Obviously, not all Democrats engaged in such conduct. Many, if not most, of those who opposed the Vietnam War did so responsibly, out of a legitimate concern that our soldiers were being wasted in a futile effort. And it goes without saying that many of our nation's most honored combat veterans, as well as numerous champions of veterans' rights, have served in the Congress as Democrats. Any listing of these exemplars risks omitting equally deserving names, but one cannot think of veterans' advocates in the Congress during and after that period without remembering Sonny Montgomery, Tiger Teague, Daniel Inouye, Bob Kerrey, Chuck Robb, John Glenn, Max Cleland, and a host of others, all of whom served our country and are held in great esteem.

At the same time, it is also undeniable that for many years the Democratic Party occupied the political center of antimilitary rhetoric in this country. And despite the Republicans' deserved reputation for harboring more than their share of "chicken hawks" who talked up the war but had "other priorities" when it came to serving, there were few in that party who spat on soldiers when they came home, labeled them as drug doers and baby-killers, intimated that they should be ashamed of their military service, or openly celebrated when the Communists finally took control of Vietnam.

In the years after the fall of Saigon, the South China Sea teemed with small boats packed with hundreds of thousands of ordinary Vietnamese who were fleeing Communism at substantial risk of death. Against this evidence, which marked the first diaspora in the long and frequently tragic history of that country, the cause for which our Vietnam veterans had fought could no longer be viewed as mindless or immoral. But even then, when the Democratic Party finally started to embrace our veterans it too often came in the form not of respect but of pity, a phenomenon that continues to this day. Unable after years of protest to remark on the justness of the war itself, the party's leadership instead focused on the emotional and physical damage that the war had brought to those who fought it. Still unwilling to call our Vietnam veterans heroes, they settled for labeling them as victims. The drug-doing, rapacious baby-killers of 1970 now became the burned-out, post-traumatic-stress-disordered, Agent Orange–drenched, unemployed, and homeless losers.

These problems did exist, as those who have remained in contact with fellow combat veterans are most keenly aware. To a certain extent they still do, for a wide variety of reasons that include the way our veterans were treated when they returned home. But soldiers returning from every major war in our history have had their share of emotional difficulties and readjustment challenges. After the Civil War, morphine addiction was often labeled "the soldier's disease" due to its prevalence among veterans. After World War II, according to a study by the National Academy of Sciences, 25 percent of returning veterans suffered from some sort of emotional difficulties. The difference is that until Vietnam such difficulties were never used to characterize one's military service, at the expense of larger and more positive contributions.

Military folks, particularly those who serve in the combat arms, tend to be pretty tough people. From a young age they learn how to get things done, to meet difficult deadlines, to conquer their fears and to face the unknown, to accept getting knocked down again and again but to keep getting back up, to live long months surrounded by chaos and frequent tragedy, to find humor in strange places, and to live up to the expectations of their ultimate judges—those who wore the same uniform in earlier times and those who will do so in the future. Many of them need help when they encounter personal or emotional difficulties. But throughout history the first people to give them that help have often been their fellow soldiers, sailors, airmen, and Marines, since personal loyalty is the coin of the realm among those who serve. And when it comes to those outside the military, veterans' greatest expectation, and indeed their most important reward, has always been to be respected by the society that called on them to take life-threatening risks and to make repeated sacrifices.

The ultimate question, especially in political terms, is this: When you look at a veteran, what do you see? Do you see a strong individual who overcame the most difficult challenges most human beings can face, and who deserves not only respect but some form of societal reward? Or do you see a victim?

Or to flip it around the other way, which actually defines the issue more clearly: If you are a soldier or a veteran and you look at a Democrat or a Republican in Congress, what do you see? From the Vietnam War until the invasion of Iraq, that question was not difficult to answer. If they were looking at a Republican officeholder, most military people began with the assumption that he or she respected and understood their service, and in some way wanted to honor them. If they were looking at a Democrat, the immediate assumption was that the officeholder might pity them and want to help them with a government program or perhaps some form of legal assistance, but that he or she did not really understand them, and thus would never be able to comprehend the dignity and sense of accomplishment that is a key element of having served.

But the times have changed. Despite this uncomfortable past, an interesting political reversal has taken place in the aftermath of 9/11, and particularly since the invasion of Iraq. And it may well account for the fact that in campaign 2006, a majority of America's veterans who were running for political office for the first time did so as members of the Democratic Party.

The historical tables have turned. It is now the Republican Party that populated the Defense Department with a cast of unseemly true believers who propelled America into an unnecessary and strategically unsound war; the Republican Party that persisted in distorting the integrity of the military's officer corps by rewarding sycophancy and punishing honesty; the Republican Party that has most glaringly violated its stewardship of those in uniform; and the Republican Party that continually seeks to politicize military service for its own ends even as it uses their sacrifices as a political shield against criticism for its failed policies. And in that sense, it is now the Republican Party that most glaringly does not understand the true nature of military service.

Combat, despite its intensity and sense of immediate purpose, is the most decidedly apolitical environment I have ever experienced. Military missions dominate the daily discussions. National political arguments may inflame the emotions now and then, but they are largely irrelevant to one's day-to-day survival. This should not be viewed as anomalous. Contrary to the insinuations of many latter-day Republican Party luminaries, few Americans enlist in the military for political reasons or in order to support specific political agendas. Most of our military people serve because they love their country, or because of family tradition, or because they enjoy soldiering, just to name a few reasons. Some might agree with a particular administration's war policies, while some others do not. But whether one soldier or Marine agrees with another's political views has nothing to do with getting the job done, because that job involves controlling the tactical battle space to which they have been assigned. The rest of it belongs to the politicians who have decided to send them into harm's way and who are charged with determining an end point to their involvement.

It is both patronizing and condescending for politicians to use our military people as backdrops or "color commentary" for their own political goals. The implications of such political posturing are even more troublesome when the military's competence becomes the sole bright spot in political wars gone awry. Between the Bush Administration and the more extreme elements in the Congress, the Republican Party has further endangered our nation's entire strategic posture through the way it has conducted the war in Iraq. Their most glaring and crucial failing has been an adamant refusal to match the sacrifices of our military with a sound, regionally based diplomatic strategy designed to take advantage of the military's performance.

Such a strategy could have, and should have, been in place as early as 2003. If the Bush Administration had followed the right approach on the diplomatic front, the combat mission of the United States in Iraq could have been ended years ago, with no damage to regional security or to our nation's international prestige. To the contrary, in terms of global strategy, international diplomacy, and the health of our economy, our country is actually at greater peril now than before the invasion, even as the war in Iraq has consumed an ever-higher percentage of our national budget.

This administration has gone to the military again and again, overly stressing our ground forces through repeated deployments with little time to refurbish and retrain, wearing down its equipment, and pushing its career force to the edge of burnout. Our military has consistently answered that call, never failing to control its tactical battle space. But over this same span of time the region, from Lebanon to Pakistan, has descended into ever more dangerous instability. Key economic indicators clearly point to the worries of the international community over this instability. The price of oil has more than tripled from $24 a barrel just before the invasion and at some times has quadrupled, reaching prices in excess of $100 a barrel. Gold, a measure of international nervousness, has gone from $300 an ounce to as high as $900. The price of silver has tripled; copper has gone up sevenfold. The value of the dollar itself has crashed, in some cases to all-time lows.

At the same time, millions of refugees have spilled out of Iraq, including many of the country's most talented professionals, some leaving the region and others heading into Syria and Jordan, threatening further destabilization there. According to the *Washington Post*, "The U. N. High Commissioner for Refugees estimates that up to 2.5 million Iraqis have fled the country," 1.5 million of them going to Syria and 500,000 to Jordan. Millions more have lost their homes and their traditional neighborhoods inside the country. Again according to the *Post*, 2.4 million Iraqis have become "internal refugees," having lost their homes inside the country, 80 percent of them women and children, many of whom suffer from disease and malnutrition. Combined, these dislocations comprise nearly 20 percent of Iraq's prewar total population of 24 million people.

Regionally, the situation is just as fitful. Predictably, Iran has exerted pressure inside Iraq from the east as it also threatens greater domination of the region. The Saudis, to the west, have been responsible for a plurality of the insurgents operating inside Iraq. Turkey has become so concerned with activities in the Kurdish area of northern Iraq that its parliament has authorized military actions inside Iraq's borders. The regimes in Afghanistan and Pakistan have both become ever more fragile and are increasingly threatened by the forces of Islamic fundamentalism and jihad. Indeed, the reduction of Al Qaeda activity in Iraq has been matched by an increase of such activity in Pakistan and Afghanistan, including the assassination by Al Qaeda of former Prime Minister Benazir Bhutto in December 2007. The potential danger of a nuclear-armed, Taliban-leaning government in Pakistan is one that many, including myself, warned about before the invasion of Iraq. Such a prospect is far more serious than any danger we might find in Iraq itself.

Most military people can see and understand these realities. But rather than openly recognizing them, Republican leaders have for years claimed that any mention of them insults "the troops" and comprises a form of defeatism that will not "let them win" in Iraq.

These patronizing litanies from politicians who shield themselves from accountability by claiming that criticism of the Bush Administration's policies undermines the troops is blatant political avoidance and not true respect. Most of our military men and women know this. A basic respect for service demands that the wars we ask our military to fight be properly designed from the outset, with clear strategic goals that include an understandable end point to our military involvement. A fundamental respect also means that after several years of war in Iraq and Afghanistan, those directing these efforts should be able to develop sensible operational policies built on rotational cycles that allow our troops enough time at home between deployments. And a true indicator of respect would be for those who repeatedly call our present-day military men and women "the new Greatest Generation" to support the same level of GI Bill benefits for those who have served since 9/11 as those given to our World War II veterans. We have seen none of this.

Except in an Orwellian world, wars are not supposed to be endless. Nor are occupations supposed to last forever. Those who claim that one cannot oppose the President's policy and still be supporting the troops should consult the opinions of the troops. Poll after poll shows that the active-duty military's views on this endeavor are largely a mirror of American society as a whole. During my Senate campaign, a poll of American troops in Iraq showed that 72 percent of them believed the United States should pull out of Iraq by the end of the year—that year being 2006. In December 2006, nearly 60 percent of our active-duty military people surveyed by the highly reliable publishers of the *Army, Navy, Air Force,* and *Marine Corps Times* newspapers disagreed with the Bush Administration's Iraq policies. And in December 2007, despite all of the administration's hyping of the so-called surge, a *Los Angeles Times*/Bloomberg poll showed that 60 percent of military families believe the Iraq War was not worth the cost, and that 58 percent believe the United States should withdraw its military from Iraq within a year or sooner.

Our military people want a win, but they also deserve an end. And so the true question facing us is: When does their win translate into an end? In a situation such as Iraq, only forceful diplomacy that takes place alongside military activities can answer that question. All of America, including our military, knows it.

How would the present challenge in Iraq be addressed by a President with a full understanding of, and respect for, our military? One need not search too far into our history for an answer, and again we can find it in the leadership of former General Dwight D. Eisenhower.

When Eisenhower ran for President in 1952, the Korean War had been raging for two years and had fallen into a stalemate with no clear end in sight. Rather than stage-managing a series of propagandistic speeches with our military men and women as backdrops, and rather than filling the airwaves with a mindless litany of focus-group-tested phrases such as "cut and run" and "let them win," Eisenhower faced head-on the hard facts of Korea and the toll it was taking on our fighting forces.

In a speech delivered on October 25, 1952, just before the presidential election, Eisenhower castigated the conduct of the Korean War and its impact on those who had been called upon to fight it. His conclusion—and his promise to the American people—should be permanently hanging on the wall of the Oval Office so that every President who sends troops into battle can be reminded of it on a daily basis.

Eisenhower said in part:

[The Korean War] was never inevitable, it was never inescapable . . . When the enemy struck, on that June day of 1950, what did America do? It did what it always has done in all its times of peril. It appealed to the heroism of its youth . . . The answer to that appeal has been what any American knew it would be. It has been sheer valor—valor on all the Korean mountainsides that, each day, bear fresh scars of new graves. Now—in this anxious autumn—from these heroic men there comes back an answering appeal. It is no whine, no whimpering plea. It is a question that addresses itself to simple reason. It asks: Where do we go from here? When comes the end? Is there an end? These questions touch all of us. They demand truthful answers. Neither glib promises nor glib excuses will serve. They would be no better than the glib prophecies that brought us to this pass . . . . The first task of a new Administration will be to review and re-examine every course of action open to us with one goal in view: To bring the Korean War to an early and honorable end.

In sum, our military members deserve smart political leadership that truly looks after our national security, respects their service, and at the same time provides a proper stewardship of their well-being.

One result is that for the first time in a generation, the Democratic Party has an opportunity to prove that it is capable of that kind of leadership, and along the way to regain the trust and the support of those who serve. To their credit, many of the party's top functionaries understand this. But many more do not. Consequently, the Republican Party's strategic failure in Iraq and in other aspects of our national defense has not automatically translated into respect for the Democrats. But the recent policies of the Republican Party have indeed brought the potential of a much-needed political reassessment inside the military and among our veterans.

It will take measurable, affirmative leadership for the Democratic Party to fully regain the respect of those who have worn the uniform. The jury is still out on whether the Democratic Party will be capable of doing that. If it does so, and if at the same time it succeeds in regaining its position as the party that stands for economic fairness, the Democratic Party will cut deeply into Republican strongholds in the South, border South, and Midwest. And if that transformation takes place, it will have a long-term effect on the political makeup of both houses of the Congress.

CHAPTER THIRTEEN

A CRIMINAL
INJUSTICE

Americans are a little strange when it comes to crime. On one
hand, we tend to romanticize criminal figures, as any number of powerful films from *Bonnie and Clyde* to *The Godfa-
ther* make clear. On the other, in the real world of our neighborhoods
we fear criminals of any sort, and we typically shun those who have
been in prison. We also tend to turn our eyes away from the truth
about how our system incarcerates people, and the impact of incarceration on their lives. It is rare that questions surrounding crime
even come up during major political campaigns. In fact, the illogical,
chaotic state of America's criminal justice system is one of the most
troubling—and least discussed—issues facing the American political
system today.

It is easy, and politically expedient, for an officeholder to be known
as "tough on crime." All across the country, we are represented by
"lock 'em all up" politicians whose reaction every time a new prison is

built is to send out a press release, and who publicly rejoice every time some flub-a-dub ex-offender's parole is revoked. But few candidates or elected officials these days even dare to mention the mind-boggling inconsistencies and the long-term problems that are inherent in the way we now define crime, sentence offenders, and fail to provide for their reentry into civil society. Indeed, to be viewed as "soft on crime" is one of the surest career-killers in American politics.

But what does it mean to be tough on crime? Most of us are in pretty firm agreement when it comes to protecting our citizens and our neighborhoods from hardened criminals. Few would disagree that law enforcement should be swift and sure when it comes to such clear societal threats as treason, premeditated violence, various forms of thievery, depraved conduct, and the intimidation of our populace through organized gang activity. But beyond that, what are the yard-sticks we should use to even define crime? Which criminal acts are of such a magnitude that we should lock people up? And what should our goals be for those who have served their time—how should we approach what the experts like to term "reentry"? Should there not be a point where we can all agree that an ex-offender has truly paid his or her debt to society and thus deserves a return to full citizenship as well as assistance in making a readjustment to a better life?

We all should look upon such concerns as part of true leadership, and concur that it is in our societal interest to focus on them.

The conditions under which we actually remove human beings from society should be profound. When we do so, we are not only taking away their freedom; the statistics are overwhelming that we are most likely changing their lives forever. And—not incidentally—we are requiring the rest of our citizenry to spend precious tax dollars on building prisons for them, clothing them, feeding them, guarding them, and in some ways even entertaining them.

To the contrary, in America the common practice in recent years has been to make incarceration an all-too-common "solution" to an ever-wider set of activities. We've come a long way since Colonial times, when much low-level criminal activity was dealt with by putting a miscreant into the stockades for a day or two and allowing his fellow citizens to pass by, throw a few rotten tomatoes, utter their disgust, and then consider the matter over and done with.

It is not considered politically wise to point this out, but over the past two decades America has gone completely jail-happy. We are locking people up at astonishing rates, often for offenses that are unevenly enforced or, to put it more bluntly, blatantly not enforced except among the disempowered members of our society. We now live in a system that is either afraid of, or incapable of, bringing big-time perpetrators to justice. Almost as a consequence, our lawmakers seem to be satisfying a concerned electorate with symbolic victories over the "widgets"—the small-time, expendable players who are largely pawns and who now fill our prison cells. Having proclaimed twenty years ago that crime could best be solved and deterred by locking up as many criminals as possible for as long as possible, our legislators have instead managed to create a vast pool that includes unnecessarily stigmatized individuals. Among other concerns, this mass of disenfranchised humanity threatens to congeal into the bedrock of what is becoming a permanent underclass.

A multitude of living ghosts walk among us today, largely unseen and unnoticed by those who occupy the highest reaches of the political world. Almost all of them are American citizens, and yet they have no right to vote. Most live below the poverty line, but they have little access to public housing and they must overcome strong barriers in finding employment. Many are habitual drug users and many more are mentally ill, but few programs are available to return them to productivity. Their notions of family and community have been devastated by long years of separation and by the stigma that attaches to their past, feeding the vicious cycle of family breakdown, inadequate education, and further criminal conduct that has caused our more disadvantaged members to fall ever further from the American mainstream.

This is not simply a racial problem, but the racial disparities are huge and are an indicator of how deeply this issue is affecting Americans of lower social status. African Americans, who make up about 12 percent of our society, comprise more than half of all our prison inmates; twenty years ago, they made up only one-third. One study shows that 13 percent of black males in America—one in every eight—cannot vote because of laws denying convicted felons the right to do so. Other statistics provided to my Senate office show that a black male without a high school diploma now has a 60 percent chance of going to jail during his young adulthood, and that a black male with a high school diploma has a 30 percent chance. Studies also indicate that once an individual of any race has been in prison, he has a two-thirds chance of being rearrested within three years and a 50 percent chance of going back to jail in that same period.

In short, for those who become ensnared in our criminal justice system, prison often becomes an alternate lifestyle. Black, white, Latino, Asian, whatever their ethnic origins, they are our own version of The Untouchables. And proper leadership demands that we focus our energies on bringing true criminal conduct to justice while reducing the ranks of the incarcerated, not only for their good but also for our own. Societal fairness demands it. And the reality is that 95 percent of those who are incarcerated will eventually make their way back to the streets. Some of them want to be career criminals. Most do not. For those who do not, in many ways the choice is ours as much as it is theirs as to whether they will become repeat offenders and societal burdens or, with proper assistance, transition into becoming productive citizens.

Twenty-five years ago, I became one of the first American journalists in modern times to be allowed inside the Japanese prison system, after which I wrote an in-depth story on Americans in Japanese jails. The system itself was harsh in terms of inmate living conditions but remarkable in its human fairness. The prisons were run by highly trained professionals for whom prison administration was a career path, not unlike the military in America. In Japan, one had to start at the bottom to reach the top, beginning with the guards who supervised prisoners in their cells and extending all the way to the wardens who ran the operations. Every guard in the Japanese prison system had to pass a competitive, nationally standardized entry examination. He then received a minimum of a year's training that taught him counseling, martial arts, and discipline, and also instilled in him the notion that he would treat the inmates firmly but with the utmost respect. This compared to an American system where the "recommended standard" was only one week of on-the-job training to qualify someone to become a turnkey in U.S. prisons.

In Japan, prison violence was almost unheard of, either at the hands of guards or between inmates. In fact, any guard who struck a prisoner received a mandatory seven-year jail term. As one warden put it, "Our guards are not oppressors. They are a prisoner's teacher, judge, and friend." Every able-bodied prisoner had a job. If one was in solitary confinement, he typically sat in his prison cell and made paper bags eight hours a day. A prisoner bowed to his guard when requesting permission to speak. Sentences in Japan were deliberately short, rarely longer than four years for even the worst of crimes. The focus of their system was on solving crime rather than retribution. At that time, the Japanese were bringing 72 percent of their crimes to conviction; America was bringing about 19 percent of its crimes to arrest.

Importantly, the entire focus of the Japanese criminal justice system from the moment of arrest to the day a prisoner was released from jail was on fairness, both to the individual involved and to society as a whole. Victims were brought directly into the criminal trial proceeding. A proper apology from the perpetrator might affect his sentence, a concept that promoted psychological healing between the wrongdoer, his victim, and society as a whole. Prison labor among first offenders was skills-oriented, allowing proper certification from the Ministry of Labor for such skills as automobile mechanics and computer repair that were honored on the outside.

The fairness and workability of this system was an eye-opener, especially when Japanese prison authorities told me that they had built their present system a century before, modeled largely on how the Americans and the Germans had designed their own. Their question for me, frequently asked, was this:

"We learned from you. What has happened to your system?"

For all the comparisons, the most striking finding, even then, was the difference in the overall incarceration rates between our two countries. At that time, I wrote with concern that America, with twice the population of Japan, had 780,000 people in jail, as compared to only 40,000 sentenced prisoners in that country. In other words, America was putting people in prison at ten times the rate of the Japanese. Given the cultural differences between our two nations, direct comparisons were impossible, but even then America had the highest incarceration rate in the non-Communist nations of what we called the "free world."

Little did I know that by 2006 our country's jail population would have tripled to more than 2.38 million prisoners, the highest reported incarceration rate in the entire world. In addition, there are now in excess of five million additional people who have recently left jail and are under "correctional supervision," including parole, probation, and other community sanctions. According to the *New York Times*, by the end of 2006 "about one in every 31 adults in the United States was in prison, in jail or on supervised release."

For some on the extreme fringes of our political debates, these numbers might represent the best way to fight crime. But they should give the rest of us serious pause. With 5 percent of the world's population, our country now houses 25 percent of the world's reported prisoners. The United States currently imprisons 737 inmates per 100,000 residents, an incarceration rate that is nearly five times the world average rate of 166 per 100,000. Russia, the country with the second-highest incarceration rate, imprisons 624 per 100,000; England and Wales imprison 148 per 100,000 people; Germany imprisons 95 per 100,000; Australia 126 per 100,000; and Japan only 62 per 100,000, a rate that still is not even one-tenth that of the United States.

The United States is now home to approximately five thousand prisons and jails, with more being built every day. Estimates prepared for a recent hearing that I chaired before the Senate's Joint Economic Committee indicate that in 2006 our state governments alone spent $2 billion on prison construction, three times what they were spending only fifteen years before. They also show that the combined expenditures of local governments, state governments, and the federal government for law-enforcement and corrections personnel now total more than $200 billion a year. Recent figures are difficult to obtain, but in 2001, the average cost of operating a state prison facility was $22,650 per inmate annually. For federal prisons it was $22,632. By some estimates, we are now spending approximately $50,000 a year for every inmate.

In the age of independent contractors, a multibillion-dollar industry has now grown around the construction, servicing, and operation of prisons, in some ways similar to the big business that has evolved around our overseas military commitments in Iraq and Afghanistan. One of the great ironies of the "outsourcing" debates, where so many good American jobs have been shipped overseas, is that for the first time in my lifetime economically hard-hit communities now actually compete to bring prisons to their local areas as a source of revenue and jobs. Prisons also require increasingly large amounts of funding for health care. According to the same report prepared for the Joint Economic Committee, in 2001 medical care for prisoners in state facilities alone was estimated at $3.3 billion.

As our prison population has skyrocketed, the political process itself has remained resolutely silent. Few politicians wish or even dare to talk about the inequities of our criminal justice system. Some are merely unaware of the situation, since its realities are remote from their own daily lives and since this issue is difficult to break apart and examine. Most know that talking about these inequities promises little if any support in the form of campaign contributions. Companies that want to build prisons or provide food services and supply new guards are often represented by lobbyists, and even those that are not frequently have access to the political process. Few who would be helped by reducing today's prison population even have money to donate to political campaigns. Many cannot vote anyway, since they have lost that right as a result of their incarceration. And in a country where the slogan "soft on crime" can ruin one's reelection chances, there is always the possibility that an opponent can run a brutally damaging political ad if a politician begins speaking out.

But while there is little advantage for a political leader to say that too many people are in jail, the hard truth is that, with such a high rate of imprisonment, there are only two possible conclusions to draw about our country's present approach to criminal justice: Either we are home to the most evil population on earth, or we are locking up a lot of people who really don't need to be in jail, for actions that other countries seem to handle in more constructive ways. And when one looks at the factors that have caused the prison population to nearly triple just in the last thirty years, it becomes pretty clear that it's the latter.

In truth, a great deal of the growth in our prison population has not been due to increasing crime rates but from other factors, many of which reflect our government's inability to reach solutions to seemingly unsolvable problems where our citizens are emotionally engaged but deeply divided. Twenty years ago, lawmakers frustrated with what they viewed as too much discretion being allowed judges decided to institute mandatory sentencing and harsher parole standards. By legislative decree, the mandatory minimum penalty for possessing five grams of crack cocaine, roughly equal to two packets of sugar, became a five-year prison sentence. Since 1986, approximately 100,000 people have been imprisoned as a result of these mandatory sentences, most of them nonviolent drug users and small-time dealers, with very few drug kingpins affected. Similarly, parole revocations are now estimated to account for one-third of all admissions to prison, twice the rate of the early 1980s.

Changing attitudes toward the institutional treatment of those who are mentally ill have created a situation where the number of mentally ill in our prisons is approximately five times the number currently being treated as inpatients in mental hospitals. The Department of Justice estimates that 16 percent of the adult inmates in American prisons and jails—as many as 300,000 people—suffer from mental illness, with the percentage of mental illness among those in juvenile custody even higher. Our prisons and jails are also heavily populated by the "criminally ill"—inmates who suffer from HIV, tuberculosis, and hepatitis.

No issue has affected the workings of our criminal justice system more dramatically, and no issue illuminates the perplexing unfairness of our incarceration policies more clearly, than that of drugs. To borrow a medical term, when it comes to this troublesome issue, American society seems clinically bipolar. On one hand, we have always been a society with a large percentage of people who have used external stimulants, from the first days of our settlements when the tradition of moonshine stills arrived along with our pioneers and became an accepted part of the farmlands along the frontier. On the other, America is imbued with a strong moralistic streak, and there are plenty of people involved in the political process who will remind us of the dangers and the evils of drug use. And indeed, for many in our society drug use can quickly evolve into drug addiction. Medical experts rightly wish to protect us and our children from the harmful effects of such products as tobacco, alcohol, and illicit drugs, as well as the addictive nature of some of these products, which are known to ruin lives.

So when it comes to drugs, the American government is in many ways trapped in an unsolvable battle that involves the reality of our recreational tendencies, the dangers of drug addiction, and the moral ideals of our most well-meaning crusaders. But the inescapable truth is that we are a nation with significant alcohol and drug use and little social stigma for such activity, and no solution to this problem will be possible if we fail to take this fact into account. Drug usage in America is pervasive. It varies from the legal, such as all forms of liquor, to the sometimes-legal but formally available, such as prescription drugs, to the illegal but widely available, including all manner of drugs whose possession and use constitute criminal conduct.

We not only like our beer, it has become synonymous with such national pastimes as sporting events and barbecues. We not only like our wine, it has become synonymous with good food and culture. We also like our whiskey, and I will be the first to say that I enjoy mine. It is also considered appropriate to ask a doctor to prescribe a wide variety of medications to ease just about any malady that ails us—reducing pain, masking depression, eliminating insomnia, or relaxing tight muscles, just to name a few.

A very high percentage of our society also has used, and continues to use, illegal drugs. According to the government's Bureau of Justice Statistics, in 2005 112 million Americans above the age of twelve indicated that they have used illegal drugs at some point in their lives. This amounts to 46 percent of our entire adult population. Not only is this percentage astounding when we consider that these are acts all of us know are illegal, but the younger the age groups, the higher the percentages tend to be. With respect to continuous use, among those aged eighteen to twenty-five, 28 percent indicated they had used marijuana in the previous year and 7 percent indicated they had used cocaine. The Bureau of Justice Statistics also indicates that among high school seniors in 2006, two-thirds had used alcohol in the past year, one-third had used marijuana, and 6 percent had used cocaine—double the cocaine usage in that age group from just ten years ago.

Selling or buying drugs is a crime, but illegal drugs are not hard to find. When the 2006 high school seniors were asked which drugs they were able to "obtain easily," 85 percent indicated that they had no problems finding marijuana, 47 percent said the same about cocaine, 39 percent said crack, and 27.4 percent said they could easily obtain heroin.

These statistics should alarm us for a wide variety of reasons. First and most obviously, they are undeniable evidence of the extent to which illegal drug use has become accepted, or certainly tolerated, behavior. Our culture's use of drugs has overwhelmed the intent of existing laws; at the same time, obtaining drugs still constitutes an illegal act. This means that one of the first "adulthood" experiences among many of our young is learning that laws are made to be broken. This in and of itself tends to blur the line between legality and criminality in other areas. Buying and using drugs is illegal and can result in prison time, but the practice is pervasive and cuts across every racial and professional group and geographical area of America.

For all the talk of the availability of drugs in Vietnam during that war, I saw far more drug use while I was a student at the Georgetown Law Center than I ever did in or around the military, and I never once saw drug use openly condemned by either a professor or another student. The typical "fact pattern" used to introduce Fourth Amendment privacy issues such as search and seizure began with a common reality: "A cop pulls you over for speeding. You've got marijuana in your glove compartment. Under what conditions is he allowed to search your car?" And this was more than thirty years ago; a full generation has passed, with little change in attitude. One would be seriously challenged to count the judges and political figures who at one point in their lives have engaged in this activity. Some, frankly, continue to do so.

So where does the judge get his drugs? And what does that say about the stability of our system?

The second reason these statistics should alarm us is that the hugely expensive antidrug campaigns we are waging around the world are basically futile when it comes to actually preventing drug use in the United States. The billions of dollars we spend on drug-interdiction programs might drive up the cost of various drugs on the streets of our cities, but they aren't stopping the overall flow. Drugs aren't used in this country because someone is growing them in Colombia or Mexico or Burma or Afghanistan. People are growing them in those places because there is a market for them in the United States.

On this point, the ironies abound. Early in 2007, the Senate Armed Services Committee held a hearing on vastly increased levels of opium production in Afghanistan, which since our 2002 invasion has reverted to an even more powerful narco-state than at any other time in recent history, including when the Taliban controlled the country. Having been in many Afghan villages as a journalist covering the American military there, the realities I had seen were in no way reflected by the almost fantasy-driven testimony of the administration's witness, or in the questions he was receiving from many of the senators on the committee.

The entire discussion during the hearing reminded me of the old parable of the blind leading the blind. Proposed solutions for reversing the massive return of opium production in that country revolved around such issues as allegations of corruption in the Afghani government, the NATO policy of trying to destroy opium crops on the ground, and the possibility of various alternate crops that might be grown by Afghani farmers. A lot of time was spent talking about improving transportation in the country so that more perishable crops might make it to distant markets, as if opium were being grown instead of tomatoes because there weren't enough trucks or good roads to get tomatoes to the consumer.

One cannot disagree that the people of Afghanistan would benefit greatly from infrastructure projects that can enable greater commerce. Nor can one deny the addictive dangers of heroin. But the reality is that the opium production in Afghanistan is an example of basic market economics at work. The Afghanis grow opium, sometimes in fields so vast that they resemble the rice paddies of Vietnam, because there is a foreign market for their crops, a market that they could not duplicate with any other known product.

If you want to reduce the opium crop, you'll have to find a way to reduce the demand for heroin at its destination point.

At another hearing, this time in November 2007 before the Senate Foreign Relations Committee, the administration came before us to justify a proposed $1.4 billion program designed to assist the government of Mexico in its antidrug efforts. Most of this money was targeted for helicopters, unmanned drones, and other expensive equipment that the Mexican government said it needed in order to intercept drug shipments heading inside the United States. And yet, only a week or so before, *The Economist* magazine had published an article indicating that "marijuana is now by far California's most valuable agricultural crop . . . worth even more than the state's famous wine industry," and that "four-fifths of outdoor marijuana plantations [in California] are run by Mexican criminal gangs."

You can give the Mexican government a pile of money to buy fancy equipment, which it may or may not use to try to chase down drug runners in a never-ending game of cat and mouse. But a whole lot of them are already across the border. And if you want to address the problem, put that $1.4 billion into busting up the gangs that are operating here in the United States.

The antidrug advocates are right to focus on the many dangers of drug abuse. The questions that come to mind, however, relate to how these dangers might best be addressed. What has been the effect of the way we have dealt with this issue in terms of criminal law? And how do we better educate our public about the health issues so that we can create more-informed citizens?

Drug offenders, most of them passive users or minor dealers, are swamping our prisons. According to data supplied to the Senate Joint Economic Committee, between 1984 and 2002 those imprisoned for drug offenses increased from 10 percent of the inmate population to approximately 33 percent. Experts estimate that the increase in the incarceration rate for drug offenses accounts for about half of the dramatic increase in the numbers of those imprisoned over that period. Nor do these convictions and mass imprisonments point to a more effective policy of breaking up the power of the multibillion-dollar drug industry. Nor have they resulted in a reduction of the amounts of the more dangerous drugs, such as cocaine, heroin, and methamphetamines, that are reaching our citizens.

Justice statistics show that of all drug arrests in 2005, 42.6 percent were for marijuana offenses. Additionally, nearly 60 percent of those in state prisons for a drug offense have no history of violence or of any significant selling activity. Indeed, those statistics show that in 2005, four out of five drug arrests were for possession, whereas only one out of five was for sales. Three-quarters of the drug offenders in our state prisons in 2005 had been sentenced for nonviolent or purely drug offenses.

When it comes to incarceration for drug offenses, the racial disparities are truly alarming. Although drug use among the races is statistically about the same, a 2006 ACLU report indicates that African Americans, with about 12 percent of our population, account for 37 percent of those arrested on drug charges, 59 percent of those convicted, and 74 percent of all drug offenders sentenced to prison. In federal prisons, sentencing records show that African Americans serve nearly as much time for drug offenses as whites do for violent crimes. And although an estimated two-thirds of regular crack cocaine users are white or Latino, 82 percent of the defendants in federal court for crack offenses are African Americans.

How do these disparities come about?

Even as I write these words, it is virtually certain that somewhere on the streets of Washington, D.C., an eighteen-year-old white kid from the Maryland or northern Virginia suburbs is now buying a stash of drugs from an eighteen-year-old black kid. The white kid is going to take that stash back to the suburbs and make some quick money by selling it to other kids (of all different ethnic backgrounds) from his high school or college or inside his social circle. His chances of getting caught once he clears the black kid's neighborhood are pretty slim. The black kid, lured to the street corner by a similar motive of making some quick cash, is probably going to keep selling drugs until he either gets shot or is caught and arrested. Since his neighborhood is more than likely a high-traffic area for drugs, it is natural that local police and other drug enforcement officials will periodically target it. Thus, his chances of getting caught are pretty high. And once he's caught he will go to jail, to be replaced by another eighteen-year-old black kid. And then the cycle will repeat itself.

The probability is also high that the white kid will soon stop his risky little side business. It is even higher that the other suburban kids who are buying drugs from the white kid will remain legally unaffected by their behavior and will go on to college. After college, many will end up as high-degreed professionals, some of them as lawyers. As they grow older, they will look back on their drug use as recreational and joke about it, laughing it off as a mere phase, just one more little rebellion on the way to a responsible adulthood.

On the other hand, as soon as he is arrested the black kid will enter a hell from which he may never recover. This hell is so familiar to many black communities that it has evolved into an ugly but predictable way of life. It is a hell that will affect his family, his community, his future employability, his rights of citizenship, and even the way he interrelates with individual members of the rest of our society. The American criminal justice system not only stigmatizes those who become enmeshed in it; it also ensures that most of them will never be free from that stigma from the moment they first walk into the inside of a prison cell.

In addition, prison life will change the black kid, harden him, mess up his mind, and redefine his self-image. And after he is released from prison, the black kid will be dragging an invisible ball and chain behind him for the rest of his life. The normal flow of his educational and social life has been interrupted. Prison has become his entryway into adulthood. Few employers of consequence will want to hire a convicted felon. Very few reentry programs are available to help him move into a responsible future. The odds are two-thirds that he will be rearrested within three years, and they are better than fifty-fifty that he will be back in jail during that same period.

By the time the white kid reaches fifty years of age, he may well be a judge. By the time the black kid reaches fifty, he will likely be permanently unemployable, will be ineligible for many government assistance programs, and will not even be able to vote.

If the laws against drug use were uniformly enforced, just for starters half of Hollywood would be in jail instead of half of Harlem. And for all the money and the effort we have spent on the war against drugs, we have not been able to crack the problem at its sources— where it is grown and manufactured—or, most tellingly, at its destination—America's seemingly insatiable demand for the product. This juxtaposition between those millions who use drugs and those few who get caught up inside the legal system and end up with wrecked lives should give us pause, for it illustrates a problem that affects all of us as Americans.

What can be done? Here are a few thoughts.

The time has come to stop locking up people for mere possession and use of marijuana. It makes far more sense to take the money that would be saved by such a policy and use it for enforcement of gang-related activities. We should also fully fund the increasingly popular concept of drug courts, where drug offenders are allowed to enter treatment instead of prison and have their drug offense expunged from their records if they successfully complete treatment. And we should do a better job of cleaning up drug-dependent Americans in and out of jail. According to one study, 53 percent of those in state prisons indicated some form of drug dependency but only 14 percent had received any meaningful treatment.

Drug addiction is not in and of itself a criminal act. It is a medical condition, indeed a disease, just as alcoholism is, and we don't lock people up for being alcoholics. Most Americans understand this distinction, even though the political process seems paralyzed when it comes to finding remedies to address it. Our country urgently needs more funding and more treatment centers for treating this disease, not more prison cells for punishing people who have fallen into conduct that, at bottom, is more harmful to themselves than it is to our society.

As for the broader aspects of our criminal justice system, America's leadership must come to grips with how costly, unfair, and impractical the entire approach to crime has become. In the future, it should be one of our highest national priorities to rethink this process, all the way from the philosophical concepts that drive it, to the conditions under which Americans are incarcerated, to the reentry procedures and programs we make available once their incarceration is completed.

We are spending trillions of taxpayer dollars in foreign adventures that have been advertised as reshaping much of the rest of the world into more democratic institutions. We need to look inward and to reshape our own system in a way that better serves individual justice, community safety, and the long-term productivity of those who have found themselves on the wrong side of the law. This does not mean surrendering to the forces of illegality. Rather, it means narrowing the numbers of those forces, as for instance the Japanese have done, and working to repair the broken places in our societal structure so that we can maximize the potential of every American.

With the right sense of urgency and the right priorities among governmental, academic, and community circles, America's best minds and most dedicated leaders could quickly redefine our system of criminal justice. Contrary to so much of today's political rhetoric, to do so would be an act not of weakness but of strength. Our political system has seen more than its share of office-seekers using this issue to establish "get-tough" credentials by boasting of how many people they are going to lock away without the possibility of parole. We need leaders who understand that true discipline in a society is measured not by how many people are in jail but by how many people are functioning productively as law-abiding citizens.

It doesn't take much to throw somebody in jail. But it takes leadership, thought, and dedication to direct their energies into positive conduct, and in the process to reshape our most blighted communities.

For those who would argue that such recommendations are an indication of lack of social willpower, I should point out that the inspiration for this philosophy actually derives from my service in the United States Marine Corps. Few organizations in the country, or for that matter in the world, can match the disciplinary environment of the Marine Corps. At the same time, "Uncle Sam's Misguided Children" have long been famous for taking in some of the most headstrong, aggressive, antiauthoritarian members of our society and changing the direction of their lives. Properly led, they learn to live with discipline and thus to develop self-discipline, enabling them to work within a demanding structure. They learn to produce results. Many also learn to lead. Those who refuse to take the discipline pay the price, and if they do so they clearly know why.

American society could benefit from a similar approach. To be an American has historically meant that we all have a chance to succeed, and that if we falter, except in the most grievous of circumstances, we should be allowed a second chance as well. We cannot advertise to the world that we live in a fair system if we are preventing large numbers of our citizens from participating in this process owing to early mistakes that involve stupidity, peer pressure, or nonviolent conduct.

America's greatness has always been in giving people something to believe in and in treating them fairly. If someone on his way to prison today is convinced that his future is now inarguably ended and that the system in which he lives does not treat all similarly situated

PART THREE

Truth and Consequences

CHAPTER FOURTEEN

WHAT THEN MUST WE DO?

On June 5, 1968, I had the honor of raising my right hand and taking the oath of office as a second lieutenant in the United States Marine Corps. Thus began a professional journey that I then believed would result in a career of service to our country in the profession of arms. Forty years have flown relentlessly by since that day, filled with unpredicted challenges and unplanned detours. I have often been surprised by this twist of fate or that, and have met my share of frustrations and disappointments. On the other hand, I have never been bored. While not exactly turbulent, my journey has encountered more than a few bumps along the road, and it has never reached what the social scientists might call stasis, either.

Personal and professional markers have dotted the varied highways of my life as those years unfurled: relationships begun and lost and others begun again, children born in three different decades, and an assortment of career endeavors connected not by logic so much as by an insatiable intellectual curiosity and a willingness to take a risk. And this must be said: I know and appreciate that I have been blessed. I have a tendency to mistrust politicians who flaunt their religious views. In the Book of Matthew it is told that when you pray, you should go into the closet and close the door, then pray to your Father in secret. I do so, regularly. My faith is deeply important to me, and not a night goes by that I don't give thanks for the life I have been called upon to live.

I could never have foreseen it all those years ago, but I know what it's like to write a book and have it make the bestseller lists, to go to the premiere of my own movie, and to give a speech accepting an Emmy Award for my television reporting. I also know how it feels to walk inside the White House and meet with the President and his key national security leaders. I have had the privilege of working as a full committee counsel in the House of Representatives, preparing legislation and moving it through the Congress, and of debating serious national issues on the Senate floor. I have met daily with, and been a key aide to, the Secretary of Defense. I have run the Department of the Navy. I have spent time with many foreign leaders, both as a journalist and as a government official.

And yet while doing such things, I can never shake the memories of how it feels to be on the outside looking in. I remember what it was like to be viewed as second-rate by other students as I sat impatiently through "dummy English" classes in high school. I have spent long months leading combat patrols into the looming unknown of sweltering tropical battlefields. I have worked alone day after day, writing my first novel (*Fields of Fire*) seven times from cover to cover on the mere gamble that I might, somehow, one day find a publisher. I have traveled hundreds of times unprotected and unattended in xichlo pedicabs as they made their way along pocked, litter-strewn streets, past carefully watching faces, into the farthest alleyways of Southeast Asia's slums.

My professional career began with an oath to protect the Constitution against all enemies, foreign and domestic, at a time when the country was riven by both external and internal conflict. It would be an understatement to say that 1968 was a tumultuous year. Only hours before our Naval Academy class gathered at the Navy–Marine Corps stadium for the long-awaited graduation ceremony, Senator Robert F. Kennedy was assassinated in Los Angeles. Only two months earlier, on April 4, Martin Luther King Jr. had been gunned down in Memphis, Tennessee. Just four months before our graduation, at the end of January and throughout much of February, the Communists' all-out Tet Offensive had brought the bloodiest fighting of the Vietnam War, leading President Lyndon Johnson to decide against running for re-election. Beginning in earnest the year before, but increasingly after the Martin Luther King assassination, the African American sections in many of America's cities had erupted in frequent violence, with much of our nation's capital itself occupied by National Guard troops. And later that summer, the news coverage of the Democratic National Convention in Chicago would be dominated by footage of the clashes between provocative antiwar organizers and heavy-handed members of the Chicago police.

The United States of 2008 is also a troubled and divided place, in a quieter but, to me, a more deeply disturbing way. Oddly, as I have outlined on these pages, one of our greatest difficulties today is in bringing the problems that most threaten our future out into the open so that they can be honestly debated. Issues such as economic fairness, fundamental social justice, the long-term strategic direction of the country, and the hardening of American society along class lines rarely make it onto the Senate floor, much less into the arena of the national political debate. It often occurs to me that, although the country was in far greater overt turmoil in 1968, the premises on which our society was founded were never really in true doubt. In 1968, the idea that our problems were eventually solvable was not in serious question, at least for most Americans. It is actually harder to make that case in 2008.

But 1968 was indeed a bloody, tumultuous year. And for those of us who stepped forward to serve, it marked the beginning of more than a decade of internal turmoil, confrontation over our service, accusations of having participated in an immoral, unjust war, and, for some, a gnawing self-doubt. Ironically, the end result for me and many others was that we learned to love our country even more deeply for all its flaws and public flagellations, because we were required to reconsider the beliefs and values that had once been handed to us as our natural legacy, indeed as a birthright. For years it was argued in the open arena of public debate that our very system was incurably flawed, but few of us agreed. And so we went through the intellectual challenge of justifying America's uniqueness on fresh grounds. This caused us to believe all the more strongly that America was at bottom a fair and splendid place; that it was the moral beacon for the world; that for all our problems we had the will to solve them, the patience to undergo the painful debates that might identify solutions, and the constitutional system that would provide for remedies and thus hold together the loyalties of our people.

Today an entirely new set of doubts exist, many of them far more fundamental to the makeup of our society and at the same time more complex than the issues of civil rights and even war itself. Some of these doubts go to the core principles on which our government has always rested. But for all the reasons mentioned in this book, we are not engaging in the kind of constructive debate that might allow us to reach a set of fair solutions. And we will only be able to do so as a by-product of reflective, thoughtful leadership that is anchored in a sense of true stewardship of our people.

I have precious few good memories of 1968 or of the years that immediately followed. But I did learn some invaluable lessons. And those lessons are capable of being applied to the challenges we face today.

As the turmoil of the antiwar and civil rights rebellions swept the nation, for those of us serving in the United States military the issues were, as they have always been, more simple and direct, and in a sense also more personally urgent. Those who were not wearing the uniform enjoyed a luxury that we ourselves could not indulge in. Despite the urgency that many of them felt, they could disengage themselves from the debate if the notion struck them. They could argue; they could protest; and they could march. Then, if they so chose, they could go home, or back to school, or decide to focus on other matters. Ours was a more restrictive world, one from which we could neither take a breather nor decide to reject. We had sworn an obligation and we were bound, both legally and in our honor. A war awaited us and it was not going away anytime soon. It was our mission—indeed our sworn duty—to prepare for that war and to provide leadership to those who were fighting it.

And so, against this backdrop of protest and confusion, we went about our tasks.

I have often remarked that there was purity in my time at the Marine Officers Basic School of the sort that I have rarely seen in any other portion of my life. That purity came from our collective knowledge that in a very short time we would be receiving orders to combat. With those orders would come the unavoidable reality that we were soon going to be responsible for the lives of hardened United States Marines fighting a vicious war, often under unimaginable conditions. Those with whom I went through that training cycle will always hold a special place in my heart. We all knew where we were going, no matter the political arguments that were happening in other places. And we all knew that many of us would not come back alive.

As the war heated up, the Marine Corps had tightened the Basic School course from thirty-two weeks to twenty-six, and then again to twenty-one, cutting out many of the classes on drill and ceremonies but adding a course on the sixty-millimeter mortar. We trained hard, six full days a week, often bivouacked or in the field for night exercises. We worked through Christmas Eve and were back on the tarmac the day after Christmas, heading out to tactical bivouacs. We trained on New Year's Eve, and were back at it again on January 2. We graduated on February 5, 1969, and for those of us assigned to infantry units, we were on our way to Vietnam by early March.

The Marine Corps takes a back seat to no other institution when it comes to combat preparation, and the Basic School reflected that. Designed and mentored by officers who had seen the worst small-unit fighting of World War II and Korea, our curriculum moved smoothly from the intellectual to the practical. Again and again we learned a weapon or a concept in a classroom, then were required to fire it or implement it in one of Quantico's sprawling training areas. By the time we finished Basic School, we had studied and used every weapon in an infantry battalion. We had also studied and conducted tactical exercises in squad, platoon, and company formations. We had worked extensively in the thick woods, mostly at night, learning and implementing different patrolling techniques. And we had spent long hours in Socratic dialogues with our staff platoon commanders, debating leadership challenges that might face us as small-unit leaders in combat.

Our instructors were handpicked from among the finest young officers in the Marine Corps. Almost all of them had been in combat. Many bore visible scars from that war. As the months went by, they repeatedly and unendingly challenged us with an age-old mantra. Soon, a sobering responsibility would be on our young shoulders, carrying with it the need to make daily, life-or-death decisions.

What do you do now, Lieutenant?

And sometimes they coached us with the kind of inside information that makes sense only among those who indulge in the intricacies of daily combat. *Forget the rule books. Remember what I'm going to tell you. This will save your life.*

Isolated moments still flit across my mind, for the reality of what we soon would face was never far away in Quantico.

My next-door neighbor when I moved into the military housing project at Thomason Park was a tall South Carolinian whose face and features remain a fuzzy, blond blur. Quick-tempered and intense, he became frustrated and beat his eight-week-old puppy after the little mixed-breed dog peed on his combat boots. I took the dog off his hands and named him Shep, after one of my favorite Elvis Presley songs. My neighbor finished his training three months before I did and headed off to Vietnam. By the time I finished Basic School, my dog Shep was six months old. And my hot-tempered neighbor was already dead.

I learned to love the cynicism and symmetry of Marine Corps humor, which permeates everything Marines do, especially their harder tasks. When things would go wrong, the jokes would quickly begin.

"To err is human, to forgive divine. Neither of which is Marine Corps policy."

"Ah, another opportunity, masking itself as a disaster . . ."

"I didn't say you had to love it, I said you had to do it . . ."

"Everybody on the left, get on the right. Everybody on the right, get on the left. Everybody in the middle, mull around!"

Late one December afternoon as we stood on the tarmac awaiting the helicopters that would take us to our latest tactical exercise, I stood near two of our staff platoon commanders, both of whom had been wounded in Vietnam. The CH-46s were famous for the ease with which the enemy was able to shoot them down in Vietnam. As the choppers scudded toward us through a bleak gray sky just above the interminable tree lines, one of the staff platoon commanders shivered with memories and shook his head.

"I gotta get out of the Marine Corps," he said.

"Why?" asked the other.

"I hate those helicopters."

"You'll never get out," said the other staff platoon commander.

"Why?"

"You'll miss those helicopters."

Just before we graduated from Basic School, a tough but insightful lieutenant colonel brought those of us who were headed for the infantry into a separate room, where he gave us the most unforgettable speech of the entire training course. His speech has stayed with me all of these years because, whether or not the colonel fully appreciated it, his wisdom transcended his subject. The speech was not a part of our curriculum. As commanding officer of the support battalion at the Basic School, the colonel was not even a member of the teaching staff. He had either volunteered or been called upon to give the new infantry lieutenants a reality check, and there were few better qualified to do so. The colonel had served as an enlisted Marine during some of World War II's hardest fighting, then as a rifle platoon commander during the Korean War, where he was awarded the Navy Cross for extraordinary heroism. And he had just returned from commanding an infantry battalion in Vietnam.

He began by telling us, flatly, to get used to the fact that a pretty large majority of us were going to be killed or wounded. He warned us that in physical terms, Vietnam was the hardest war the Marine Corps infantry had ever fought. For the infantry the combat operations were continuous, giving the war no beginning and no end. There were no creature comforts—no hot food, no barbed wire, no tents, no toilets, no cots, no jeeps, indeed few roads. He advised us that physical ills were frequent in "the bush," as we called the infantry areas of operations: malaria, shrimp fever, shigella, sun poisoning, hookworm, ringworm, oozing infections that could erupt after a mere scratch against reeds or sawgrass. And he urged us to become the ultimate stewards of our troops' well-being. In the Marine Corps tradition of "loyalty down," we would be not only their commanders but also their advocates to the higher-ups, who might not understand the daily conditions under which they were operating.

"Take care of your Marines."

And then he gave us the truest challenge, the warning that echoes in my memory almost every day. He began by recounting a story of a fight in Korea that went incredibly bad, where for all his combat experience he made an error in judgment while under fire. "I had the enemy pinned down on a ridge," he said. "There was a tree line on our right. I set up a base of fire, and sent thirteen Marines into the tree line in order to envelop them. Thirteen Marines went into the tree line, and all thirteen were killed. And gentlemen, there is not a day that goes by when I don't think about that."

The colonel then spoke of the inalienable bottom line of combat leadership: While all Marines are equally in harm's way, it is the leaders who must make the decisions about what to do, then live with the results. What he may not have realized is that he also spelled out the timeless, inalterable responsibility that in less dramatic ways sits on the shoulders of all who choose to exercise leadership as a way of life. It is impossible to quote him directly after forty years, but this was the colonel's message:

"You are in the business of fighting, and every day you are going to make decisions, often under pressure and under fire. Your decisions will have consequences. No matter how good you are, people are going to get killed. Sometimes it will be the enemy. Sometimes it will be innocent civilians. Sometimes it will be people you care about, people you trust, and people who trust you. You can't escape this. It is the burden of command. For the rest of your life, there will be times when you wake up and look into the mirror and wonder if you could have made a better decision. You can't turn back the clock, gentlemen. Keep your mind in the game, because you're going to have to deal with the results of your decisions for the rest of your life."

In the long months I spent as a twenty-three-year-old rifle platoon and company commander in the infamous An Hoa Basin west of Danang, the colonel's admonition resonated again and again. During the Vietnam War, the South Vietnamese government categorized villages from "A," meaning completely government-controlled, to "E," meaning completely controlled by the Communist Viet Cong. And they also had a separate category—Category Five—for those that were regarded as politically hopeless. Most of the villages in the An Hoa Basin were Category Fives, making them so-called free-fire zones.

We constantly operated in these blown-out populated areas, moving from village to village and digging new company perimeters every few days. We lived in the villages, patrolled through them, fought inside them. The enemy used the villages for routes of ingress and egress from their base camps in the mountains as they conducted their own combat operations. They also viewed them as major supply points, since the villagers in these areas supported them, and since many of the men from the villages were with the enemy in the mountains. Air strikes and artillery missions on populated areas were the order of the day. On one operation, the American high command ordered B-52 "arc light" strikes on top of a heavily contested peninsula called Go Noi Island, leaving craters twenty feet deep in places where a day before there had been thatch-roofed homes. Our rifle company did the Bomb Damage Assessment, or BDA, of these areas after the B-52 mission. The landscape was churned and lifeless, what one might imagine if he were walking on the moon.

The An Hoa Basin was a bloody, morally conflicted mess.

Enemy contact came in every imaginable form in the Basin, from small cells of local Viet Cong to regiment-size North Vietnamese army units. Over time, dozens of my Marines became casualties from a wide array of weaponry, ranging from mines, hand grenades, rifle and automatic-weapons fire, mortars, rocket-propelled grenades, and large-caliber recoilless rifles. And every day, we who led the squads, platoons, and companies were required to make decisions. Many of these decisions addressed moral dimensions that would have confounded discussions in the seminars on ethics and philosophy at the universities where some of our peers now grappled intellectually with the war we had been sent to fight. For us, these decisions became routine, as normal as walking. But they often involved a Hobson's choice, as there are few clear answers in combat. And they had moral, as well as mortal, consequences.

Here's a routine, daily choice. You are crossing a mile-wide stretch of rice paddies, heading toward thick tree lines interlaced with small villages. You know on the one hand that people live in these hamlets. On the other, you know that the enemy has long ago dug narrow fighting trenches, moatlike, at all the village edges. If the enemy is in the area, they can watch and prepare for an hour as you cross the paddies and head toward the tree lines. One of their favorite tactics is called "grab and hold," where they wait until you are nearly on top of them and then open up an ambush.

If they ambush you from their trenches and spider holes when you are in the open, they will cut you to pieces. But if you "prep" the tree line with a mortar or artillery mission in order to preclude, or as we used to say "loosen up," an ambush, innocent civilians may well be killed. And of course, there is no guarantee that the enemy is actually in the tree line, while you know full well that civilians are in the villages. And for all of this back-and-forth, it is not a rote process. As you approach the tree line, you search for telltale signs that might indicate the enemy is near. Are the water buffalo out in the fields? Can you see any children playing?

But this is intellectual dabbling. You are walking in the real world, with Marines around you and a weapon in your hand, not sitting in a college class on moral philosophy. You have to decide, and your decision must come before you are within a few hundred meters of the tree line.

What do you do now, Lieutenant?

You take care of your Marines. You prep the tree line. And you accept that you are going to live with the consequences.

Sometimes such moral dilemmas become deeply personal. I could choose among many, including several involving the Marines whom I commanded. But much of life is better examined in microcosm, so let me use one.

While I was a rifle company commander, a South Vietnamese army unit made daytime contact with a North Vietnamese army (NVA) unit in the eastern sector of a particularly troublesome area called the Arizona Valley. Outgunned, the NVA broke contact and headed west toward the mountains. On short notice, we were ordered to relocate to a thin string of villages in an attempt to set up a blocking position and cut off their retreat. We packed our gear and moved quickly across a wide rice paddy, reaching a village and sweeping on-line through it. At the far edge of the village, our lead platoon immediately set into a blocking position facing another open paddy where the retreating NVA might cross.

The follow-on platoons then began "clearing" the village bunkers. This was a normal process when we were facing enemy contact. Every thatched "hooch" in the Arizona Valley had a family bunker next to its porch, with a rabbit hutch–like double entrance. When firefights broke out, the families would head into their bunkers, which were strong enough to withstand artillery shells. But it had become a common tactic for enemy soldiers to hide inside the bunkers as well, often allowing them to come out and open fire on Marine patrols from behind. And so a routine had developed, which both the Marines and the villagers understood. Marine fire teams would move carefully from bunker to bunker, calling *"lai day"* three times, telling the villagers in Vietnamese to come out from their bunker. After that the Marines would throw a grenade into the bunker, and one of them would enter it, making sure it was clear.

At the far edge of the village, our lead elements were firing at the tail end of the retreating NVA unit, which was now breaking away from our hasty sweep-and-block. Inside the village, one of our fire teams had cleared one of the family bunkers, but the Marine who jumped inside following the grenade blast found that three people had not come out. A younger man in black pajamas, probably a local Viet Cong afraid of exiting, had been killed. Hardened by combat, we shrugged that one off. But the other two stopped my heart even in the mind-numbing repetition of tragedy that so defines war.

A wispy, gray-haired, bearded old man in white pajamas, probably a grandfather, was dead, having wrapped himself around a small boy in order to protect the child from the grenade blast. Why had he not come out of the bunker? Were he and the boy too slow to move once the Marines called for them? Was his voice too frail to be heard if he had answered the Marines who were calling for him to come out, as villagers often did before exiting their bunkers? In any event, it was clear that his final thoughts were of the boy. His shocked, opaque eyes and his still-curled body were the very definition of love and human sacrifice. The boy was still alive, although barely.

At the far edge of the village, our lead units were still firing at the NVA. I walked through the village with my platoon commanders, deciding where to set up defensive positions, since dusk would soon be upon us. I called in a position report to our battalion commander. And all the while, the corpsman from the platoon I had commanded before taking over the company followed me, cradling the little boy in his arms. The corpsman and I had now served together through seven months of hard combat. We had both seen a mountain of tragedy, and we kept nothing from each other. But this one was getting to each of us, and he was insistent.

"Skipper, if you don't get this kid out of here right now, he's going to die."

I called for a medevac, but I knew what the answer would be. Emergency medevacs were available only for Marines. The Arizona Valley was a high-risk landing zone for any helicopter. Vietnamese civilians could only be given "routine" medevacs, when landing zones were calm and all Marines had been taken care of.

What do you do now, Lieutenant?

I couldn't lie to my chain of command. There weren't any Marines to be medevacked. I made my case for the boy, and lost.

"They'll only bring it in as a routine," I told the Doc. Both of us knew that this could take hours and possibly into the next morning.

"All right," he answered, clearly exasperated. "Then you watch him die."

The Doc put the small child on top of a wooden box, right next to where I had set up the radios for my command post. Over the next half hour, as I spoke repeatedly on the radio and set up the poncho hooch where I would spend the night, the boy lay quietly, never making a sound, all the while watching me. Nor could I stop watching him. And as we stared at each other, he slowly died.

I was left with the same feeling as when we took our own casualties. The boy's death had to be set aside, compartmentalized, put inside a mental box. There was no time either to reflect or to grieve. I was commanding a rifle company in the Arizona Valley. We were in a new village. Marines were digging into our defensive perimeter, so there were lines to check. I needed to walk the edge of our perimeter and examine nearby terrain features so I could decide where to put artillery and mortar fire in case we were attacked. Somewhere in the village a water buffalo had broken out of his pen and was rampaging near my company's fighting positions. Night came. We rotated the watches on the radios and in our fighting holes. The next morning, we were gone. And, as Sonny and Cher liked to sing, the beat went on.

But there are still moments when I look back and see the little boy's soft brown eyes, and the curled corpse of the old grandfather whose last living thought had been to save him. I will never forget either of them, nor should I. The An Hoa Basin filled all of us with a lifetime of such stories. Some of them happened to our Marines, some to the enemy we fought; many more happened to the villagers caught in between. My memories of those days are one reason that I have traveled so many times to this region in my return visits to Vietnam, which began in 1991. The villagers in these contested areas paid a horrible price. No matter one's feelings about the war itself, or which side they might have been on, we owe them.

What was the microcosm I mentioned? When you have personalized death, looked into the eyes of innocent people as the life drained out of them, watched human lives torn apart not once but hundreds of times—friends, enemies, and those caught in between—it brings not only sadness but also an oddly stubborn wisdom. When you have watched an enemy fight with ferocity and often with honor, you tend to conclude that on some level you have more in common with those you were trying to kill than you do with people who view wars only as an intellectual debate. And when you have served among good people, fellow Marines, some of whom you came to love with the same intensity as you do your own family, there are few others you will meet in your lifetime who can ever gain that same level of trust and respect.

To state the obvious, all of this wrapped together makes you a different person. Like most people who shared this existence, I have often been worried since those days, sometimes been frustrated, and now and then been angry, but I have never really been afraid. Whatever can be done to me, physically, mentally, and emotionally, has already happened, other than to take my life. The challenges I faced, and the decisions I was required to make every day, did make me tougher. But they also imbued me with some hard-earned insights and enabled me to consider other aspects of life with a different kind of clarity. And above all, they intensified my resolve to take care of those who for a variety of reasons have been less fortunate than I.

There are no instant replays in life, no reset buttons, no rewinding of the reel. We cannot undo that which has already been done. But we do have a duty to remember, and to live our lives with a sense of invigorated purpose that might counterbalance the tragedies we have seen.

As the colonel intimated, such a sense of personal accountability is the burden of true leadership, whether in combat or on Capitol Hill. Few issues have the immediacy of combat, but the principle holds in any situation. When you are given the authority to make the decisions, you also inherit the responsibility to accept the consequences, as well as the obligation to use your authority for the common good.

What has this got to do with the politics of today?

Everything.

Our country is in the middle of a profound, many-headed crisis. This crisis is rooted in a number of causes, but much of it has been brought about by poor leadership decisions at every level of government and in every major philosophical arena. Our nation was maneuvered into invading and occupying a country that was not directly threatening us, by political thinkers whose Trotskyite worldview is so far to the left that some think they are on the right. Our voters have been manipulated by the false emotional debates of the extreme far right, from Jerry Falwell and Pat Robertson to Karl Rove. Our senior leaders, Democrat and Republican alike, have failed to grapple effectively with the major political issues of the day, from international relations to monetary policy to basic economic fairness among our citizens. Our electoral process itself is dominated by powerful financial interests that, to put it mildly, are threatened by the very notion of true reform.

Elections shouldn't be media circuses; nor should they be auctions where a candidate sells himself to the highest bidder. They should be moral contracts between those who wish to lead and those who with their votes are consenting, if not demanding, to be led. And nor will any true leader ever allow himself to become just another franchise of some special-interest group.

In that context, the burden of leadership is to make hard choices, to tell the truth, and to take responsibility when hardship follows. Those who have participated as national leaders as the present crisis evolved should either accept accountability for their acts, and in some cases for their failure to act, or call it a career. The leadership of both parties should come to an agreement that our national debate is taking place under the sobering reality that the United States is at more risk, strategically, economically, and culturally, than at any time since the combination of the Great Depression and World War II. We cannot solve our problems by petty obstructionism, or by manufacturing silly "gotcha" votes that amount to nothing more than emotional distractions. Both sides are guilty of this, and the Bush Administration is guiltier still. Politics will always involve deeply held views and strong disagreements, but the frustrating one-upmanship that now characterizes both the administration and the Congress is insulting to the dignity of our heritage and is causing the United States to rapidly lose its place at the head of the community of nations.

If philosopher Will Durant were alive today, he might be observing with wry irony that we are on the verge of an inexact but useful historical mirror. To analogize, Rome is slowly burning. The Emperor Nero wakes up every morning, distracts his imperial subjects with dark warnings about the dangers of the barbarians, praises his legions who are chasing the Vandals and the Goths somewhere on the far-flung frontier, and then goes back to playing with his fiddle. The Senate, unable to command the Emperor's attention or respect, is paralyzed with emotional, unproductive debates. From its chambers we hear, daily, a fount of sound and fury, impotent diatribes that signify little more than its own inability to govern. The whole body of government, Emperor and Senate alike, turns its eyes away from the forces that are bankrolling its tenure while selling off the Empire for personal profit. And the citizens, alternating between disgust, apathy, and fear, know that their way of life is unraveling before their eyes and see that their leaders are either powerless or disinclined to act.

The situation is timeless, as cyclical as history itself. And the question is eternal:

What, then, must we do?

In one form or another, this question is asked daily in every country, indeed in every community and in almost every thinking household around the world. In some authoritarian societies it is necessary to whisper it, hoping for some as yet undefined, dramatic change that might bring greater fairness and free up the human spirit. In others it is vigorously debated. And in the America of today, we quite frankly find ourselves doing a little bit of both.

Permit me a moment of literary reflection, for truth is often found in fiction. In the film *The Year of Living Dangerously*, the dwarf photojournalist Billy Kwan (played in an Oscar-winning performance by Linda Hunt) is obsessed with this question as he travels through the darkest slums of Jakarta, Indonesia. The film, set in 1965, depicts the months leading up to an attempted coup d'état sponsored by the Chinese Communist government, designed to depose Indonesian strongman Sukarno.

Filmmaker Peter Weir's underrated masterpiece, shot on location in the Philippines, is in my view the finest film ever made about Southeast Asia. It is also one of the most nuanced movies ever made about the struggle between individual conscience, personal loyalty, and governmental power. Viewers are overwhelmed by the blending of Weir's intimate directorial style with the haunting music of the incomparable Maurice Jarre (*Lawrence of Arabia, Doctor Zhivago*), until the sights, sounds, and indeed the very feel of Southeast Asia all seem palpable. That combination itself would have made for a first-rate film. But Weir's ability to deftly juxtapose Java's history and culture, as well as its people's hopeless strivings and masked resentments, alongside the veneer of luxury in which the country's rulers and many of its well-off westerners reside, makes it in this writer's mind a classic.

Kwan the dwarf, the eyes and voice of the film and frequently its narrator as well, links all of these pieces together. Often working with Western journalists, most of whom he despises, he finds a friend and possible soul mate in the new, ambitious Australian journalist Guy Hamilton, played by Mel Gibson. At the outset an unabashed supporter of Sukarno, in whom he increasingly loses faith as the film progresses, Kwan personalizes his concern for the poverty that surrounds him by attempting to assist the dying child of a prostitute, visiting the child regularly and bringing money to his mother. In a quiet, symbolic struggle, Kwan repeatedly urges the mother to use the money for medicine, wanting the child to live. But the mother pockets the money, sensing that the child is so weak that it will die anyway.

Early in the film, as they walk along packed streets crowded with misfits and beggars, Kwan justifies his feelings to Hamilton. "And the people asked him, saying, what shall we do then? It's from Luke, chapter three, verse ten. What then must we do? Tolstoy asked the same question. He wrote a book with that title. He got so upset about the poverty in Moscow that he went one night into the poorest section and just gave away all his money. You could do that now. Five American dollars would be a fortune to one of these people."

"Wouldn't do any good," Hamilton answers Billy, surveying the poverty that surrounds them. "Just be a drop in the ocean."

Kwan answers knowingly. "Ah, that's the same conclusion Tolstoy came to. I disagree . . . I support the view that you just don't think about the major issues. You do whatever you can about the misery that's in front of you. Add your light to the sum of light. You think that's naive, don't you?"

"Yep," Hamilton answers.

As the film progresses, Hamilton betrays Kwan, as well as the woman they both love, in order to advance his career. In a separate incident the child dies, sending Kwan into a grief-stricken bout of despair. The despair extends to Sukarno, whom he now has come to blame for the people's suffering. Back in his small studio, Kwan types the words over and over, growing mad with despair.

What then must we do? What then must we do?

Kwan has lost all his anchors. His friend has betrayed him; the boy he was trying to save has died, possibly through the deliberate misfeasance of his mother, and his faith in Sukarno has ended. Deciding to do something—anything—that might add to the sum of light, he finally dares to hang a sign from a hotel window as a pomp-filled Sukarno motorcade approaches in the street below. The sign says simply, "SUKARNO FEED YOUR PEOPLE." It is pulled down by Sukarno's security agents before the motorcade arrives, so that the strongman never even sees it. The agents also kill Billy Kwan, whose gesture did not even allow him his one moment of justice, that small light that might in a way inform, if not the world then at least Sukarno, that his heavy-handed ways were devastating to Indonesia's people.

And still the question haunts us. What do we do, in any society, when leaders turn their heads away from the people who have no power and from the problems that truly confront us?

Billy Kwan mentions Tolstoy, and also quotes a passage in the Book of Luke that refers to John the Baptist. John the Baptist's answer in the scriptures is not unlike Billy Kwan's: If you have two coats, give one of them to a person who has no coat. If you have extra money, do likewise. Biblically this is profound, and it defines the message of the New Testament. But in terms of government such altruism has the obvious limitation of being impractical—not to mention that John the Baptist ended up with his head on a plate at one of King Herod's dinners for, among other things, fomenting egalitarian thoughts among the masses.

The Russia in which Tolstoy asked the question was marked by a prolonged resentment among the intellectual and working classes toward those who had too much power and wealth, centralized and untouchable—the members of the same aristocracy to which Tolstoy himself belonged. This resentment exploded in an ill-fated revolution in 1917, only seven years after Tolstoy's death. Designed to bring about a redistribution of income and power to ordinary people, the Russian Revolution instead quickly became a savage and corrupted dictatorship that also openly sought world dominance.

As Arthur Koestler's 1940 novel *Darkness at Noon* so brilliantly portrayed, the governing structure of the new dictatorship was composed of cutthroat apparatchiks from the very classes that had so deeply resented the old aristocracy. A line from a 1970s song made popular by the British group The Who comes quickly to mind: "Meet the new boss / same as the old boss." America and the free world lived with the dangerous reality of that revolution throughout my young life and into my middle years. And we are still feeling its implications in our foreign policy today.

In America, the question still begs an answer. But our situation is far different.

The American system was built and refined by innovators who replaced individual despair with individual rights, who promised to cut off the heads of tyrants rather than allow tyrants to cut off the heads of dissidents, and whose own revolution produced not new savagery but a guarantee of balanced government, replete with intricate checks and balances. The challenge, and indeed the responsibility, of each succeeding generation has been to preserve these rights, to preclude the concentration of power into the hands of a privileged few, and to ensure that our country maintains a careful but energetic role in international affairs.

In short, our problems are not systemic, as in those other countries where despair, tyranny, and revolution became the order of the day. The American system itself is not only sound, it is brilliantly constructed. Our challenges are not in repairing our system of government but in improving the way we have been selecting our leaders. Not accidentally, too much time is being spent in the American political process in distracting our citizens from the true issues that concern our future in favor of the emotional issues that actually mask the difficulties we face.

The cynical manipulation of people's emotions is as old as politics itself. For generations it was believed that the American South was divided purely along racial lines. In truth, the long history of the American South was that of a small veneer at the top, deliberately keeping less fortunate whites and blacks at each other's throats to the point that neither group could fully comprehend the extent of what was happening above them. And this is precisely what is happening on a larger scale in American politics today.

Let me speak the obvious. Those who do not want significant reform in America enjoy the emotional arguments that occupy untold hours of political commentary while keeping our citizens distracted from the issues that truly threaten our future. Should we imprison people who burn our flag? Should gays be permitted to marry? Can you love the troops and still hate the war? Should Britney Spears be allowed to keep her kids? Did Charlie Wilson really use cocaine?

We need to get past these artificialities and focus on the long-term good of the country. And today, the inalienable bottom line of solving

America's many problems is, simply, to find good leaders and to hold them accountable.

There are such leaders among us. Some already hold office in our government, including many who are my friends and colleagues. Others would be willing to step forward if they felt confident that the opportunities of serving would outweigh the heavy price that today's emphasis on negative politics requires them to pay. To that group I would say, quite simply, that your country needs you. And I would ask you to please realize that those who do not want significant change are very happy that you're still sitting on the sidelines while they advance their own controllable candidates into the offices that you yourselves should be holding.

And to the American voters I would offer this small piece of advice: Be just as shrewd and ruthless in your demands on our leaders as the political wizards who are running these campaigns are in their strategies designed to get your vote. Do your part to send to Washington people who truly want to solve the problems of this country, from the bottom up.

You won't regret it. You will benefit from it. And the stakes could not be higher. Sometimes the business of politics seems silly. At other times it can be infuriating. But you must stay in the game, because you and also your grandchildren will be the inheritors of both our successes and our flaws.

ABOUT THE AUTHOR

JIM WEBB, Virginia's senior United States senator, is an Emmy Award–winning journalist and the author of nine books, including the bestselling cultural history *Born Fighting* and the classic novel of the Vietnam War *Fields of Fire* as well as *Lost Soldiers, The Emperor's General,* and three other novels. As a Marine in Vietnam he received the nation's second- and third-highest awards for combat heroism. He served as Assistant Secretary of Defense and Secretary of the Navy during the Reagan administration.

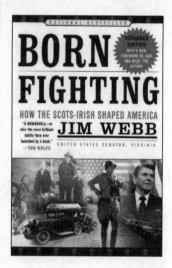